# OLIVER TOMKINS

# OLIVER TOMKINS

*The Ecumenical Enterprise, 1908–92*

Adrian Hastings

Published in Great Britain in 2001 by
Society for Promoting Christian Knowledge
Holy Trinity Church
Marylebone Road
London NW1 4DU

The publishers acknowledge with thanks permission to reproduce extracts
from the following:

John Betjeman, 'A Subaltern's Love Song', *Collected Poems*,
John Murray (Publishers) Ltd.

G. K. Chesterton, 'The Higher Unity', with permission of A. P. Watt Ltd,
on behalf of The Royal Literary Fund.

British Library Cataloguing-in-Publication Data
A catalogue record for this book is available from the British Library

ISBN 0-281-05441-X

Typeset by FiSH Books, London
Printed in Great Britain
by Bookcraft, Midsomer Norton

# Contents

*The photographs will be found between pages 88 and 89.*

# Preface

I first met Bishop Oliver in Cambridge in the autumn of 1975 shortly after his retirement from Bristol. We became friends and I visited Oliver and Ursula from time to time in Worcester but I don't think I learnt much about his past life. He mostly listened. It was always part of his nature to exercise a gentle reticence about his own role in things. It certainly never occurred to me that I would later write his biography.

In July 1991 Rupert Bliss asked whether I would consider writing the biography of his wife Kathleen who had died two years earlier. She was a remarkable and influential person and the idea intrigued me, so I turned to a number of people for advice, including Oliver. They were born within a month of each other and had been friends and co-workers through much of their adult lives. Oliver replied, 'We were contemporaries at Cambridge and I kept in touch with her right up to the time of her death ... I think that her biography could be an illumination of the religious and social history of the period 1930–1990 which could be just up your street. She touched life creatively at such a lot of points.' So he urged me to accept. It was probably the last letter I received from him. However, I decided against the idea on further consideration: not only had I never met either Kathleen or Rupert but I found that Kathleen had kept no journal and had written only one short book. There seemed no large cache of unpublished material to hand. I felt that in these circumstances it would be too hard to come to understand her. Nevertheless the suggestion had made me feel that I would quite like to attempt one carefully researched biography. So when Canon Trevor Page, Oliver's son-in-law, spoke to me in 1993, a year after his death, about the possibility of a biography, I felt attracted by the idea of undertaking it. The decisive question in my mind was once more the availability of papers. A quick visit to Ursula in Dorking convinced me that there were more than enough, above all three volumes of journal, but also other notebooks listing sermons preached, books read, expenses incurred. It is upon all of these, together with six bulky files of personal papers, that this life is primarily based. Two of the six files are marked 'Personal Letters' 'A–L' and 'M–Z', the other four are marked respectively 'Personal', 'Bristol', 'Ecumenical (Personal)' and 'Varia'. The last includes *The Ring of Light*. Other files contain selected sermons. Through extensive use of all of this I have endeavoured to give the book in some way the character of autobiography.

I have, however, also attempted to make of it what Oliver himself suggested in reference to Bliss, 'an illumination of the religious and social history of the period', in particular of the ecumenical movement, both internationally and in Britain, of which Oliver was for long a central figure. It has, in consequence, something of the nature of a group biography, the group of people who led the ecumenical movement up to the Uppsala Conference of 1968. To ensure a unifying theme other activities have, inevitably, been somewhat marginalized. One volume of limited size about a very long and full life must necessarily be selective. While sticking for the most part to the genre of history, rather than theology, I have tried to make of it a history of theological thought as well as of events and organizations and, furthermore, to reflect at various points, particularly in the final chapter, more theologically and in my own voice. How far was the enterprise which was so close to Oliver's heart to be accounted a failure and, if so, how far could that be related to specifically theological causes?

First and foremost, I owe a huge debt of gratitude to Ursula and her four children for the invitation to write Oliver's life, for entrusting me with his most personal papers, for being patient with the long delay in bringing the work to completion, for spending a fascinating weekend with me in Dorking in June 1996 to go together over the family's story, and for reading my typescript and making numerous suggestions. I have been greatly assisted by the two small books edited by Oliver's daughters: Monica Cleasby, *Oliver Tomkins by his Friends* (1995) and Oliver Tomkins, *Asking God: A Pocket Book of Intercessions*, edited by Deborah Page and Andrew Teal. I was also much helped by conversations with Trevor Page.

Numerous other people have much assisted me by recalling aspects of Oliver's life either through interview or by correspondence, as also by lending me papers. They include Lord Runcie, two close friends of Oliver's now dead, Bishop Lesslie Newbigin and Bishop Robin Woods, Bishop Patrick Rodger, Alan Webster, Michael Paton, Bob Jeffery, Henrietta Woods, Francis and Margaret House, Bishop Daniel Wilcox, Alfred Jowett, Eric Saxon, Peter Wills, Winifred Young, Anne Pakington, Mary Gill, Diana Gunn, Mary Tanner, Keith Clements, Ruth and Martin Reardon. I benefited from a group discussion at Sheffield chaired by Professor Clyde Binfield and another at Worcester with Joan Harcombe, Rosemary Stevens, Robert Loveless and Winifred Young. In Bristol I owe a very special debt to Bishop Barry Rogerson and Olga Rogerson for their hospitality and unlimited helpfulness, and also to their staff and the numerous people they arranged for me to see: Bishops Freddy Temple and Peter Firth, Jean Gray, Monsignor Joseph Buckley and Canons Edward Bailey, Dick Bennell, John Wilson, John Ware, Malcolm Widdecombe and George Mitchell. Francis House, Martin and Ruth Reardon, Alan Webster and Horace Dammers have read all or parts of the typescript and I have much benefited from their comments. If mistakes remain, I alone am responsible.

Besides the considerable collection of his papers which have stood on the shelves of my study in Leeds, I have made much use of further papers in Lambeth Palace Library, both ones already deposited there by Oliver and others in the Fisher, Ramsey and Groser Collections together with John Moorman's diaries, and am grateful for the help of Richard Palmer, Melanie Barber and the library staff. I have also made use of papers in Bishop's House, Bristol, in the Bristol Record Office, in the Hunter Collection in Sheffield City Archives, others in the SCM archives at Selly Oak, Birmingham, and again in the World Council of Churches archive in Geneva, as also in the Mott Collection at Yale Divinity School, New Haven, Connecticut. I am deeply grateful for much assistance in all these places.

I have tried to indicate sufficiently but not excessively the location of papers I quote or refer to through notes. Where there is no reference, a quotation comes normally either from Oliver's journal or from a letter in his personal collection held with the journals.

Finally, I owe a great debt to Susie Millard for typing and retyping the book as it progressed.

Bishop Oliver once remarked that an ounce of imagination was worth a ton of experience. The ton of experience on which this book is based should be clear enough – thousands of pages of archival material and numerous interviews. I can only hope that the ounce of imagination is there as well.

# 1

# Oliver Fellows Tomkins

In March 1873, the year David Livingstone died in Central Africa, Oliver Fellows Tomkins was born in Great Yarmouth, one of 11 children of Daniel Tomkins, a Congregationalist schoolmaster. Two were children of his first wife, Frances, and nine of his second, Carrie (Caroline Fellows), whom he married in 1869. Daniel represented *par excellence* the middle-class Nonconformity of the Gladstonian era at its most benevolent and successful. Descended from a Somerset farming family, he had settled in Yarmouth in 1847 on appointment as head of its 'British School'. Sixteen years later he opened his own school, Great Yarmouth College, a popular and well-run institution in which French was learnt from a 'Mademoiselle' and German from a 'Herr Professor', who also taught drawing and outdoor sketching. Music, the study of wild flowers and the art of good handwriting were among many other prominent features of the curriculum.

Daniel was deacon and secretary of the Congregational Church of Middlegate Street for 40 years as well as being Superintendent of its Sunday School and one of Norfolk's representatives on the Congregational Union of England and Wales. He also enthusiastically supported every other good cause that came his way, from the British and Foreign Bible Society and the British and Foreign Sailors Society to the Temperance Movement, on account of which he wore on his breast the blue ribbon of a teetotaller. He was no less active in politics than in religion. A staunch member of the Liberal Party, which he had found in Yarmouth in a pretty disorientated state, he set about its reorganization, becoming at different times both Secretary and President of the Yarmouth Liberal Association. When Gladstone visited the town, it was Tomkins who presented the congratulatory address. He was also the first Nonconformist to be elected to the Town Council and became both Chairman of the School Board and a JP. He was, indubitably, a man of substance. His library contained more than 5,000 volumes and his house was packed with oil paintings and watercolours, stuffed birds, antique furniture and old china.

Carrie, so far as one can tell, was Daniel's perfect partner. Besides mothering a large family and presiding over a still larger household, she headed a girls' school of her own from 1877, Sutherland House on the Marine Parade, run in conjunction with her husband's establishment and no less successful. She was also the author of various little books of devout poetry, *Hymns for Quiet Hours* and *Twilight Verses*. The life and home situation of the Tomkinses was kind, comfortable, cultured, even humorous, a very mellowed and rounded version of English Nonconformity at the peak of its political influence and numerical strength. Certainly the portrait of Daniel in old age, sitting with his collie dog in his flower garden, painted by a very young Alfred Munnings, is as assuredly pleasing as could be. Munnings had been recruited in his teens by Jack Tomkins, Daniel's son by his first marriage and managing director of the Norwich firm of Caley's Chocolates, to paint pictures to adorn the tops of chocolate boxes. This charming portrait of an old gentleman at rest would do that very well.

Successful as they were in this-worldly terms, Daniel and his wife were motivated throughout by the highest sense of religious, moral and social duty. One sees it not only in his mountain of ecclesiastical responsibilities, but, perhaps even better, in what people seemed to remember most about Daniel – his plainspokenness in a long fight against corruption in local government. And one sees it in what in the end mattered most to the heart of Carrie – the missionary movement in non-Christian lands. The late nineteenth century was an age notable for its missionary enthusiasm, fuelled by a steady flow of biographies of Evangelical heroes. There seemed no better way to be a Christian in the quickly expanding world of late Victorian imperialism than to preach the gospel in some far-off country. If that task was often conceived in the very simplest of terms, the gripping sense of urgency, a spiritual responsibility to share the message of salvation at whatever cost, is unmistakable.

Carrie Tomkins prayed every night for many years that one of her sons would be a missionary. She had done so ever since her firstborn had died in infancy. Her prayer seemed granted when Oliver, her eldest surviving child, volunteered to join the London Missionary Society, whose most famous member had been David Livingstone. Tall, strong, intelligent, notably gentle, with a frank, open face and pleasant voice, Oliver had, an admiring young cousin wrote many years later, 'the look of an athlete in the pink of condition'. He had once rescued a boy from drowning in the sea at Yarmouth. Undoubtedly, in deciding to be a missionary he had been influenced, like other young Evangelicals of his generation, by attendance at the annual Keswick Conventions. He was identifying with the spirit of a movement at the high tide of its public enthusiasm and yet it is no less to be noted that the number of missionary volunteers of his calibre, men especially, remained very far from excessive. O.F.T., as his family have come to call him, may not have been unusual in his ideals – they were common enough to his time and class – but he was unusual in the firm, yet unassuming, clarity with which he carried them through. 'I do not want to run in front or fall behind God's purpose for me,' he wrote very soberly while in training at Harley College. Apprenticed by his father as printer and bookbinder before going to Harley – for Daniel was firmly of the opinion that everyone should have a skilled craft – Oliver had a far less flamboyant Evangelicalism than the more upper-class Cambridge men, no less Keswick inspired, who did so much to create the image of the 1890s' English missionary. Once four years in college were completed, Ollie, as he was often called, was ordained at Princes Street Congregational Church in Norwich, where his parents had moved in retirement, and left for New Guinea in December 1899.

The list of new missionaries sent out that year by the LMS is as follows: Dr Ruth Massey and Miss Bateman for China, the Rev. W. Hatch, Dr Alice Hawker, Dr Ernest Lewis, Miss Stringfellow, Miss Barlow and Miss Hopewell for India, Miss Ella Sharp for Africa and the Rev. O. F. Tomkins for New Guinea. Seven women and three men. Three doctors, two clergymen and five teachers or nurses, they hardly represented any very vast response to the challenge of a new century and a world lying more open to the West and to the Christian message than it had ever been.

New Guinea was still an unusual destination for a missionary and Oliver was going to join a very unusual man. James Chalmers was second only to David Livingstone in the pantheon of nineteenth-century Protestant missionary heroes. He had left Scotland for the Polynesian island of Rarotonga with his first wife in 1866. Eleven years later he was moved to New Guinea whose coastal cannibals he began to evangelize with the aid of Rarotongan teachers. His first wife, Jane, died in 1879 and in 1888 he married again, Lizzie Harrison. Each was worn out by the spartan life and exuberant energy of a strangely magnetic, tyrannical, volcanic husband. He was a mix of ceaseless and quite homely devotion to the people he evangelized and a flamboyant self-confidence which could appear both egoistic and dismissive of others – Europeans especially. To his people he had a special name, 'Tamate'.

> If I went to the natives and said, 'Who is the king?', remarked Dr Doyle Glanville much later, 'Tamate' was the reply. If I said to them 'Who is like a father unto you?', they would say 'Tamate'. If I said, 'What is maino (peace)?', they would say 'Tamate'.

In a world of constantly warring cannibalistic groups 'making peace between the tribes' was, Chalmers himself insisted, one of the best ways to 'preach the gospel'.

If Chalmers was a quintessentially early- or mid-Victorian missionary character, the self-made, charismatic, working-class, whisky-swigging adventurer who enchanted Robert Louis Stevenson and could infuriate more recently arrived colonial officials, Tomkins personified instead the late-Victorian missionary ideal, middle-class, more professionally trained, no less interiorly confident but definitely less colourful. Temperance was now very much part of the package. Yet they got on very well together. Tamate was ageing and tired. Never before had he had an assistant and Tomkins was both competent and eminently respectful. 'He will do, send us two more of the same sort', Chalmers wrote home three days after Oliver's arrival. Mrs Chalmers found this very proper young man 'a bit too straight-laced'. She had, after all, confided to a friend a couple of years earlier that she and Tamate were 'not at all like sober middle-aged folk should be'. But she was in fact increasingly ill, worn down by the strains of climate and daily life at Saguane. She had only returned to New Guinea in August 1897 after five years in Britain. Tomkins joined them there in February 1900. While he found the language extremely difficult and had none of Tamate's outgoing ebullience, he could help Mrs Chalmers in the school when her husband was away on his constant field-trips with little but a 'toothbrush, pyjamas, hair-brushes' and a walking-stick. Oliver wrote regularly home in his meticulous copperplate handwriting, stressing, to reassure his family, the ordinariness of his existence. In July he even sent a nice letter from his New Guinea dog Tip to his parents' dog at home, named Trimmer. 'My master often tells me about you and says I am something like you… when my master can take photos at all decently I will send you one of myself.' The last thing that Oliver wanted to suggest about his life was the heroic or the exotic. Saguane, he implied, was not really so different from Norwich. Three months later Mrs Chalmers died, leaving a tired and at times discouraged Tamate alone with Tomkins for the last months of ministry together – the failing prophet and 'son Timothy' as he liked to describe this exceptionally loyal young man whom he recognized as now quite indispensable, a blessing 'as if sent direct by God'.

On 3 April 1901 Chalmers wrote to a friend, 'We leave tomorrow for the east, as far as Cape Blackwood and expect to be away a fortnight.' The next day they sailed in the mission boat, Tamate and Tomkins, nine mission students, Navagi, the chief of Ipisia, and Jimmy Walker, a mixed-race mission employee. They were going into an area known for its unfriendliness, nowhere more so than the island of Goaribayi, where they arrived on Easter Sunday, 7 April. Oliver wrote a long entry in his diary that night:

> We had been sailing in the open sea since Good Friday morning and this afternoon we drew towards our destination viz Risk Point (we anchored at 3 o'clock in a fine harbour and we're just having a short service with the

crew). This district has only been visited once before, and that was 5 years ago when the Government steamer came here and tried to civilize the native by the gentle persuasion of the rifle. So we did not know what sort of a reception we might get...Before the service was over several canoes appeared in the distance coming towards us. They were all small canoes, some with only one man, others with three or four. As they came nearer the wonder was how they balanced themselves standing up in less than half of the trunk of a tree hollowed out and no outriggers to keep them steady. By this time there must have been twenty or more. They hesitated as they got nearer to us, till we were able to assure them that we meant peace. Gradually one or two of the daring ones came closer and then alongside till at last one ventured on board. Then in a very few minutes we were surrounded by canoes and the vessel was covered with natives. One of my earliest impressions of missionary work was gathered from a picture of the missionary jumping ashore with a book presumably the Bible in his hand from which, the picture leads one to suppose, he is forthwith going to instruct the natives who are to be seen crowding round. I have wondered since, if this depicts the missionary's first visit to some heathen tribe, and if so in what language the Bible is written and how the translation was obtained. On this our first visit we were able to do really nothing more than establish friendly relations with the people. They stayed on board about three hours examining everything from the ship's rigging to our shirtbuttons.

They tried hard to persuade us to come ashore in their canoes, but we preferred to spend the night afloat and promised we would visit their village in the morning.

It was the only entry of any length in Oliver's diary. Its comments may suggest a missionary greenhorn, yet the length and care of the entry may also hint at an underlying unease and the intention to provide a record of the visit up to that point, whatever should happen next.

They went ashore the following morning. Tamate had tried to persuade Oliver not to come with him and they had quite an argument until Oliver got into the boat with the words, 'If you go, I go. If you stay on board, I stay on board.' They landed together. So far as is known they were clubbed to death a few minutes later and then they were eaten.[1] Before he had left England there had been rather a lot of jokes about Oliver and the cannibals. The missionary *Home Magazine*'s journalist had an interview with him and was able to report:

After shaking hands with him, I said: 'Well, you are going out amongst the cannibals.' 'Yes,' he replied; 'at least to the few that are left.' I could not help remarking, in a jocular way, as I looked at his jolly English face and honest blue eyes, 'I hope you will be somewhat wasted before you get out there, for I am afraid the cannibals will think you are a very tasty dish!'

Comedy had turned too quickly to tragedy, but it could not be seen as a matter of tragedy and no more. It cried out indeed for theological interpretation. How could the devout commentator not find in it an almost redemptive meaning? 'They were clubbed and *eaten*. In this way they were allowed to give their flesh, like the Master, for the life of the world.' Or, again, to quote words from the London Missionary Society itself, Oliver had been called in 'a chariot of fire' to the Master's presence in Heaven. Killed in all the innocence and unalloyed enthusiasm of youth and health, he could become henceforth a sort of patron saint of Evangelical mission. Fifty years later one of the children playing amid that cannibal feast was a deacon of the Congregationalist Church.[2]

Glorious as it may sound in retrospect, what had happened could not but be shattering for the Tomkins family. He had been at work for hardly more than 12 months. Saguane was not like Norwich after all. His father was dying, his mother nearly overwhelmed, nearly but not quite. 'My dearest Leo,' she wrote to her second son on 22 April. 'So it seems our dear Oliver has gone home – got a martyr's crown. It seems as if I could not believe it... I know it is *well* but so mysterious... Best love, dear old boy.' O.F.T. would remain for the family a sort of marker for shared idealism, someone of whom they could be unequivocally proud – a gentleman and a martyr – but, with time, someone they could smile about too. Singing the hymn 'Oft in danger, Oft in woe' became an inherited expression of this feeling, a family joke with a secret double meaning they could enjoy sharing. For others too the story of the missionary eaten by cannibals had become, in the drawing rooms of Edwardian civilization, something of amusement. In Chesterton's mocking lines:

> He gave, if not the gospel-feast,
> At least a ritual meal,
> And in a highly painful sense
> He was devoured with zeal.[3]

There was a perennial joke in the theme not suppressible by the reality. Leo had a particularly lively sense of humour, so, perhaps, even he would come with time to smile at it. The immediate effect of his brother's death was, however, simply to confirm his own missionary commitment. Two years later, 1903, he was already on his way to a mission in China, by sea to Shanghai and then overland to Hangchow. When, in 1908, his son was born in Hangchow, he was inevitably named after his murdered uncle, Oliver Tomkins.

# 2

# From China to Cambridge

One day in the autumn of 1889, Leo Tomkins, then a schoolboy of 15, received a letter from his elder brother who was studying at the time in Switzerland. 'I think mother told you some time ago that since I have been here I have been saved. It is about that that I want to write just a few words. Mother and I have been praying for you ever since that God will open your eyes to see what a great salvation he has prepared for all of us... Do not be afraid to tell dear Mother all about it.' It seems a quaintly simple model of 'salvation', yet one conforming entirely to conventional Evangelicalism and it would have been hard for Leo not to respond affirmatively. A little later he was able to write back to Oliver to assure him that 'This afternoon Mother spoke to me about it and then we knelt down and I saw that I need only to come to Christ and simply trust Him. Do go on praying for me that I may not go back from Jesus.' Already in this early letter one gets a sense of what Leo was like. A shade less self-confident than Oliver. Slight in build, gentle, thoughtful, easily amused, then and for long he would follow dutifully the road his mother and brother had traced for him. His father had, however, insisted that he complete an apprenticeship as an engineer before doing anything else, and he was indentured in March 1891 for four years until he reached the age of 21 and was employed in two iron works. Only after that could he turn to acquire a London BA and to study for the ministry. He was already at the Congregationalist College at Cheshunt when the news of his brother's death arrived. He immediately offered to the London Missionary Society to replace Oliver in New Guinea once he was ordained. They chose instead to send him to China, to the great inland city of Hangchow.

Leo, like his brother, was ordained in Prince's Street Church in Norwich, declaring in the service that 'he was going forth in a spirit of sympathy, believing that God had partly revealed his truth by heathen religions, but had made his full revelation in Christ'. That was a surprisingly liberal declaration of faith for a young evangelical missionary in 1903. He arrived in Hangchow late that year and was soon busy learning the language, supervising more than 30 'out-stations', some of them in large towns, acting as superintendent too of the workmen engaged in mission-building projects and struggling to get over typhoid – all the dreary, down-to-earth complexities inseparable from missionary existence. He was also able to marry. He had met Katey Stratford while studying at Cheshunt. She ran a local post office, took care of her mother and attended missionary gatherings. In 1906 she wrote to tell him that her mother had now died. 'Come and marry me,' he replied. Two months later she arrived in China and they were married with all the solemnity English society could provide in the cathedral of Shanghai that December. Seven years older than Leo, Katey was clearly a woman with considerable determination. She had little education, but plenty of romantic vision. Like many a Victorian of simple religious convictions, she imagined the non-Christian world would soon be on fire in response to the preaching of missionaries.

Perhaps even Leo had once thought it might be like that. 'The Evangelization of the world in this generation' – the Evangelical watchword of that age – seemed a wonderfully large challenge to young people of Christian faith in the opening years of the century. The reality of the work once you reached your appointed destination could be very different. What strikes one from the records is the sheer apparent insignificance of so much of the activity of a mission in inland China among small groups of very unimportant but frequently quarrelsome people about whom one understood very little, the tiniest minority within the great towns of inland China. It could become so much a matter of keeping the peace among one's converts, reconciling quarrelsome preachers, Mr Hu with Mr Hsu. All in all it must have been hard to keep one's spirits up, far away from any major centre of achievement. Nevertheless, from the historian's vantage point, and a realization of how extensive and deep-rooted the Chinese churches have become meantime, despite 50 years of Communist counter-attack, it is possible to evaluate the apparently pretty ineffectual struggles of the evangelists of a century ago far more positively than, at the time, may have seemed plausible to anyone other than the committed.

Oliver was born in Hangchow on 9 June 1908, his sister Sibyl two years later at Hwang-Pi, to which her parents had by then moved. Katey was ill from dysentery at the time and she never fully recovered from the accumulated ill-health of those years. Their address was now simply 'London Mission, Hwang-Pi'. It was London, capital of the world's principal imperialist power, that identified them. But in 1911, with the collapse of the Imperial government and the advance of the Republican Army all British people were advised to leave and British missionaries followed the advice of the British Government as much as anyone else. It was, perhaps, with a certain relief that at dawn one morning the Tomkins family hurriedly boarded a boat at Hwang-Pi and set out for Hangchow, Shanghai and England. The memory of it which survived, however, was the story of how, as they went to the boat, three-year-old Oliver was nowhere to be found. They hurried home to discover that he had quietly returned there to finish his breakfast.

The feeling of relief Katey felt already at Hangchow when she saw the Union Jack flying above the British Consulate was understandable enough, but both the feeling and the flag were expressive of that still very colonial age of missionary endeavour. The missionary romance had, for her at least, been transformed only too rapidly into a certain revulsion with the incomprehensible reality of China, a mix of disdainful superiority and contemporary confusion. Back in England in 1911 the high hopes with which Leo had left in 1903 and Katey in 1906 had clearly not been fulfilled. However, 1910 was, in the mythical version of mission history, a moment of elation, a strategic high point when the great International Missionary Conference in Edinburgh both formulated further programmes of action across the world and set in motion the whole ecumenical movement of the twentieth century: the pursuit of unity, it would be claimed, derived from the experience of mission. It was true in a way and Oliver's own life with its missionary roots and ecumenical branches and fruits might be used, a half-century later, to illustrate the saga effectively enough. But the immediate reality for the Edwardian missionary foot-soldier could be vastly depressing. It is hard not to think that for the Tomkins family, arriving back in England the year after the Edinburgh Conference with Katey in poor health, the few possessions they had managed to pack left somewhere in a trunk which would only arrive years later, an apparently ineffective missionary life behind them and no very obvious future ahead, what was uppermost quite frequently was a sense not of elation but of depression. What kept them just on top of things was Leo's quiet sanity and exceptionally strong sense of humour, together with their great devotion to one another.

Could they ever return? Leo at least probably wanted to. He had learnt a lot of Chinese. Why not build on that by pursuing the study of the language academically?

They went to Cambridge and he studied for the Tripos, the very first person actually to take the degree in Chinese. However, in the summer of 1913 he resigned from the LMS. Katey's poor health made a return to China unrealistic and, instead, they moved to Fowlmere, a village just to the south of Cambridge where he became minister in an old Congregationalist pocket of countryside. The local squires, heirs, maybe, to a long Cromwellian tradition, were still Nonconformists. So at five Oliver became a country boy, attending a Dame school, Carlton House, Melbourn, in the neighbouring village and learning to ride both a bicycle (his own) and a pony (that of his friend, the farmer's son). A year later and the Great War had begun. Some time in its latter part the Fowlmere ministry ended when Leo went to France to help with the YMCA and to act both as Welfare Officer for the Chinese Labour Force and as censor for its letters, surely one of the odder occupations in the great unsettlement. Oliver was dispatched for a while to his uncle's prep school in Yarmouth.

When the war was over, Leo came back from France bringing with him another final large shift in the family predicament and one which would prove of quite decisive importance in the life of his son. Though the child of such staunch Nonconformists as Daniel and Caroline Tomkins, he had decided to enter the Church of England. Apparently it was the conduct of Anglican chaplains at the front which had so impressed him into deciding that he would like to join them. This may hardly seem of itself a very adequate explanation for conversion from Congregationalism to the Established Church. But Leo had been changing with the years. His initial calling, like that of his brother, had been to a missionary apostolate in some other continent. Congregationalism hardly entered into it. Moreover, China and France between them had brought about a quiet widening of vision to make the old entrenched divide between Dissent and the C of E seem insignificant. Perhaps it was itself a case of missionary experience producing a new evaluation of unity. Why should Protestant Christians remain divided? Congregationalism, once one of the great strengths of Victorian England, was almost everywhere in steep decline; it is noticeable how many Free Church people moved to Anglicanism in the 1920s and 1930s. Leo was a Protestant and remained a decidedly Protestant Anglican, his core religion being what Oliver much later described as a 'generous liberal Evangelicalism'. Crossing the divide into the Established Church may not have seemed half as significant to him by 1919 as it would have appeared to his father. He spent a year of training at Westcott House, a theological college in Cambridge, and was ordained once more, this time episcopally. In 1920 he became a curate in Sheffield.

Oliver's remembered life really began with residence at the Manse in Fowlmere. From China, where he had been only three and a half when they left, little survived in his mind: an impression of his baby sister sitting on a verandah step, an impression of himself wearing a topee and stumping around the garden with a long bamboo, 'hunting lions', an impression of Chinese faces over a garden wall beckoning him to join them. Like his uncle he was nicknamed 'Ollie' by his parents. Chinese servants turned it into 'Holi' (pronounced 'Hawley') and 'Holi' his parents called him ever after –'My darling Holi boy'. That was his principal Chinese legacy, that and the trunk which after some years of travelling eventually arrived at Fowlmere. He retained it till his death, still marked 'TOMKINS HANKOW CHINA'. It contained all that survived materially of his parents' China years – egg-shell thin tea cups and two big peacock-blue vases, a pen-vase with a curly dragon, a mother-of-pearl and black clay tray, a wedding presentation scroll of white silk and red Chinese letters, some Chinese pictorial versions of the parables, the Prodigal Son and his swine, some albums of photographs. It was just enough to maintain the sense of a Chinese background, for Oliver and Sibyl, the feeling that they were indeed the children of a missionary marriage.

Detailed memories, however, began with English country life – the harvesting of Hundred Acre Field and the clubbing of rabbits which went with it, the fascination of watching the village blacksmith forging a horse-shoe, learning, with his father's help, to ride a bicycle, and the kindly habit of Mr Johns, the elderly squire of Fowlmere, who provided visiting small boys with a putter and golf ball with instructions to see how far away from the house they could drive the ball.

The Tomkins family spent only two and a half years at Fowlmere. They remained almost certainly by far the happiest years of Oliver's childhood, indeed the only at all settled years, and in retrospect they seemed far longer than they were. If they ended when he was still only eight, they had been sufficient to provide something of the magic of childhood and to act as a counter to the otherwise shifting, unsettled existence produced by their return as homeless refugees from China, the requirements of war and of his father's two periods of study in Cambridge. His mother's ill-health and a shortage of cash were, however, the really permanent features of his childhood and they impressed on Oliver an underlying sense of insecurity, a tendency to worry, hidden anxieties about health and income, from which in life he would never entirely escape.

Formal education started at Cambridge in the autumn term of 1913 at the Perse Preparatory School. Oliver was just five. There were six boys in the class and Oliver came third, though their average age was almost a year more than his. His first term report was good, his 'general progress' was said to be 'rapid', his writing improving. He had been late for school 45 times. By the spring term his late arrivals were down to ten and, while when he was just five it could only be said in regard to Geography that 'he does his best', by the time he was five and a half he was reported to 'show great interest', and his arithmetic was 'good for his age'. He then moved to Carlton House and by Christmas 1914 he had made 'a very good start' in dancing while his crochet work was 'very fair'. However, after only one term at Carlton, he moved again, this time for two and a half years of boarding at his Uncle Billy's school in Great Yarmouth, where he began in January 1915. Only his writing now seemed unsatisfactory. The Carlton House mistress had reported it to be 'very slow', at Yarmouth it was simply 'bad'. By the summer of 1917, however, he was once more in Cambridge and back at the Perse, aged still only nine. Perhaps he had slipped a bit with these comings and goings for he was now put in a class whose average age was well below his own. The General Report of his work and conduct was, as ever, 'good on the whole', though as to knitting it was remarked that he 'talked too much to do good work'. By the time he left the Perse Preparatory School in the summer of 1919, aged just 11, he had reached third place in a class of 23, his writing was 'very much improved', he had done 'excellent work' in drawing and the arithmetic was getting better. He then transferred for a final Cambridge term to the main Perse School where his form master found him 'too dreamy'. History, reading aloud and French seem from these early school reports to be the areas in which he most consistently shone.

In 1920 Leo moved to a curacy in Sheffield and Oliver to a boarding school in Worksop, St Cuthbert's. One year later, in September 1921, aged 13, he began his secondary education at Trent College, just outside Nottingham. He was to remain there for six years, just as his parents were to remain in Sheffield, only a few miles away. Here at last was stability in sharp contrast to the changes and uncertainties which had overshadowed life ever since they had fled ten years before from Hwang-Pi and the army of the revolution.

Trent College stood close to the River Trent in Derbyshire. It had been founded by a group of local low-church gentry in the 1860s as a thoroughly C of E and Protestant school in evident reaction to the Tractarian character of the Woodard Schools which were arising at that time. Trent would instil the spirit of the 'Old Church of England', devoid of modern Anglo-Catholic tendencies but not too emphatically Evangelical either. It was also intended to be cheap. Unendowed, it had depended greatly on its founding fathers and when they passed away it was in some danger of collapse, with large debts, few amenities and a declining number of boys. From that fate it was saved by a new head-master appointed in 1895 at the age of 27. John Savile Tucker retired 32 years later, in 1927, a man who must 'rank among the great Headmasters', Tarver, the historian of Trent, concluded. He saved, enlarged and reworked the school, a man who never spared himself and was frequently on the verge of a nervous breakdown, single-minded in the determination to root out 'indiscipline and evil'. He was, Tarver commented, 'a grand commander in an emergency but a bit of a nuisance in the piping times of peace'. Oliver had him as headmaster throughout his years at Trent, Tucker's final period.

> Oh! It's not the nerve or sinew,
>    Or learning's store alone,
> That Trent upon her sons bestows,
>    Which stamps them for her own.
> 'Tis manhood's gleam in boyish eyes,
>    Steadfast and true and keen.
> The heart that never quailed at need
>    The soul that ne'er was mean.
>       Live for ever, falter never,
>       Live for ever, Trent!

The Trent school song had to be learnt by heart by every new boy and was sung on all appropriate occasions. And it was not, by any means, the only Trent song. There were songs for all special activities, like Sunday Walks, Paper Chases and the Cadet Corps. The latter began as follows:

> We've been hard at work all day,
> But we've not come out to play,
> But to learn to fight for England and the King...

While such songs date from the beginning of the century, they were still part of the stock of school life in the 1920s. Trent was certainly strong on Tory values, on games, on the Officer Training Corps, in which Oliver was a sergeant, but it found time for other less predictable things as well, like long country walks and gardening. Here the Rev. G. J. S. Warner was chiefly responsible. He had joined the Trent staff in 1907 and was there throughout Oliver's time. Natural history, snakes, bugling, digging a complex labyrinth of trenches during the war for the OTC to practise in, planting trees, even constructing temporary bridges across the River Trent – these were the varied passions he succeeded in sharing with generations of boys. The great August school walks to Land's End and John O'Groats had taken place well before Oliver's arrival but long tramps, camps at Eastnor or on Exmoor and the planting of trees remained the Warner enthusiasms of the 1920s. For Oliver he always remained 'Daddy Warner'.

At Trent and in his father's Sheffield parish Oliver imbibed his lifelong Anglicanism, an Anglicanism of middle England, middle-class, middle church, even geographically middle, and educationally middling too, respectable enough, somewhat undistinguished, yet still including occasionally a slightly mad gleam in Mr Warner's eye.

Six years is a long time to be at one boarding school and Oliver was 19 when he left Trent. Even then he did not quite leave. He had failed to secure the Oxford scholarship for which he had been working. Unfortunately he also failed the Higher Certificate. In consequence he went to teach for a year (1927–28) at Bramcote Hall, Trent's Prep School, just five miles away.

Trent suited Oliver well enough or he would hardly have been willing to spend the extra year at Bramcote, but its stimulus, at least in its upper forms, seems painfully limited. He enjoyed reading Chesterton, Masefield, Shaw and Wells – all popular but not too demanding writers of the time. He started to write himself and enjoyed signing his pieces backwards – REVILO SNIKMOT.[1] He joined in the normal range of school activities, became a prefect, even Head of School in his final year, so he must have personified what Tucker's Trent wanted of Tridents well enough. Yet he could still view this little world of minor privilege and invented tradition which he had inhabited so long with an amused but critical eye. Of Tucker he could report that 'The Old Man is going on as strongly and as inexplicably as ever' – he had just succeeded in linking cricket with Whitsun – of Tarver, his Form Master, that he 'still comes into chapel punctually five minutes late, his gown still in the small of his back'. The Trent ethos had more to do with 'The Public School Spirit' than with Christ, he came to feel after the heady experience of his first Student Christian Movement Conference at Swanwick in his final summer term. A year earlier he had written home, 'I realise more and more what it is costing and has cost you both to keep a son who is merely being turned into a "gentleman" at very great expense, imbibing tradition, conservatism, and prejudice and enjoying all the other advantages of a Public School Education.' Remarks like this should, obviously, not be overplayed. Passing observations in letters home could be phrased a little daringly but with tongue in cheek as well. Oliver enjoyed Trent and the leadership role it offered him. He surely sang 'Live for ever, falter never, Live for ever Trent' over and over again with gusto, conviction and just a slight smile. After leaving school he long remained an active and loyal Trident, attending school reunions and Trident gatherings in Cambridge. Never in life would he display an unkindly critical response towards institutions to which he belonged. It was not part of his nature, yet it is difficult to feel convinced that the 'very great expense' was worth it for a poor parish priest, though in the eyes of his parents anything spent on their son, on whom they and his sister increasingly doted, was well worthwhile.

One must wonder too about the Trent tuition which proved inadequate both for Oxford entrance and the Higher Certificate – especially on the Latin side. It necessitated the additional year at Bramcote working on the required Latin texts. It may well be that a highly conscientious fulfilling of his duties as Head of School had affected his studies. Anyway the next year it was all right. He travelled up from Bramcote to Christ's College, Cambridge, thoroughly prepared to pass the entrance examination and could write home before he sat it: 'I'm not fretting about this exam. I've been through the darn book four times, I've done 13 unseens from it, and I know Ovid's life backwards. I can open it at random and translate any 10 lines anywhere. If I don't pass, I shall chuck scholasticism and take to duck farming.' That hardly commends either college entrance requirements or Oliver's vision of 'scholasticism', but Christ's offered him a place and the ducks were left to themselves.

As in many another small boarding prep school, the experience of a young man on the staff at Bramcote proved a depressing one. Evelyn Waugh's *Decline and Fall* was published that very year. How much Bramcote had in common with the preposterous prep school there described we cannot know but Oliver undoubtedly found it both morally and intellectually dreary: 'No depth, no kind laughter, so many sneers, so much cheap wit, so much futility – but thank God for the boys.' And he did enjoy having a room of his own. 'When my Latin lines have been polished off earlier in the day, I love to go upstairs after dinner, and undress, and put on my warm silk dressing gown and jazz pyjamas, and with my feet on the mantelpiece, a cup of tea, a pipe, a good book, to read or talk myself sleepy, then tumble straight into bed.'

The other side of life throughout these years was holidays in Sheffield. We hear little about them but one image kept coming back in later years. The parish of St Stephen's, to which Leo was appointed in 1925 after five years of curacy in a more middle-class area, included rows and rows of grimy back-to-backs in sordid streets called Daisy Bank and Mushroom Lane, all long ago pulled down. Here Oliver, as he later recalled:

> saw –and smelt – poverty and disease and felt the Church as somehow rele-
> vant. I remember, as an older school-boy, wanting to share my father's job,
> visiting a dying woman in an ill-lit room. As I entered the door, I was
> puzzled that her face should be covered with a black handkerchief; but
> when I came near the handkerchief got up and flew away in the angry buzz
> of a hundred flies.

That seems to have been one of only two truly memorable experiences of this lengthy period. The other was attendance at the SCM (Student Christian Movement) conference at Swanwick in Derbyshire, just a few miles away from Trent, and listening there to a leading Evangelical, Edward Woods. Woods had been Vicar of Holy Trinity at Cambridge, a friend and patron of Leo's, and Oliver had been taken to listen to his sermons as a small boy. A typical Cambridge Evangelical, comfortably upper class and married into the banking family of the Barclays, Woods was an SCM man all his life, one of the many who nearly became a missionary overseas, but not quite. Immensely kind and lovable, father of a large family, always, it was said, 'on the side of the angels', passion-ately devoted to the Boat Race, the Inter-Varsity Hockey Match, and grouse shooting, Woods generated an optimistic, uncritical confidence in the truth of Christianity and the essential soundness of a world presided over by the British Establishment. Enthusiastic and liberal-spirited but definitely Protestant, he was just the person to inspire an adoles-cent Oliver, desperately loyal to his parents but still in need of a new vision, and he did just that. Woods was an activist in the Faith and Order wing of the ecumenical movement, one of the only Anglican bishops at the time with real enthusiasm for what was then still a young movement. It proved for Oliver the moment of conversion to a lifelong passion. 'My own personal commitment to the cause of Unity,' he wrote much later, 'came I suppose when as a schoolboy I heard Edward Woods, by then Bishop of Croydon and a hero of my youth, speaking with infectious enthusiasm and hope about the conference on Faith and Order at Lausanne (1927).' Oliver never forgot this debt and when Woods died, now Bishop of Lichfield, he was persuaded by the Woods family to write his life, a diffi-cult thing to do acceptably as in many ways he had passed well beyond the Woods approach. He did it reverently, a little reticently, still profoundly loyal to the appeal of the inspirer of his youth.

By the time he left school, Oliver felt fairly sure that he wanted to be, like his father, a parson within the Church of England, but he had thus, and almost at the same moment, been infected too with the pursuit of Christian unity. About neither of them had he actually thought very hard. In a way, then, the course of his future life was already set – at once Anglican and ecumenical – and it seems to have been derived, almost too easily, from loyalty to his father and to the circle his father encouraged him to enter. Yet it was also true that Trent itself had largely failed to broaden his horizons and that, for a quite intelligent young man of 20, he appears intellectually under-developed. Certainly it was Cambridge, rather than school, which furnished his mind with a sense of the sort of world he would ever after inhabit, but for Oliver there was no significant shift of direction as he moved from the one to the other. He went up to Christ's College in September 1928.

He was provided with rooms in Jesus Lane, not far from Christ's but a good deal cheaper than living in college. Money was a great preoccupation. His parents had next to none. Leo, well over 50, had only just been given a parish of his own and in a very poor district of Sheffield. They had no way of increasing their income other than through letting rooms in the vicarage but they seemed unable to succeed even in this and the unlet rooms became a recurring subject in Oliver's letters home. The problem was undoubtedly exacerbated by his mother's poor health. An anonymous 'Sponsor' provided £55, there was a college scholarship for £50 and the diocese of Chelmsford (to which he had committed himself) was also contributing something. A first letter home from Cambridge sets the note of financial stringency clearly enough:

> I've bought a cap and gown and surplice! The former two I've actually worn. I got them second hand too. Among the twenty-three circulars waiting for me in my rooms when I arrived were 11 from tailors who wanted to sell me these at prices varying from 27/6 to 22/6 and square 7/6, and surplices from 11/6 to 13/6, but I got a very decent gown, not at all disreputable really, for 7/6 and a square which is the shape to start with that mine would have been in a week, for a bob. My surplice though cost 5/-, but I suppose it's as good as new. So there's the whole outfit for 13/6, the price of a surplice.

If he gained on these, he lamented that he was going to have to pay no less than 7/6 a term to garage his bicycle; furthermore it had already cost him 3/6 to bring it on the train from Sheffield. A relative had sent him five pounds which he wanted to put towards the £7-17-6 needed to become a life member of the Union. He felt this a good idea but still needed to ask his parents: 'Write and tell me if you think that would be justifiable.' He much enjoyed seeing Shaw's *St Joan* at the Festival Theatre. He got a 2/4 ticket for the first night with a rather poor seat where he could all the same see 'the greater part of the play'. He enthused on both the play and the acting. 'It *is* a good play – Shaw's best, I always feel, though its presentation depends an awful lot on the part of St Joan. Have you ever read it? You really must do so if you haven't.' The brittle superiority of a Cambridge 20-year-old undergraduate writing a little patronizingly home to his 50-year-old parents is very much there in such remarks, to be followed in a subsequent letter by the details of his weekly bill – the shilling for two baths, the extra 9d now being charged for breakfast, the 1/6 for crested postcards. 'That visit to the Festival Theatre was a piece of blatant extravagance I shan't repeat yet awhile.' Financial considerations involved moralizing too:

> I do feel grateful to God and all those He has made so unselfish and generous to enable me to come here. Believe me, I do understand a bit the

struggle that it has been for you to have had me so well educated so far, and now we must try and kill utterly that sin of Satan's -- pride – and be honestly thankful to any who are in a position to enter with us into an agreement even though their side is wholly financial. Honest gratitude and humility sincerely applied can discharge any debt of money that we so sneeringly call 'charity'.

Clearly, a sense of 'the fact of poverty' was something Oliver felt acutely in these years and his parents may have felt it even more. Its impact on his mind was never wholly overcome, though when, in 1930, his father was offered a living in London, the pressure was considerably lightened.

It did not, anyway, impede him from sharing in the round appropriate to a Cambridge student. The first thing, undoubtedly, was rowing. 'I'm a rowing man', he was soon able to report home. Enthusiastic Evangelicals generally were. 'Rowing men', he told his parents, 'are considered the salt of the earth, nice fellows to know and it's a grand sport – so I joined.' However, at first he 'did everything wrong', yet his coach, a member of the College Crew, 'didn't even laugh at my crabs. If he is typical of the rowing spirit, I shall like it.' By mid-October he could report that the coach remarked 'a great deal better than yesterday, Number Four, a great deal better', and Oliver had himself come to feel that 'there's a thrill in thrashing through the water that you don't get on the track or in any ball game'. College races were soon beginning: 'Must go to the boathouse now', the next letter concluded apart from the postscript, 'No 2 caught a crab and couldn't get his oar out again for 10 strokes so we lost by two strokes... Thank goodness I'm not 2.' This sort of thing did not last; Oliver's spirit was too profoundly uncompetitive. But he enjoyed undergraduate life, liked parties, made plenty of friends, among them a rather good musician and cartoonist, the future correspondent from America, Alistair Cooke.

One Sunday afternoon early in his first term at Christ's, Oliver was invited with three other freshmen to lunch with the Master. He had, understandably enough, looked forward to it with some trepidation. Instead it turned out well. The Master remembered his father and mother. It was impressive to lunch in a room built in 1504, to enjoy the oak-raftered ceiling and moulded panelling, the beautiful furniture, but it was the walk after lunch around the Fellows' and Master's Gardens which affected him most and his account of an autumnal garden is worth the reading.

> [It was] beautifully tinted now. Slightly neglected in appearance (no gardener could compete with the endless drift of leaves) both gardens had that air of having lived and died and lived again in undisturbed serenity, so independent, and yet always suggesting past rather than present care, that no garden, whose four walls had seen no changes but nature's in hundreds of years, could help feeling. When we slipped through the yew hedges to look at the tranquil bathing pool, with stone busts at one end gazing with boredom at the neglected seventeenth-century summer house at the other, or down at the thousands of leaves floating on top or drowned at the bottom of the pool, I felt that we were the first people to steal there since Milton, gazing into the water, contrasted the lot of the thoughtful and the cheerful man; or, just possibly, Darwin, copying a tadpole or waterboatman, recognised a near relation. October I think is the only month that could give that impression.

Here already is the imaginative eye of a poet, good with words even in a letter to his parents, and fond of interpreting the visual present through historical allusion to detect therein some underlying meaning.

At this stage we hear little of the more studious side to life. It was natural for a future priest to study theology and Oliver had just received from the great Albert Schweitzer the present of a book inscribed 'Oliver Tomkins, a young theologian, from Albert Schweitzer, an old theologian'. Yet he actually felt more interest in history, which he liked and was good at. Even before coming up this problem had been sorted out with the help of a college adviser: take Part I history in two years, then a part of the Theology Tripos for another two years, to be followed by one year in theological college. By so doing, in his adviser's view, he would steer 'a middle course between the futility of reading history for three years and then starting at zero for two years at a theological college and the appalling possession of a theological mind (the outcome of doing all theology) which mistakes small things for great and means for ends'. Oliver's undergraduate mix of history and theology was certainly reflected throughout his life. Perhaps it meant that he missed the academic mastery of either subject but whether he would later have agreed that the 'theological mind' is indeed 'appalling' in mistaking 'small things for great and means for ends', one does not know. Maybe in his heart of hearts he would always have concurred.

It is difficult to gauge the progress of a mind and, most certainly, Oliver was anything but bent on acquiring a 'theological mind'. He mentions early essays on the unemployment problem and the organization of English trade in the fourteenth and fifteenth centuries, but almost the only surviving evidence of his academic ability as a student is a none too convincing one, a paper read to an undergraduate society in March 1932 – his fourth year at Cambridge – in which he begins by saying that it is to be 'about Barthianism' but having 'dropped that bombshell' goes on at once to admit that he knows nothing of Barth and has never read a book of his. Most of the paper Oliver later threw away so we do not know in what its central argument consisted. In retrospect he thought that only beginning and end deserved to survive, which does not say much for the rest. Here and elsewhere one senses an intellectual slackness, a deep psychological reluctance to take academic matters too seriously. 'For a whole year,' he wrote in old age, 'a small group of us construed the Greek New Testament to a don in his dotage with the English text on our knees under the table.' The Cambridge theology of the time he found minutely analytical: 'Every drop of doctrinal pond-water,' he wrote, 'swarmed with unsuspected microbes.' He found it impossible to be enthralled. Only Clement Hoskyns taught his students to use, not only 'a critical microscope', but a 'telescope as well'. Sir Edwyn Clement Hoskyns was Dean of Corpus Christi. He is a hard person to evaluate. An Anglo-Catholic under heavy German influences and a social conservative, he had rediscovered New Testament study as a matter more of theological insight than textual criticism. He generated more enthusiasm than clarity. The Cambridge Divinity Faculty did not care for that sort of thing and isolated him. A young man named Michael Ramsey had obtained a First in theology the year before Oliver came up. For him Hoskyns was a great inspiration and so he was for Oliver: 'Under him we discovered with amazement that theology is about God.'

For Oliver at Cambridge what mattered was less the intellectual than the moral and spiritual experience which he found, above all, in Holy Trinity Church and the Student Christian Movement. As we have seen the SCM had already impinged quite centrally upon his life with his 'First Swanwick' in 1927 and his 'Second Swanwick' in 1928. Hearing E. S. Woods at the one and Dick Sheppard at the other was what had really moved him. Returning from Swanwick to Bramcote in 1928 he had written, 'it has affected me even more profoundly than last. I have found you again, dear Christ, just a little more nearly and a little more clearly than ever before.'

He came up to Cambridge, then, an SCM man and it was in the SCM from the start of his university life that he found both his sense of purpose and his closest friends – Frank Woods, for instance, Edward Woods's son, Kathleen Bliss, Eric Abbott and Lesslie Newbigin. Almost immediately he was reporting home on 'a splendid SCM meeting in John's Hall'. Eric Abbott had contrasted what the SCM might be in Cambridge, 'a spiritual fellowship and a spiritual force', with what, he claimed, it actually was, 'a safe and unexciting body, often vaguely intellectual admirers of an easy-going God'. SCM membership at Cambridge stood at the huge figure of about 650. Oliver wondered whether an appeal of this sort might not cause a drop in numbers but thought that might be 'all to the good'. Abbott remained a friend for life and if they both soon got beyond such rather youthful contrasts, the fact remains that Oliver would pursue the goal of making SCM a spiritual fellowship and a spiritual force pretty single-mindedly for the next 12 years.

Lesslie Newbigin recalled his first contacts with Oliver when Lesslie was still hardly a Christian. He found SCM exciting just because it was open. Within it he was drawn into belief little by little until he became almost as active as Oliver himself. What with the daily midday prayer in Great St Mary's, missionary breakfasts, preaching parties during the vacation,[2] pre-terminal retreats at Shelford, and, above all, the annual conference at Swanwick, being SCM was already close to a full-time way of life. Lesslie and Oliver came up to Cambridge the same year. If one compares Oliver with Lesslie, or again with Michael Ramsey, one notices at once a large difference. Newbigin and Ramsey appear as wrestling with the whole contemporary world of agnosticism, politics, conflict secular and religious. With regard to his personal life, there is no sign of anything comparable in Oliver. His mental world was that of a rather easily convinced, intellectually unadventurous, young Evangelical. He appears to have wrestled neither with faith nor with theology, but to have been an almost natural believer, though never a rigid one. If the young Oliver could fairly be classed as an 'Evangelical', it was of an innately liberal kind. His exact contemporary at Cambridge, Donald Coggan, illustrates the opposite type. He read Oriental Languages – Hebrew, Aramaic and Syriac – and got an excellent First, but his life and thinking were at the time strictly bounded by the frontiers of CICCU (Cambridge Inter-Collegiate Christian Union), the Conservative Evangelical student union, which refused to have anything to do with the wishy-washy SCM. The paths of Oliver and Donald, in consequence, may never have crossed. Oliver preferred history to theology, openness to exclusivity. In academic terms he was quintessentially a Second, as Donald was a First. But they were both Evangelicals.

Oliver, moreover, seemed psychologically immune to the world of decisive religious experience. Sudden conversions were not for him. He did not need them. Already in 1931 he could write about himself in his spiritual diary:

> I don't seem to get these shattering crises that form the religious experience
> of so many. I have just been talking to A- C- , whose way of working seems
> always to be bringing him into contact with the climacteric, the sudden
> conversion, the that-night-in-that-room-he-found-the-Lord kind of experi-
> ence. He has been telling stories of such miracles in missions and
> discussions, of startling testimonies given and sudden revolutionary deci-
> sions reached. Such things are outside my personal experience, and only to

a limited extent have I seen them in others. I am timid and conventional, and
too much of a Hellene in my religion.

He saw things, he went on, not in black and white but 'more in chiaroscuro than in
contrasts'. It would be so all his life as he, almost tiresomely, continued to repeat his
undergraduate discovery that he was a 'both-ander' not an 'either-orer'.

Oliver's lack of partisanship, his balance, coolness and humour, his obvious huge
commitment to the SCM together with the natural leadership qualities which had made
him Trent's Head of School now brought him the Presidency of the Cambridge SCM. A
good listener, a practical organizer with high ideals and no apparent doubts or difficulties,
it is not surprising that fellow students found him 'an outstandingly good president'.[3]
Sixty years later Newbigin remembered especially his sense of fun and of how the
Committee was once discussing who was to be invited to speak on Church Unity. The
choice lay between Bishops Bell and Headlam. After prolonged and indecisive discussion
Oliver at length broke in: 'Come on chaps, make up your minds, is it to be Hell or
Bedlam?' They chose Bell. The SCM had come to enfold almost his whole life. He was
succeeded as President by Newbigin and Newbigin was succeeded by Robin Woods,
Edward's younger son. They would all be friends and allies ever after. And they would all
become bishops.

Secretly all his life Oliver thought of himself as a poet, a crafter of words. Maybe it was
that self-appreciation which tells us best the sort of person he was. He was never inclined
to reveal himself too widely in this light, but if we are to discern any sort of originality in
this very nice, tall, athletic, slightly self-satisfied and not obviously profound young man,
it is here that we may do so. His 1930 poem, 'The Dog Lover Argues with the Broad-
Minded Bishop' is a place to begin:

> '"Dogs in heaven" you ask?
> Well, not exactly dogs, for heaven's no place
> Of geographic certitude, where time and space
> Make their accustomed rules, as our good
> But undeniably mistaken fathers
> Anthropomorphically supposed –'
>> The kindly head out-thrust, that even unadorned
>> Supported a mitre as its due, the well-formed
>> Gaitered legs comfortably crossed, with pulpit poise
>> The Bishop amiably enlarged
>> Upon the findings of our new theology.
>
> 'The ultimate values, those clean virtues which demand
> No further explanation, but by their nature can command
> Allegiance, these make heaven;
> The sphere, you understand, where we,
> The infinite in us, can enter in
> And be at one with them and that great "Wholly Other"
> (As Otto says) from whom they spring. And so our Brother
> Body and his attributes are left behind.
> And so with dogs – devotion, honour,
> Unquestioning obedience and blind trust,
> These things we see in dogs, and they are real; they shall last
> And be the dogs of heaven.'

He smiled, and slowly passed
A ringed hand over his silk-apron,
Content that he, at least, had reconciled
Man's childish cravings with the Higher Thought.
I looked down at furry brown-ness, dozing at my feet,
Black nose twitching at some phantasmal bone, the heat
Of dreamt-of chasing quivering down
His flanks, to flutter in a stirring
Of his limply-lying paws, and was not satisfied.

'These may be values...but they are not dogs. The shock
Of a damp nose, friendly-thrust into my hand; the cock
Of one furred ear when walks are promised;
The track of muddy feet on new-washed floors;
The cheerful morning bark; the tangled coat,
Matted with goose-grass, as foiled once again, he crawls,
Back from rabbit-hunting, through a tangled hedge; old tennis-balls
Rolled with imploring nose towards my feet.
The scatter and the scamper and the sin; these things,
May not be values, but they are my dog.
Is there no room for these in heaven?'
    The Bishop smiled dissent.
He was grown old in theology, and had no dog, so was content.
But if a House of Many Mansions has
No gardens, where a dog, purged perhaps
Of the sin of chasing cats, at least can walk
Inquisitive and questing on ahead, there's something wrong
With heaven – or with the Bishop.
                    'Walkies! Boy – come along!'

Oliver was placed in the second class both for his History Part I in 1930 and for Theology in 1932: a respectable but not exciting result. His heart was elsewhere and no one will have expected any better. By the summer of 1932 two decisions had been taken. On the one hand he was to go straight on to Westcott House for his theological college year. He had long wanted to do so. His father had been there only 12 years before and his father's Principal and friend, B. K. Cunningham, was still Principal. The bond of *pietas* was once more decisive. But, on the other hand, in the summer of 1932 he was also approached to join the full-time staff of the SCM, working from London. The post was officially described as the secretaryship of the SCM and Church of England Co-operating Committee and it would begin once Oliver had finished his Westcott year.

The diocese of Chelmsford agreed to second him to this work for three years (in fact it went on for seven). Ordination was put off in consequence and for an extra couple of years Oliver remained a layman precisely in order to serve ecumenically. His commitment to the 'cause of unity' and to the SCM – at the time easily the principal organ of the ecumenical movement – began, as we saw, in May 1927 at Swanwick under the inspiration of Edward Woods who was then about to attend the Lausanne Conference on Faith and Order. That commitment grew and grew, characterizing and unifying the following 12 years of his life. There was certainly no tension for him between being an Anglican and a priest, on the one hand, and being ecumenical and SCM devotee, on the other, but it was the intensity of the latter commitment which, at the time, made him unusual and which, for a while at least, took precedence over even the development of his Anglican and priestly ministry. Later in life he often recalled the first time he had met the word 'ecumenical'. It was at a conference of the World Student Christian Federation in Switzerland in 1930. If the ecumenical movement remained throughout life at the centre of almost all he did, it is not surprising that the first hearing of the word itself was something very special in his memory: not so much an unforgettable moment of conversion but, at least, one of recognition.

The impression of unruffled continuity is almost frightening. It may be harder to comprehend the apparently undeviating, genial tranquillity of the young Oliver, than, for instance, young Michael Ramsey, President of the Cambridge Union, Liberal activist and younger brother to the brilliant atheist Frank, deciding after helping to host both Asquith and William Temple that eternity matters rather more than time, and religion more than politics. Instead of being a Liberal Party candidate he chose ordination. There is no such shift within Oliver's maturing. He may have toyed with the idea of volunteering for overseas mission, indeed it would have been almost unthinkable for a committed SCM man in the 1930s not to have done so. The movement was still geared in its underlying mystique to the recruitment of missionaries. And there was the example of uncle and father. A missionary interest had remained very much part of his home culture. His parents had been hosts to Dr Albert Schweitzer from Lambarene when he visited Sheffield to give a lecture and organ recital in 1928. Again Oliver's Cambridge friend, Lesslie Newbigin, little less caught up in an SCM world, also went on to a full-time SCM secretaryship but was soon off to India, ordained as a foreign missionary. The interplay between missionary movement and ecumenical movement was a continual one and, in the early 1930s, the latter was still very much the younger partner. Oliver's personal loyalty, however, was clearly to the new arrival rather than to the senior movement.

The year at Westcott filled out his sense of Anglican identity, under the guiding hand of B. K. Cunningham, widely regarded as a model for theological college principals.[4] He was a person of great perceptiveness, a master of wise advice offered both face to face and across a vast correspondence, a teacher not of theology but of a sensibly pastoral spirituality. Like Oliver, B. K. was allergic to theology of an academic sort, but he was none the less steeped in the reading of the New Testament. There was, admittedly, a certain naiveté in his preoccupation with maintaining the Anglican tradition of the 'English gentleman in Holy Orders' and, like many another English gentleman, he spent his summers fishing and shooting in Scotland. At Westcott, as at Trent, the preoccupation of middle-level Anglican echelons with being stamped as gentlemen is hard for the observer to suffer kindly. And it could be damaging enough both to the pursuit of justice and a spirit of prophecy. But for B. K. being a gentleman meant, principally, being courteous, accessible and loving. He managed to make of Westcott House a very charitable place. Mervyn Stockwood could describe it as 'the most loving and caring community in which I have ever lived'.[5] Caring means tolerance, and tolerance is one of the virtues most needed for an ecumenical vocation. 'He gave us our freedom,' Eric Abbott insisted years later at his memorial service. He respected the self-respect of other men and taught many hundreds of Anglican priests to do the same, Stockwood, Abbott and Tomkins among them. Oliver certainly found both Westcott and B. K. extremely congenial. Cunningham did not expect his students to fish and shoot in Scotland, but his friendship, even his sense of upper-class belonging, may well have been psychologically just what Oliver needed, secretly still over-sensitive about poverty and Nonconformist background, to enhance his Anglican self-esteem. B. K.'s always sensible letters of advice to his 'Very dear Oliver' were treasured ever after. Certainly Cunningham became a 'beloved friend and guru' – perhaps more than anyone else in his life.

The year at Westcott was no less important in strengthening his awareness of everything in Christianity that may be included under the term 'Catholicism'. His father and mother were decidedly Protestants, with a good deal of fear both of Anglo-Catholicism and of Rome. It is here that he begins to travel well beyond their reach. It began with experiencing Anglo-Catholicism both through worship and through friends. If Hoskyns was an Anglo-Catholic, so was Wilfred Knox, the delightfully odd New Testament scholar and brother of Ronald and Evoe, the editor of *Punch,* who set Oliver to work weeding the garden of the Oratory of the Good Shepherd while bombarding him with a fusillade of wit. He found High Mass at Little St Mary's 'with its incense-clouded mystery and speech-free silence' a new world of religious inspiration. A letter to his father in March 1933 was clearly replying to parental misgivings. Indeed, he agreed, 'The Roman Church has some very grievous charges to answer,' yet, Oliver thought, it was better at producing saints than Protestantism though less good at raising the general level of morality. Protestantism 'cannot shew a roll of names to compare with St Francis, or Dominic or Bernard or Benedict or Anselm and the rest of the long tale... the Catholic system is often, for the very reason that it "makes" those who are strong enough to bear, no more than a very heavy burden on ordinary folks.' This looks like an example of the 'both-and' approach. While not questioning the strengths of his own Protestant tradition, he has come to appreciate the very considerable riches of the Catholic. It was not just a remote admiration. He would remark later that he had either to marry or become a monk.

By the end of the year at Westcott this hitherto pretty typical 'Liberal Evangelical' had come to see that the monastic and the mystical mattered a very great deal. Baron Friedrich Von Hügel had helped him here. It was at Westcott that he began to read Von Hügel. Later he would like to recall that the only time he met Dietrich Bonhoeffer – it was in 1939 on the stairs of the Athenaeum – he had made one remark which he could never forget: 'If you English would read Von Hügel, you would not need Karl Barth.' Von Hügel was the totally European English Catholic layman, at once critical and mystical, at once the sympathetic student of all religions and the firm assertor of the transcendence of God and the unicity of Christ, some sort of mysterious amalgam of Troeltsch and Barth – the historical width of the one with the faith of the other. For Oliver, Bonhoeffer 'meant that in Von Hügel the sovereign grace of the Eternal God over the proud pretensions of man was so richly expounded by a liberal Roman Catholic that the same message from a conservative biblical Protestant was made redundant. From Von Hügel I learned an analysis of reality not just of religion, which has never left me.' Von Hügel was, it is worth reminding ourselves, a very conservative liberal, just as he was a very liberal conservative: the terms in fact cease to signify for so profound a thinker. For Oliver, as for others of his generation, Von Hügel offered the best guidance available for an almost systematic reconciliation of modern scholarship and orthodox belief. He gave him what the Cambridge school of theology had failed to provide.

In this final Cambridge year he also won the Winchester Prize – for Reading! He had put in for it rather as a joke. All day he attended at the Senate House with, at the start, some 40 other contestants, to read aloud from *Paradise Lost* and Dean Church's *Oxford Movement, Coriolanus,* Psalm VIII, *Henry V,* Gibbon and the Book of Common Prayer. For the piece of his own choice he read Shelley's ode 'To Night'. Ever since prep school he had been commended for his reading in public. Now he had proved his excellence. The prize of £20 worth of books seemed to overwhelm him: 'Whatever shall I do?' Such riches had never come his way.

In the summer of 1933 Oliver was 25. He had spent five years in Cambridge and gained from it all he could. As President of its SCM he had already been a member of a national working party, including people like William Paton and Gabriel Hebert, to explore the issue of Intercommunion and he had presided over the national summer conference at Swanwick, so his Cambridge role was of itself already evolving into something far wider. He was now to earn his living by doing very much what he had already chosen to do unpaid. His office would be at the SCM headquarters in Golders Green, his salary £250 a year, and he would live with his parents in Paddington.

# 3

# The SCM in the 1930s

In the summer of 1935 a friend at the headquarters of the World Student Christian Federation (WSCF) in Geneva sent Oliver 'a simply lovely parody of "The Church's One Foundation"' which he had just heard from the lips of Wim Visser't Hooft, at the time its General Secretary. Its first verses went as follows:

> The Church's one foundation
> Was Bluff King Hal, her lord;
> She was a new creation,
> Made by his royal word.
> To dodge the Pope he sought her,
> When he would change his bride;
> And Bess, his glorious daughter,
> What he left out supplied.
>
> 'Mid strife and litigation,
> And fierce internal war,
> She suits the British Nation;
> What can you ask for more?
> Till with the vision glorious
> Her longing eyes are blest –
> The Union Jack victorious
> O'er North, South, East and West.

It was, wrote Oliver's correspondent cautiously, 'for very private circulation only'. A group of people may sometimes be better understood by their jokes than by their more solemn and pompous statements. The first thing to remember about the SCM in the 1930s is that it was a group of lively youngsters, keen to mix 'prayer and argument, blasphemy and piety'.[1] They liked to laugh at their respective churches pretty freely, often only too aware that they were well out of line with the general run of clergy. As David Paton, one of the more fiery of SCM staff, wrote to Oliver (22 January 1937):

> I begin to realise what people like Leslie Hunter mean when they castigate the clergy. Does not membership of the SCM staff spoil you for anything else? Criticism is there, but in love. And we trust each other; and we all think rather differently. What is it like to come off the staff into the sort of curacy X has got, where anything like the conditions we know is impossible from the start...

Perhaps that was part of the reason why David volunteered for China. Oliver was unlikely to have expressed himself so fiercely. Nevertheless if we are to have a sense of the

movement he was part of, heart and soul, as full-time as could be, from 1933 to 1940, it
needs to be in terms of a group of highly committed young radicals, far from united in
terms of theology but all feeling the winds of Barth, Niebuhr, Dodd, even Maritain, upon
the one hand, and of a steadily worsening political state of the world on the other. SCM
Christianity involved, among other things, a lively political concern, generally of a
Socialist sort. 'For the SCM politics seems to mean Socialist politics,' George Every of
Kelham wrote complainingly to Oliver in 1937. He was right. Though its socialism took
a variety of forms, there was little room in it for what Every called 'intelligent Tories'. Yet
an 'exceptional combination of conviction and openness'² was what distinguished the
SCM at that time. They argued vigorously over 'neo-orthodoxy', pacifism and much else,
but they were very much aware that, while their influence with students was considerable,
the contrast in mind-set between them and the general run of the clerical world was enormous, keen as they were to rally when they could behind senior ecclesiastical figures like
William Temple, the Archbishop of York, or Leslie Hunter, Archdeacon of
Northumberland and soon to be Bishop of Sheffield, both long-standing allies of the
movement. Influential as Temple was, in terms of ideas Reinhold Niebuhr (Reinie to his
friends and admirers) was probably all in all the SCM's primary guru in the late 1930s.
*Moral Man and Immoral Society* had been published in 1932.

> The true believer
> In Reinhold Niebuhr
> Is apt to mention
> The fact of tension.

The author was Oliver.³ Niebuhr generated a sense of passionate confrontation where
Temple generated a slightly facile sense of peaceful agreement.

The 1930s were, for the SCM, something of a golden age – in the size of its membership, the number and quality of its staff, the enthusiasm with which it threw itself into
providing an intelligent alternative to either Communism or Fascism and thus filling the
spiritual vacuum produced by the rapidly worsening state of the world upon the one
hand, the lack of an imaginative and confidence-inspiring leadership in Church and state
upon the other. That enthusiasm was also a response to the sudden shift in theology away
from 'liberalism' to 'neo-orthodoxy' and to interminable discussions on Barth. For
decades the British SCM had been most efficiently run by Canon Tissington Tatlow, its
finances had been placed upon a sound basis and 'Annandale', a large new headquarters
building, opened in Golders Green. Tatlow retired in 1929 and from then on the General
Secretaries, like the rest of the staff, were expected to be young and not stay too long. The
SCM's special sort of vitality could best be kept on the boil by a rapid turn-over, despite
the dangers this inevitably engendered in a lack of continuity. Most staff members were
recruited from the ranks of the student membership immediately following a first degree,
few were ordained at the time, and they acted as stimulators more than leaders. Not many
stayed much longer than three years, though some effective junior secretaries returned a
few years later at a senior level. In such circumstances much depended on the leadership
skills of the General Secretary. Robert Mackie, a Scottish Presbyterian with a very light
touch, was General Secretary from 1929 to 1938. He had come to the job from the post
of Scottish Secretary and left it to become General Secretary in Geneva of the World
Student Federation.

Secular student unions were weak at this period and denominational chaplaincies
hardly existed outside the Anglican appointments in Oxford and Cambridge colleges, so

the SCM, with its rather inclusive note and well-structured organization, picked up a considerable membership, much of it only rather weakly committed to the concerns that moved its leading minds. In 1935 its official membership stood at 11,500 out of a total student population of 72,000. Stricter Evangelicals were already hiving off at most colleges to join SCM's rival, the Inter-Varsity Christian Union, a fundamentalist body founded in 1928 as an extension of CICCU (Cambridge Inter-Collegiate Christian Union) and committed to avoiding the contamination both of liberal theology and of social concern. Where the SCM word was 'discuss', the Christian Union's word was 'proclaim'. But the very size and openness of the SCM continually threatened its effectiveness. Eric Fenn, a staff member from 1926 to 1937 and one of the wisest minds SCM ever fostered, remarked that it was clear to him that 'many of the interests in which the movement was involved at the top were the interests of the senior secretaries rather than of the Movement, and one of Robert Mackie's gifts to us was his thrusting of such things back into the minds of student committees to test them out as true interests.'[4] Mackie was a listener and an enabler, moved more by poetry than by theology. There can be no doubt that his special kind of gently charismatic, warm, relaxed, personally perceptive leadership was crucial to the health of the SCM in the 1930s and to its successful selection of outstanding staff. As one of them, John Mackay, later wrote:

> I once heard it said that when Robert Mackie came into a room it was as though a light had been switched on which wasn't on before – and that metaphor comes as close as any is likely to do to convey the effect of his presence. It is very hard to distinguish how much of the marvellously enriching and liberating effect of membership of the Student Movement was due to particular people, for all the senior members of the staff in the 1930s contributed richly...If others played significant and indeed indispensable parts, however, there was no doubt that Robert was the producer of the play, the conductor of the orchestra, *primus inter pares*.

Or again, in the words of another young staff member, Alan Booth, Mackie and Eric Fenn presented

> the religious equivalent for our generation of Morecambe and Wise – each partner feeding the other with opportunities to score in accordance with his own particular talent...How to be religious without apparently trying, how to serve God with devotion without making a profession of it, how to keep your feet on the ground and your prayers in heaven, how to be wholly committed and find the whole thing hilarious – it was a formidable agenda.[5]

Mackie handled the personal relations, Fenn provided the ideas. After 1937, when Fenn ceased to be Study Secretary, his intellectual role was taken over by Alan Richardson who ran very effectively the annual fortnight-long theological reading party for all SCM staff at Grindleford in Derbyshire. But the entire existence of SCM staff, particularly those based at Annandale, may well be imagined as a sort of continual seminar. This was where Oliver, like many others, really learnt his theology. Let us list just a few of the names of Oliver's colleagues, SCM secretaries of the 1930s, and then consider briefly what some of them later did: Gilbert Baker, Alan Booth, William Greer, Gilbert Hort, Francis House, Kathleen Bliss, Hugh Lister, Dick Milford, Lesslie Newbigin, David Paton, Ronald Preston, John Ramsbotham, Ambrose Reeves, Alan Richardson, Robin Woods.

Hugh Lister, besides becoming a London curate, was chairman of the Hackney Wick branch of the Transport and General Workers Union and an indefatigable organizer of strikes and flying squads. It was unusual activity for a C of E priest. However, when the war came, he enrolled as an officer in the Welsh Guards and was killed near the Dutch border in September 1944. Gilbert Hort, Lesslie Newbigin and David Paton, all three exceptionally brilliant, went as missionaries to Asia. Hort, who joined the Delhi Brotherhood, died the same month as Lister, suddenly struck down by infantile paralysis, to the dismay of a church particularly in need of his sort of contribution. Paton went to China and later, after all missionaries in China had been expelled, wrote his *Christian Missions and the Judgement of God*, a blistering critique which most missionary writers have tried to forget about ever since. Newbigin went to India, became one of the first bishops in the new Church of South India and, over 50 years, the writer of many influential books and finally an Evangelical elder statesman, hyper-active far into his eighties. Reeves became Bishop of Johannesburg, one of apartheid's fiercest critics in the 1950s, and was deported from South Africa after the Sharpeville Massacre in 1960. Dick Milford became Vicar of the Oxford University Church of St Mary's, the principal founder and first Chairman of Oxfam and, later, Master of the Temple, upsetting many of its members by testifying for the defence in the *Lady Chatterley* trial. Ronald Preston, the SCM Industrial Secretary 1935-8, went to a slum curacy in Sheffield before returning to the SCM to help its post-war revival as Study Secretary and editor of *The Student Movement*. By the 1960s he was Professor of Social and Pastoral Theology in the University of Manchester and the leading authority on socio-political theology in Britain. Alan Richardson, the principal theological educator within the 1930s SCM, became in due course Professor of Theology at Nottingham and Dean of York. He was probably responsible for more books and on more subjects than anyone else in the group including, in later life, a massive *Dictionary of Christian Theology*, edited by him and largely written by him too. Newbigin, Reeves, Milford, Preston and Richardson all represent distinct facets of the 1930s SCM which each developed in his own way by the 1950s into a highly personal contribution to the national and international life of the churches of exceptional quality.

Francis House is, however, the member of this group whose interests most closely paralleled those of Oliver and a long glance at his career in this period will both help an understanding of the SCM and provide a useful comparison with that of Oliver. Just three months the latter's junior in age and, like him, a vicar's son, Francis entered Oxford to study history at Wadham in 1927, which he followed with a fourth year doing 'Modern Greats' (Philosophy and Political Economy, 'PPE'). In 1931 Robert Mackie suggested he join the SCM staff. He had been the international secretary for the Oxford SCM in 1930 and his involvement in the European student world steadily grew. It was an involvement which inevitably meant coming into ever closer contact with a virulent Nazism and anti-Semitism. At a conference in Brno in Czechoslovakia which he attended in 1933 one of the ablest speakers was Dr Fritz Beck, a Catholic German student leader. In June 1934 Beck was murdered by Nazis in the 'night of the long knives'. In the summer of 1933, just a few months after Hitler came to power, House had had the strange but educative experience of sharing in a Nazi 'labour camp' for German students in East Prussia, with its spartan conditions, very hard work, highly political lectures and comradely evening sing-songs. At the time he struggled to stress the good side of what he thought he saw – the youthful self-sacrifice, personal self-discipline, national pride, an orchestrated upsurge of resentment against the injustices of the Versailles settlement. That, of course, was what many Christian leaders in Germany, including Martin Niemöller, first saw in Nazism as well. The news, a year later, of the murder of Fritz Beck helped disillusion him quickly enough.

After ordination and a couple of years in a London curacy, in 1937 Francis was invited to join Wim Visser't Hooft and Suzanne de Diétrich in Geneva at the headquarters of the World Student Christian Federation. Francis replaced Ambrose Reeves as the team member with special responsibility for the Balkans. This took him to Budapest, Bucharest, Athens, Belgrade and elsewhere, but much of his time was spent, as was Wim's, analysing the worsening situation in Germany and giving what support they could to the Christian Student Movement there, until it was formally banned in August 1938. Francis was in Munich on 9 November 1938, the *Kristallnacht*, when hundreds of synagogues were burnt and thousands of Jewish shops looted. He saw it happening. In consequence of the closeness of his personal encounter with this orgy of race-hatred and the grim realities of Nazism, he had a less ambiguous attitude to issues of international politics than most liberal-minded British Christians in the late 1930s, including Oliver. Francis continued to be based in Geneva and even to visit the Balkans until the Fall of France in the summer of 1940 when he returned, just in time, to Britain, to a curacy in Leeds and then, somewhat later, to work with the BBC.

To detail Francis's life at this period so extensively may seem something of a digression, but he was the only other English SCM person of Oliver's generation to develop a really close involvement with the European Churches – an involvement, indeed, even deeper than Oliver's – and it helps to contextualize Oliver's career to see it against that of Francis, who had been greatly helped in all of this by his fluency not only in French but in German and his willingness to try many another language as well, from Russian to Hungarian. Slightly senior to Oliver within the SCM staff, he represented its internationalist dimension highly effectively. Where Francis led, Oliver was to follow.

Every SCM secretary had a defining area either thematic or geographical. Oliver's first assignment in 1933 was to the SCM/C of E Co-operating Committee. To that was added the Theological College Department and the Student Campaigns Committee. By 1935 he was also an 'Assistant General Secretary' and in 1937 he took over from Eric Fenn the editorship of *The Student Movement*. He was also one of the Directors of SCM Press. If one asks where his main contribution lay, it is not so easy to say. He was certainly not the special conduit for new theological ideas in the way that Fenn and Richardson, the Study Secretaries, were expected to be and in fact were, nor even in the way that near-Barthian 'rampageous Evangelicals' like David Paton could be. Oliver, even as a young man, was never swept off his feet by the excitement of a new orthodoxy, feeling himself already to be quintessentially 'central' rather than either Evangelical or Anglo-Catholic, in any of their forms. It is hard for centrality to be exciting. Nevertheless his role throughout his SCM years as secretary to the Theological College Department as well as to the SCM–Church of England Committee drew him to the more theological side of SCM work – Faith and Order rather than Life and Work. Late in his time at Annandale he produced a courteously phrased but pretty scathing memorandum for the Archbishops' Commission on Training for the Ministry in which he criticized the Anglican theological colleges for their 'lack of interest in theology': 'It is not so much an academic interest in theology that is lacking... but the whole expectation that the learning of theology will make any real difference. A parson is just a good chap, ordained.' He found no concern for the contemporary: 'Such issues as the false conceptions by which men live today or the struggles of the Church in Germany, the Far East, or even nearer at hand, are studied neither for themselves nor for the sake of revealing the vitality of the past history of the Church and its doctrine.'

If Oliver quickly came to be appreciated as one of the most effective members of the SCM team, it was because within its culture of committees and a seemingly interminable round of meetings he was such a very good listener to what everyone else was saying, because of a certain clarity of judgement when he finally expressed his opinion, because of the reliable hard work he put into carrying out policies and explaining them to others – a combination of balance, efficiency and pleasantness. He was the natural editor. Once Fenn left the staff, Oliver, now in his fourth year, became also something of a deputy leader, very widely known to outsiders in a way comparable to the General Secretary himself. His style of leadership matured in a mode very close to Mackie's.

What turned into Oliver's special expertise grew little by little out of the regularity of his visits to the continent and the conferences he was invited to attend – both specifically SCM ones and, then, an ever-widening range of other ecumenical meetings. The close personal relationship he established as a result with a number of outstanding European ecumenical figures – Wim Visser't Hooft, Pierre Maury, Leo Zander, Nicholas Zernov, Reinhold von Thadden and others – would be one of the most important things in his life. It was in these years of the 1930s that Oliver became, like Francis House and George Bell, and quite unselfconsciously, that rather rare bird, an Anglican European. This was much helped by a reasonable fluency in French. The chief 'new frontier' of the 1930s was unquestionably that of Europe, its ideological conflicts and headlong descent into open war. It is understandable that the person within the SCM who had, almost by chance, become the closest it possessed to a European expert should come to occupy a position of special importance in the field of the interpretation of European Christians to British ones.

His first visit to Geneva was for a WSCF conference in 1930. By the beginning of 1934 he had got as far as Sweden and Denmark and was in January a delegate to a conference at Lund at which he listened to the Czech theologian Josef Hromadka, as well as to Hanns Lilje, the General Secretary of the German SCM, who had already made a considerable impact on the British SCM as a principal speaker at its 'Quadrennial' conference in Edinburgh in the summer of 1933. Lilje was a friend of Martin Niemöller and of Dietrich Bonhoeffer, a leader already in the struggle to retain the Church's freedom from Nazi control yet not exempt too from a certain admiration for what Hitler appeared to stand for. In this he was closer to Niemöller than to Bonhoeffer and, like Niemöller, would later be imprisoned by the Nazis but escape with his life. So, 1936 saw Oliver in Berlin, Sofia, Paris, Geneva and Ireland. And each place produced a widening circle of continental acquaintances from Wim Visser't Hooft and Suzanne de Diétrich in Geneva and Leo Zander in Paris to Professor Zankov, Dean of the Theological Faculty in Sofia, and Pastor Niemöller in Berlin. His relationship with Wim would become little by little something central in his life. If it began with the Geneva Conference of 1930, it was much deepened a few years later when he acted as Wim's lieutenant in an English tour. Most memorable was a clergy gathering in Bishop Barnes's home in Birmingham where Wim was to address the meeting on Karl Barth's theology, something still hardly heard of in Britain at the time. Barnes was well known both for his extreme Modernism and for his antagonism to Roman Catholicism. Visser't Hooft began his lecture: 'Karl Barth is fighting against two things, which are at bottom the same thing, Roman Catholicism and Modernism.' Nothing was better calculated to set the cat among the pigeons! Oliver was never a Barthian; he could well be thought a bit of a Modernist and his fondness for Catholicism was increasing. But his loyalty to Wim was unstinted.

Particularly interesting must have been a highly confidential conference held at Bièvres near Paris in March 1937 in which Oliver and Wim were included in a group of Protestants in discussion with Roman Catholics. As Oliver noted in a letter to his father, all the continental Protestants were 'Barthian or near-Barthian' these days with 'no single defender of Liberal Protestantism'. The four Catholics included Yves Congar, whose epoch-making *Chrétiens désunis* was published that year. The conference topics centred on all the main themes of classical theology and its worship included Anglican Evensong, a Russian Liturgy, Mass in a nearby Dominican convent. At a further meeting in 1939, Congar was joined by Jacques Maritain and Gabriel Marcel – a remarkable trio – but Oliver's place was taken this time by Francis House. The typical format of a post-Vatican II ecumenical meeting of the late 1960s was already here in place in the 1930s and Oliver, still in his twenties, could experience its restrained excitement.

While the World Student Christian Federation was preparing throughout these years for its World Conference of Christian Youth to meet in Amsterdam in July 1939, the ecumenical movement as a whole was focused on two meetings which took place in 1937 – the second conference of the Life and Work Movement in Oxford in July and that of Faith and Order a month later in Edinburgh. These two conferences, especially the first, both crystallized the best Christian thinking of the time in regard to the central crises of world society and established a framework for the ecumenical enterprise in the future by deciding to bring into being a 'World Council of Churches'. The whole subsequent history of the ecumenical movement flows out of what happened in 1937 and would probably not have happened if it had not been for a small handful of people, mostly British. The parameters of almost everything most enduringly significant in Oliver's life were shaped in 1937. William Temple, Joe Oldham, William Paton and George Bell, all four Oxford graduates, were the principal founding fathers of a world and a mission which he, more than any other English person, came to inherit, and his relationship with them must now become the focus of our attention.

The ecumenical movement had continually sprouted new international organisms as the twentieth century advanced and the sense of Christian unity and its needs surmounted the barriers of denominational separation in one area after another. Much of it sprang from early cooperation within the YMCA and YWCA, lay organizations dating back to mid-nineteenth-century London. A number of the principal ecumenical leaders of the twentieth century, including John Mott and Visser't Hooft, began their careers in the YMCA. Some of the new urgency derived from the requirements of missionaries, of a host of varied denominations, faced in Asia or Africa with their own tiny flocks up against a huge non-Christian majority – the denominational divides of the West paled into insignificance in that context. Much again came from intellectual and political pressures affecting all the Churches within modern Western society which seemed to undermine the point in most of their long-established divisions, but of which the academic and student community tended to be particularly aware. Christianity was under challenge as never before and it was natural for believers to feel the urgent need to draw together and cooperate in a multitude of ways.

The World Student Christian Federation, established at a meeting at Vadstena in Sweden in 1895, was the first major new organism, with the indefatigable American Methodist John R. Mott as its principal founder and first General Secretary. Nevertheless, the World Missionary Conference, held in Edinburgh in 1910, is often regarded, a little simplistically, as the starting point for the modern ecumenical movement. It was undoubtedly a particularly well organized and well publicized event, and does mark the beginning of a new level of organized international activity. Mott was its chairman and J. H. Oldham its executive secretary. From then until the 1950s Mott would remain the tireless and spiritually persuasive, if intellectually banal, elder statesman, while Oldham would develop into a very lay *éminence grise*, the far-sighted planner and arch-intriguer with a rare ability to make his plans come true. The First World War prevented an immediate translation of Edinburgh's continuation committee into something sounding permanent, an International Missionary Council (IMC) but this came about in 1921. It was based at Edinburgh House in London with Oldham as its secretary. For the first time in its history, there existed in consequence a network linking the leaders of a large part of non-Roman Catholic Christianity in a continuing and effective exercise of intercommunication and mutual assistance but it was a network which, while involving Churches in the non-Western world, only included missionary societies and their backers in the Western one.

In 1925 a 'Universal Christian Conference on Life and Work' was held in Stockholm hosted by Nathan Söderblom, the Archbishop of Uppsala. Its catch phrase, 'Doctrine divides while service unites', was good in opening up the ground for ever wider types of cooperation but, inevitably, raised unavoidable question marks for churches which were, after all, identified principally by their doctrines. Only a couple of years after Stockholm, an alternative strategy produced the 1927 Faith and Order Conference in Lausanne, presided over by Bishop Charles Brent of the American Episcopalian Church, its principal instigator. He had been present at Edinburgh and grew restive at its determined avoidance of the underlying issue of Christian division. Doctrine may indeed divide but that is hardly a reason not to face up to it, if one is seriously pursuing unity. Each conference had its continuation committee. Each cost more money than its backers, at the time of the great recession, could well afford. Moreover, many ecumenically minded people had a hand in both, as also in the International Missionary Council which held its own major 1920s' conference in Jerusalem, a year after Lausanne.

By the early 1930s it was beginning to appear obvious to the more far-sighted that this could not go on. A single over-arching body was needed which, without claiming authority over the churches, could be representative of all of them in regard to every field of common concern. William Paton, a highly efficient first secretary of the new National Christian Council of India, had returned to Britain in 1927 to assist Oldham at the IMC and then take over the Secretaryship from him. This freed Oldham to move across to Life and Work to make the most decisive of all his ecumenical contributions – the preparation of the 1937 Oxford Conference and the agreement to inaugurate a 'World Council of Churches'. Suggestions that something like this was now opportune had been made in several quarters, but the crucial meeting was probably a confidential little gathering in 1933 when about ten people met in York in Temple's home of Bishopthorpe: Temple himself, Oldham, Paton, Visser't Hooft, two influential Americans, William Adams Brown and Samuel Cavert, both principally Life and Work men, and two or three other Europeans. What is striking at this point is the dominance of the British contribution, something which had in no way existed in the 1920s. A combination of factors brought this about. Brent died in 1929 and Söderblom in 1931, both unexpectedly, and there were no equivalent figures on the Continent or in America to replace them; moreover, the tensions produced by Fascism and Nazism were tending to undermine any wider ecclesiastical leadership, particularly in Germany. American isolationism also did not help. Yet the main factor was the sheer quality of the British personalities involved, Oldham and Temple above all. It is hardly too much to say that between them these two men brought the World Council into existence and that without them it would probably never have emerged. Almost certainly no decision would have been taken prior to the Second World War.

The British contribution was, however, very much a team one and much of its forma-tion was due to chance. There had in fact been rather little British interest in Life and Work in the 1920s. George Bell, who went to the Stockholm Conference, was very much an exception. In 1929 he became Bishop of Chichester and, when Söderblom died, he effectively led the movement for the next few years and was chairman of its Council for several of them. This both provided him with a platform from which to offer support to the Confessing Church in Germany in its struggle with Nazism and enabled him to put Oldham in charge of the preparation of the next Life and Work conference. The British take-over of Faith and Order was almost equally accidental. The leading figures here had been Bishop Brent and another American, Ralph W. Brown, its General Secretary, whose office, previously in America, had been moved to Geneva. Then Brent died suddenly in 1929 and William Temple was elected to succeed him as Chairman of the Lausanne Continuation Committee. With the financial slump the American funds behind the move-ment disappeared, the Geneva office had to be closed and in 1933 Brown offered his resignation. A little earlier Leonard Hodgson, a canon of Winchester, had been appointed Theological Secretary. With Brown's resignation Hodgson was asked to act temporarily also as General Secretary. Thus both Life and Work and Faith and Order were in reality being directed from England, just as the International Missionary Council was already run from London by Oldham and Paton, although Life and Work, better funded than Faith and Order was able to keep its office in Geneva open, staffed by a German, Hans Schönfeld and a Swede, Nils Ehrenström.

Both Life and Work and Faith and Order were planning to hold conferences ten years after Stockholm and Lausanne. It was now agreed that the two should be in 1937, the former in July, the latter in August, and both should be in Britain, the one in Oxford, the other in Edinburgh. Everything was thus being set in place. Representatives of the two movements met in the summer of 1936 with a memorandum of Oldham before them:

> The holding of the ecumenical conferences in 1937 provides an opportunity which will not recur for many years, of having the whole question of the future of the ecumenical movement examined afresh...In the historical crisis in which the Church finds itself there is need of facing these questions with the greatest deliberation and of bringing to bear upon them the best statesmanship that the Church can command.[6]

Who could refuse such a challenge? As a result, a joint committee of 35 was established to work out a plan, but in reality at every point that mattered both the plan and the strategy to achieve it were Oldham's and Temple's. Backed by Paton, Bell, Mott and Visser't Hooft, the whole proposal was proving irresistible. Visser't Hooft was the one European whose cooperation seemed absolutely vital: he had been marked out by Oldham in particular as principal executive for the new body.

Quite apart from the agreement to establish a World Council of Churches, the Oxford Conference, in particular, was important for the maturity and width of its approach to its chosen theme, 'Church, Community and State'. It had been immensely well prepared by Oldham and his chosen assistant, Eric Fenn, who had moved from his post in the SCM to undertake it. It was the quality of the exceptionally wide range of contributors which made the conference's achievement possible but they too were there largely because Oldham had inveigled them into coming. They included without doubt many of the leading theological figures of the time. Eric Fenn described Niebuhr at the conference as 'a volcano in constant eruption'. Brunner, Kraemer, Dodd and the like all played their part but it may rather have been the contribution of the lay academics and other eminent figures marshalled by Oldham, such as Sir Walter Moberly,[7] Sir Alfred Zimmern,[8] R. H. Tawney,[9] A. D. Lindsay,[10] Ernest Barker,[11] Lord Lothian,[12] T. S. Eliot,[13] Viscount Cecil of Chelwood,[14] John Foster Dulles[15] and others which made the Oxford Conference so exceptional. Here too the English intellectual contribution was preponderant, while the British SCM was adequately represented by Billy Greer, Eric Fenn and Alan Richardson.

The great absentee was the German Evangelical Church whose delegates were, at the last moment, prevented by the German Government from attending. Martin Niemöller was arrested just 12 days before the Conference opened. This may much have helped to concentrate minds on the great issues the Conference addressed – the relationship of Church and state, economic power, the Church and race, war and peace, the international order. The Oxford Conference offered no easy answers in any of these areas but it laid down the markers for a Christian doctrine of society in modern times with an authority and a lasting value which have seldom if ever been surpassed.

The Edinburgh Conference of Faith and Order the following month was less creative. Temple presided and Oliver attended as a member of the 'Youth Group'. A certain amount of opposition to the idea of a World Council, led by Bishop Headlam of Gloucester, was deftly outflanked, but succeeded in insisting on Faith and Order retaining a separate identity until the World Council was actually inaugurated. Life and Work, on the other hand, was simply merged into the World Council at once so that its Genevan office and staff could be taken over by the latter. The survival of Faith and Order with a distinct identity, something much resented by Oldham at the time, would become in due course the foundation on which much of Oliver's ecumenical life would be based. The following May, a meeting in Utrecht, chaired by Temple, agreed upon a provisional constitution and elected a provisional committee with Temple as its inevitable head. It was to have offices in Geneva, London and New York. It would have a letter-head of its own: 'World Council of Churches', written large, 'in process of formation' written small. And it would have two General Secretaries, Wim Visser't Hooft and William Paton, one in Geneva and one in London. No one anticipated that it would be a full ten years before the 'in process of formation' could be dropped, but the onset of international conflict proved too quick for its planners.

At the start of 1939, Wim was to give up his post at the World Student Federation, which would be taken over by Robert Mackie – yet another example, it is worth noting, of the extent of British leadership in the international ecumenical movement at this decisive time. Paton, on the other hand, would work only part-time for the World Council, retaining the General Secretaryship of the IMC. No attempt was made to draw the latter into the World Council at this point. It was recognized that opposition would be too great. For one thing the IMC was a much stronger body, better organized and better financed than Faith and Order or Life and Work. For another, its clientele was very different: missionary societies on the one hand, non-Western Christians on the other. It is true that Bishop Azariah of Dornakal was both at Oxford and at Edinburgh. He was indeed one of Oxford's six Conference Presidents. There were a few Chinese, Japanese and other Asian delegates at both but their presence still appears marginal, whereas it was absolutely central to the IMC's Conference at Tambaram the following year. Moreover, some at least of the missionary societies deeply committed to the IMC would never have considered entering the World Council with its far wider range of theological view. However, that is not the whole picture. Paton was a fairly autocratic executive officer of the IMC but he was wholly behind the World Council and one of its first two General

Secretaries. The intention surely was that he would at the right moment pull off a shotgun marriage. The war and his sudden death in 1943 prevented that from happening. The marriage, which must have been seen as inevitable by World Council supporters from the start, was deferred until 1961.

The staff of the British SCM could not but be caught up in the huge excitement and sense of ecclesiastical transformation which these developments produced, set as they were against an even more sombre international situation. But for Oliver in particular the conferences of 1937 seem to have been decisive in providing orientation for the rest of his life. He at once accepted a sort of personal responsibility for the furtherance of their message. In the first week of January 1938, 200 theological students and 80 ministers and members of college staffs met at Swanwick for what was probably the most important and best-prepared Theological Students conference ever to be held. Its theme was to consider 'in the light of the issues raised by the Oxford and Edinburgh conferences the significance for the Church of the situation facing us in the world today'. It was chaired throughout by Oliver who also gave the opening address. His chairmanship, reported Daniel Jenkins, 'gave both spiritual and intellectual unity to our proceedings'.[16] The speakers included William Paton, Sir Alfred Zimmern, Sir Walter Moberly, Professor John Baillie, Joe Oldham and Leslie Hunter while Wim Visser't Hooft provided the closing address. Mrs Hunter was the conference's official hostess. If there was one moment in Oliver's life when he graduated into the ranks of senior ecumenical leadership, it was surely at Swanwick in January 1938 at the age of 29.[17]

From then on, if not before, he was clearly recognized by Temple, Oldham and Paton as the providentially destined heir to their endeavours. Temple regularly invited small groups of SCM secretaries to spend a weekend with him at Bishopthorpe to share ideas and be exhilarated by his high-toned infectious laugh. On such occasions he was able to inspect and select the best the SCM could offer, draw them into his confidence and give them a sense that whatever he was doing, they must carry forward. Of the many young men he had his eye on, probably no one was more special than Oliver Tomkins but with him were others such as Eric Abbott, Francis House, and – from a rather different, non-SCM stable – Michael Ramsey.

Nothing shaped Oliver more profoundly in these later years of the 1930s than the friendship of Temple. Temple's qualities were such as to give him a quite unrivalled position within ecumenical circles. As Archbishop of York, and the son of an Archbishop of Canterbury, he had an ecclesiastical status and a lovely home which made him the natural figurehead for every movement and host for every confidential gathering. But as an academic and writer of distinguished works of theology and philosophy, he had an intellectual weight far beyond anyone else. No other ecumenical leader of the period, after Söderblom's death, could conceivably have been asked to deliver the Gifford Lectures. Yet he was also not only a masterful chairman of meetings, but an extraordinarily accessible person, always good-humoured, quick to notice lesser folk and to inspirit them with a word of encouragement. The Archbishop was such a frequent speaker at SCM gatherings at Swanwick and elsewhere that the opportunities to meet were many, but the core of their relationship was provided by the SCM–Church of England Committee established in 1933 with Temple as chairman and Oliver as secretary. It met twice a year and neither Temple nor Oliver ever failed to attend. Oliver was soon turning to Temple for personal advice. Already in February 1935 Temple could write, 'My dear Oliver, I have often had your prospects in mind...I do not think your ordination should be postponed until 1938.' Temple took him to Faith and Order committee meetings; he chose him as his assistant when he led the mission to the University of Leeds; he even rang him up at Annandale to invite him to dinner and to see a play in the West End together – always a somewhat embarrassing experience as Temple's almost uncontrollable, high-pitched laughter turned heads in the rows around! One of Oliver's most vivid memories of Temple was from a meeting of the Faith and Order Continuation Committee at Clarens in 1936. He told Temple that as he listened somewhat uncomprehendingly to the discussion he was reminded of an old lady he knew who, listening to the brilliant conversation of her grandchildren, used to say 'I do wish I ever quite understood anything', to which Temple replied 'Wouldn't it be awful if one did.'[18] After a day on the Leeds mission they drove back to Bishopthorpe and the Archbishop showed Oliver to his bedroom and said goodnight with an affectionate hug round the shoulders which would never be forgotten. It was Temple's 'gift for releasing the best in others'[19] that, years later, he would recall most warmly.

Oliver became, and remained throughout life, a disciple of Temple but he was also in the two years after the 1937 Conference deeply influenced by Oldham. Once more the older man picked him out as a sort of acolyte. Oldham was well into his sixties, rather deaf, not at all someone to preach missions to the students of Leeds. For years he had influenced the policies of Church and state especially in colonial and missionary affairs through knowing the right people, dining with them in the Athenaeum, but always appearing better informed and more far-sighted than anyone else, the mandarin who could be a guru as well. He shared with Oliver a devotion to Von Hügel as well as the ability both to listen and to plan.

The Oxford Conference had demonstrated Oldham's skills to the utmost. But where to go now? He had an idea – the establishment of a sort of inner parliament of 'the best minds', the most intelligent Christians in sight. They would meet several times a year for long discussions which would somehow reveal the road to what he liked to speak of as 'the New Christendom'. This gathering he called 'The Moot', it began in 1938, and it says a lot for the esteem in which he was held that a number of fairly outstanding people were prepared to join it.[20] But he needed a bright young man as dogsbody and prophet's assistant. For the preparation of the Oxford Conference he had had Eric Fenn but Fenn had now graduated beyond this role and was about to be appointed Assistant Director of Religious Broadcasting at the BBC, though he remained the Moot's secretary through its nine years of existence. So Oldham needed a replacement. He thought first of Leslie Hunter, but Hunter distrusted the vagueness of Oldham's plan and refused to be caught. He thought next of Newbigin whom earlier he had tried hard to persuade not to go to India in order to work with him on the Oxford conference, but Newbigin was perhaps a bit too hard a Barthian and too outspokenly opinionated to suit his needs as well as being set on a return to India after convalescing in Britain,[21] so Oliver was drawn in to work on Oldham's various plans, service this eminent gathering and share in the discussions. For the first six months of 1939 it was actually Oliver's primary occupation and at the start undoubtedly excited him. 'This work with J.H.O.', he wrote at the start of his journal in January, 'sometimes fills me with a desperate hope. It's such a fantastic gamble – "a new Christendom" indeed! but it's a gamble God is driving us to make. Christians must never look for "Catacombs to let".' To further the gamble and enable Oldham's dream to materialize, Oliver hastened round the country talking to people like Dodd and Raven in Cambridge, T. S. Eliot, Dorothy Sayers, Donald MacKinnon and Austin Farrer, all of whom were apparently enthusiastic supporters of the idea, though not all actually joined in.

The Moot held three meetings in 1939, at all of which Oliver was present. Each was intended to last three days. The first in Haywards Heath was in January, the second in Beaconsfield in April, the third at Annandale, 23–24 September. Other people who attended all three, besides Oldham and his wife Mary, included T. S. Eliot, Professor John Baillie of Edinburgh, Walter Moberly, Alec Vidler, who had recently become editor of the monthly *Theology*, H. A. Hodges, Professor of Philosophy at Reading, Eric Fenn and Karl Mannheim, the Moot's main intellectual star throughout its course, an agnostic Jewish refugee with a brilliant sociological mind. For Mannheim, attendance at the Moot was a pleasant way of mastering the English establishment viewpoint. The minutes of the January meeting take 38 pages reporting the discussion. It began with a consideration of Jacques Maritain's *True Humanism* and various comments made on it, as also of a sort of draft statement Oldham had produced to clarify their purpose. 'The central task,' he declared in discussion, 'was to draw together the best Christian minds in a new adventure of thought.' 'What mattered was the Church within the Church…the essence of the experiment consisted in asking the institutional churches to give the living church a free field.'[22] At the Easter meeting he stirred the Moot by quoting Kierkegaard's challenge, 'It is very dangerous to go into eternity with possibilities which one has oneself prevented from becoming realities.' Splendid as such challenges sound, what really was the Moot expected to do, especially as the international scene darkened by the day? Oldham next suggested the forming of an 'Order' of no more than 60 committed souls, two-thirds of them to be lay, but when Moberly and others asked how the 'Order' was to differ in purpose from the 'Moot', except in being rather larger, Oldham had little of an answer. His dream was a new kind of religious establishment, lay, liberal, devout, capable through a combination of intelligence and religious commitment of continuing to guide society in a way the bishops could no longer do. Christopher Dawson, the Catholic historian and political thinker whom Oldham much admired, published in January 1939 his latest book, *Beyond Politics*. Theoretically he was a member of the Moot, though he rarely attended meetings, but his view of its basic philosophy is revealing: 'it tends towards that alliance of religion and politics which seems to me definitely the wrong path'.[23] Whether or not the 'wrong path', the Moot's discussions were at a high, perhaps rarefied, intellectual level, which the participants appreciated, yet Oldham's plans themselves in regard to its purpose were delusory. What he could achieve in the field of British colonial policy in the inter-war years in the corridors of the Athenaeum through a mixture of moral authority, reliable information and a gently persuasive Oxford voice could not be replicated or turned into a system or an 'order'. Nor had it any practicality in the world of 1939. At Oliver's last Moot attendance, three weeks after Britain's declaration of war, the numbers were somewhat enlarged – including Reinhold Niebuhr, R. H. Tawney and Billy Greer – but the discussion appears not so different from that of the SCM staff held also at Annandale ten days before. It may be that the experience of listening for a second time that month to a rather confused debate about a Christian approach to the war helped convince Oliver to attend the Moot no more, or it may be that Oldham simply dropped him from the list of invitees because he contributed too little, just as he dropped Paton. The unexplained absoluteness of the severance seems strange, but it is certain that Oldham warmly welcomed Oliver's appointment to be Assistant General Secretary of the World Council five years later.

Anthony Hanson once composed a piece of ecumenical self-mockery entitled 'The Modern Oecumenical'. The central stanza runs as follows. Had he Oldham partly in mind?

I know how ill-adapted to the radio the Te Deum is,

And also how essential to the church the Athenaeum is;
For sanctity a substitute I've found, it's Sociology;
I write for Niebuhr's Quarterly, 'The Presbyter', 'Theology';
      About the B.B.C. I can be fashionably cynical
      I am the very model of a modern oecumenical.

As one reads through the papers and minutes of the Moot, one might start to feel that Oldham was becoming a bore, with a rather pompous and altogether too elitist conception of 'the living Church'. Already in February William Paton wrote to Visser't Hooft: 'I am full of apprehension about the prospects of Oldham's scheme. Everyone admires him so much that nobody seems to have the courage or the ability to tell him quite plainly where the scheme is obviously defective.'[24] The Moot did indeed represent the point at which Oldham gently faded away from leadership in the central line of ecumenical advance, though he would continue to provide at times the stimulus of his highly prophetic, yet also systematic, thinking.

Oliver's Moot (and mostly mute) participation did not last long, though he took away from it an enlarged vision of the nature of the Christian task. Studying Maritain's *True Humanism* had a lasting effect in helping him recognize the necessary autonomies within human experience and the consequent need, not for theological domination but a 'harmonising of the autonomies'. There was no money to pay for his services and he 'reverted' to the SCM in July. While he arranged for the September meeting to be held at Annandale, he does not appear to have continued to belong to the Moot after that – perhaps because he was thinking of an alternative with a younger membership and a more theological agenda. Once again, however, he had listened a lot but said rather little. It must certainly have been an education to attend the Moot, or, perhaps better, a 'finishing school' after his six years of full-time work within the SCM. World war was beginning. Reflections about the shaping of a 'New Christendom' could hardly hold the minds of most people at such a moment. Yet Oliver seems not to have perceived the oddity of their discussions, any more than did Oldham. They could not really sense what was about to happen, largely because they could not quite comprehend the scale of evil contained by Nazism. The senior figures in the Moot mostly shared a slightly old-fashioned 'liberal' theology, uncomprehending of any of the new orthodoxies of the Continent, and in an odd moment Oldham actually suggested that the statement he wanted them to adopt should be seen as a sort of *Mein Kampf*. That comparison at least was not appreciated.

Oldham's contribution to Christian thoughtfulness, however, was not yet over. Once the war started, he founded the remarkably influential *Christian News-Letter*. Published weekly and then fortnightly, with a circulation of many thousands, it raised the issues which Christians in war-time needed to be pondering. It came out under his name and probably made him more widely known than he had ever been before. The next year Kathleen Bliss joined him as the ideal collaborator and, from May 1945, replacement as editor. The last phase of serious Oldham influence became in consequence the first phase of that of Bliss, heir to his characteristic note, a theologically well-informed but emphatically lay viewpoint focusing much more on world and less on Church than was the case with almost all their clerical contemporaries, Oliver included.

Oliver had one final, highly memorable, pre-war experience: the World Conference of Christian Youth in Amsterdam in July. The World Alliance of YMCAs, YWCAs, SCMs and what have you were all involved. It had been prepared for years to begin on 24 July 1939. Could it now take place? War might begin at any time, but its organizers decided bravely enough to go ahead. Some 1,500 young people from 67 countries were gathered for a moving final fling of 1930s ecumenism, and they parted exactly a month before Germany invaded Poland. The atmosphere, Oliver felt, was one at once of apprehension and jubilation: 'it was such fun having so many people from so many different places' though that hardly decreased the difficulty of discussing such themes as 'International Relations, Nature and State, Race' in 42 study groups in August 1939.[25] The Conference Message declared defiantly, 'The nations and peoples of the world are drifting apart. The Churches are coming together...' For its participants, Oliver among them, the unifying authority of God above the divisive ideologies of men seemed self-evidently true and overwhelmingly important. A huge banner – 'splendid and audacious' is how Oliver remembered it – *Christus Victor* hung above the concert hall in which they met: 'Was it a hope only? Was it a delusion? Was it a slogan to cheer our own faint hearts? Or was it perhaps quite simply *true*?'[26] *À Toi la Gloire* they sang at the closing meeting with unforgettable intensity. Many returned from Amsterdam, whether to Britain, to Germany, to Lithuania or to Japan, with a sense of having received their marching orders from Christ the Lord. But where, in the real world of Hitler, Stalin and Mussolini, were they now to march?

# 4

# The war and Sheffield:
# Learning from Leslie Hunter

The SCM was often jokingly described by its members as the Society for Courtship and Marriage. Robert Mackie, Eric Fenn and Francis House among others all married within its ranks. Ursula Dunn was five years younger than Oliver. She was a Travelling Secretary for the north from 1935 to 1938 and an Assistant General Secretary 1938–9. As a Travelling Secretary she had nowhere to live except a suitcase, 40 colleges to serve – including the universities of Liverpool, Manchester, Newcastle, Leeds and Sheffield – and a salary of £119. As an Assistant General Secretary she worked at Annandale and shared a flat. She had wanted to be a nurse but her father had judged it unsuitable so she studied instead at the King's College of Household and Social Science in Kensington to gain a BSc at the University of London in 1934. Later that year she joined other pacifists in a major peace march to protest against rearmament.

Ursula came from a more Anglican, more well-to-do, background than Oliver. Her father too was a priest, who had spent the whole of his working life in the diocese of Southwark. After many years in Clapham, where Ursula was born, he finally ministered at Kingswood in Surrey, at that time the one really rural parish remaining in the diocese. Her grandfather, Andrew Hunter Dunn, had also been a London priest, deeply involved in social work in South Acton before becoming a bishop in Canada. Her uncle was the Archbishop of the West Indies. Ursula's mother, Freda, was the daughter of a successful wine merchant, Frederick Portal, who possessed a fine house and splendid garden on Sydenham Hill. The Portal background was Huguenot. His wife Marion had come from Australia with her father, John Wallace, an engineer turned parson. John Wallace's father-in-law, Francis Greenway, had been a Bristol convict shipped to Australia for forgery in 1814. He was also a stonemason and an 'architect of genius' to whom 'Sydney will always owe an irreparable debt for its finest historic buildings'.[1]

Ursula did not dissent from the ecclesiastical religiosity of her family, despite occasional feelings of impatience. Its clerical certainties, liberal and socially concerned as they undoubtedly were, could mildly irritate but never drove her to rebellion. They were, after all, laced with the certainties of the wine merchant and the near-romantic memories both of Huguenot ancestors and of the convict stonemason who had begun to construct Sydney on the lines of a capital city. All her life churchiness offended but religion soothed. She remained throughout a loyal camp follower with just an occasional hint of ecclesiastical rebelliousness. Oliver recognized more emphatically than she did herself her faith and loyalties. So, slightly surprised, she had accepted a Travelling Secretaryship in the SCM when invited to do so despite her protests to Robert Mackie that she knew next to nothing about the Bible. She enjoyed the responsibility and put up with the rigours of incessant travel from college to college, squatting uncomfortably in every little room in which she was accommodated.

Every few weeks she returned home to wash her clothes and recuperate. And then there was regular attendance at Swanwick Conferences and countless sandwiches whose production was thought to require supervising by a female member of staff. She was also one of a delegation of British SCM members, led by Mackie and including Dorothy Emmet, Alan Richardson and David Paton, who went to America in the summer of 1936 to share a joint 'Reading Party' with American and Canadian SCMers in New Hampshire. There were holidays too. One summer she spent ten days on a walking tour in central France with her first cousin, Joan Hunter Dunn, rendered immortal by John Betjeman's ever popular *Subaltern's Love Song*:

> Miss J. Hunter Dunn, Miss J. Hunter Dunn
> Furnish'd and burnish'd by Aldershot sun
> What strenuous singles we played after tea,
> We in the tournament – you against me!
>
> Love-thirty, love-forty, Oh! weakness of joy,
> The speed of a swallow, the grace of a boy,
> With carefullest carelessness, gaily you won,
> I am weak from your loveliness, Joan Hunter Dunn.

Joan's father was a doctor, the younger brother of Ursula's father, and their home was nearby, at Farnborough, just beside Aldershot. Joan and Betjeman met at work in 1940 at the Ministry of Information where she was part of the catering staff during the Blitz. His poem was published in *Horizon* in February 1941. She had fluttered his heart just a little and years later he described her to an enquirer as 'a lovely, sturdy, creole type with curly hair and strong arms and strapping frame and jolly smile and a soft laughing voice, a girl to lean against for life and die adoring'.[2] As cousins of the same age living near together, it was natural enough for Ursula and Joan to be for a time close friends, though the winds of war and marriage would soon blow them apart. For neither of them would the world of Surrey tennis tournaments remain their own.

Oliver and Ursula encountered one another at many a committee meeting of the SCM, at which neither spoke a great deal. Otherwise they seldom met. Both were attentive listeners. Ursula listened while continuing to knit. 'You know nothing about me at all,' she remarked when he proposed marriage. 'Yes I do,' he replied. 'I have watched you knitting and you always stop when something really important is said.' She had in fact known that she wanted to marry him for the last six months when, yet another meeting over, they had walked together in St James's Park and he had asked her to do so. That was 27 April 1939. He had only taken her out once before and when they did go to a dance together a little later his inability to dance made it a bitterly disappointing experience. That he had never learnt to do so tells one quite a lot about someone who had been a popular and handsome Cambridge undergraduate. Nevertheless the intensity of their love – so little worked upon, discussed or asserted before the very moment of commitment – proved singularly passionate and enduring. 'Love has been given to me today,' wrote Oliver in his journal, 'beyond anything I knew could exist.' Ursula hurried off from St James's Park to Cambridge for an engagement. Next morning she woke in her college guest room pressed against the ceiling, levitated by sheer joy. So real was the sensation that she never understood how it could be, what actually had happened! She was engaged to Oliver and the wonder of it had permeated her body so totally that for a moment it had transposed her very consciousness of place.

Ursula's birthday was 7 April. In 1939 it fell on Good Friday and Oliver, three weeks before their engagement, had already written for her the first of a long series of annual poems, though she did not know it at the time.

> His death thy life; thy birth
> Apart from Him is unto death.
> Lilt-laughter, raptured breath,
> The gay inconsequence of mirth,
> Love-lit eyes, quick-moving form,
> Dream-dance instinct with grace,
> The many-mooded mirror of thy face –
> All move towards the worm.
>
> Who took Him for the gardener, heard
> Her name, and knew that death
> Could not enthral. The Earth
> Is raised, by raising of the Word
> That was made flesh. Draw breath
> By mercy of thy truer birth.

She gave up her job in consequence of her engagement, compelled to do so by SCM rules. The graduate worker who had proudly slaved for four years on a pittance never had a full-time job again. When asked in widowhood whether that had been the case she said yes, but no one had ever referred to it before. In the SCM men and women were felt to be equals (except that the women had to resign their posts on marriage, unlike the men – a very big exception!). In the Anglican clerical world, on the other hand, women had almost no place at all. The sacrifice of a career for marriage was then so much a matter taken for granted that the unaggressive feminist had still to accept it without the expectation of question or comment.

They had intended to marry in the new year but then on 3 September the war began and it seemed sensible not to delay. The wedding took place in the same month, on the 27th, at Kingswood with Ursula's uncle, the Archbishop, officiating. William Temple had agreed to do so but was finally unable to come. He had a meeting at the Foreign Office that day, so one Archbishop stood in for another, but it was Temple's desire to come which mattered most. He wrote on the 24th that he was 'bitterly disappointed' that he could not make it. Oliver wrote immediately after the wedding to tell Temple about it and the Archbishop replied on the 30th 'How charming of you to write'. Oliver had worked so closely with him over the last few years and their mutual affection had grown so considerable that it seemed entirely natural that the immensely busy Archbishop of York, by then easily the most influential ecclesiastic in the world bar the Pope, should want to preside over this small country wedding of a little known young priest. Perhaps Temple himself already sensed that in the line of succession of ecumenical leadership here was the most promising candidate in sight.

'To have been married now for five months,' wrote Oliver in February, 'with all the fathomless joy of it and inexhaustibility of its opportunities, has taught me things a bachelor could never know.' Henceforth uxoriousness would always be a characteristic of Oliver's. In the early years it would flow out, at times a little embarrassingly, even into his sermons. Perhaps the joy of it helped blind him to the changed realities produced not by his marriage but by the war, though such blindness was common enough throughout the unrealistic months of 'phoney war'. In Oliver it took the form of thinking he could and should still continue in the SCM. He had worked for it for over six years and was, in fact, in terms of service by the end of 1939 easily its most senior staff member. Moreover, at 31, he was ceasing to be age-wise an appropriate student organizer. Early in December the Bishop of Southwark wrote offering him the Rectorship of Woolwich – an amazing challenge for a man of his years but an entirely suitable one for Oliver, especially in the war: here was 'a tough piece of work' needing someone young and vigorous, a parish including a large working-class population but also considerable opportunity for playing a wider social and civic role. Oliver turned it down: his period of service with the SCM was not due to end until late in 1941. Billy Greer, the new General Secretary, had only been on the staff for two years. Oliver felt that he alone had lots of 'senior contacts' and that Greer 'would feel badly forsaken' if he left the staff. A somewhat taciturn, reserved Ulsterman with slightly old-fashioned manners, Greer was very different from Mackie, but Oliver established no less cordial a relationship and they remained close allies for life. However, in the summer of 1940 France collapsed, Britain was isolated and Oliver found himself 'at a loose end', looking for a job. The SCM budget and the work its staff could do had, quite inevitably, been severely cut by the war once conscription got fully under way. One can hardly help but feel that, not for the only time, Oliver failed to respond charismatically to a call of great potential produced by the opportunities of a new situation. His diffidence and a sense of loyal responsibility to carry on existing work prevented him from seeing both that he himself needed a change and that the war situation prioritized pastoral demands very different from those of peace.

Almost his final task at SCM was to initiate a 'Theological Club' of 24 members, half Anglican, half Church of Scotland and Free Church, to meet once a year in the first week of July and hold together the younger theologians who had come up through the ranks of the student movement.[3] In between annual meetings dialogue would be carried on through a series of circular letters. The idea was first suggested to Oliver by Daniel Jenkins but one suspects that for Oliver it represented an alternative to Oldham's Moot from which he had quietly withdrawn. A group met to plan it in the first week of July 1940 at Annandale and the subject of the opening circular was to be 'on the Church facing the danger of being identified with our national cause'. Oliver chaired the club's meetings, held at Regent's College, Oxford, for the next three years. It was probably his chief extra-parochial and extra-diocesan activity in the years of war. His circular letter announcing the Club's formation was dated 19 July. It also announced that he was leaving the SCM for a parish in Sheffield.

How that was arranged we do not quite know. The Bishop of Southwark suggested the Wardenship of the Trinity College (Cambridge) Mission in Camberwell, a populous slum parish and one where plenty could be done especially given the support of Trinity, something guaranteed by a letter from the college's Senior Tutor. Yet again Oliver declined, accepting instead the apparently less demanding parish of Holy Trinity, Millhouses, on the south-west side of Sheffield. Millhouses was totally middle class and Oliver repeatedly said that he would have preferred to serve the poor. It also seems a somewhat pedestrian appointment for a clearly successful and widely respected high-flier at the moment when the nation was facing its gravest hour. Why did he choose it? Doubtless because Leslie Hunter, recently appointed Bishop of Sheffield who had pressed him to take it, was a good friend and an old SCM hand, bent on building up far more of a working team than was usual in a diocese of that era. Maybe too because he felt himself, in his own words, 'a fledgling of a clergyman', self-critically unsure of his capacity, without any previous parochial experience even as a curate, to carry the load of a large working-class London incumbency with the Blitz beginning. Maybe, even, because his father had begun his Anglican parochial ministry in Sheffield and Oliver's exceptionally developed sense of loyalty made it seem appropriate for him to start there too. Anyway he went to Sheffield.

In 1960, near the close of his 23 years as Bishop of Sheffield, Leslie Hunter wrote a little book about the diocese entitled *The Mission of the People of God*. When he came to discuss 'Relations with other Communions' and the change that had taken place in their regard over the previous 50 years, from hostility, or at least avoidance, to increasing cooperation, especially with Methodists, he chose to single out one parish in particular: 'In Millhouses, to take an outstanding example, since the time when Oliver Tomkins was vicar, there has been a spiritual sharing at a deep level between groups in both churches, and a growing concern for unity'.[4] This testimony from a man widely regarded as the most imaginative pastoral strategist of his generation to a young vicar who had spent only four and a half years in a Sheffield parish, and that more than 15 years earlier, appears remarkable.

Oliver was 'collated' by Bishop Hunter to the parish of Holy Trinity, Millhouses, on 31 August 1940 at the age of 32 and he left it at the end of January 1945 to take up the position of Assistant General Secretary of the World Council of Churches. These years, Oliver's only period in parochial work, may well appear the least significant in his *curriculum vitae*, anxious as he had been to be a local pastor and sad as he was never to be so again. He was, in feeling like that, as in so much else, a temperamentally somewhat conventional priest, wanting to do the real work any good priest sees himself as primarily ordained for – the cure of souls. He liked to insist on his ordinariness. Yet in point of fact Oliver was already, beneath the surface, a far from conventional Anglican priest of his generation: someone formed by long years of quite exceptional ecumenical experience in the SCM, both nationally and internationally. He came to Millhouses, then, with a double persona. On the one side he appeared to be a typical young priest keen to throw himself into the full round of parochial work; on the other he was the formed ecumenist, longing to try out at the grass roots of a local church ideas which he had been imbibing for years in the more esoteric atmosphere of a student movement and, indeed, of the high-powered theological consultations he had frequently attended.

We have, then, to observe the meeting between Oliver and what was a fairly typical middle-class parish of an industrial town, but we have, too, to locate that meeting at a very special point in time. There was a war on, and Oliver arrived in Sheffield at one of its worst moments, a couple of months after Dunkirk and the Fall of France. The Blitz was just beginning. The speed with which everything had changed may be illustrated by one rather bizarre little example. The final issue of *The Student Movement* to be edited by Oliver was dated June 1940. While noting the invasion of Belgium and Holland and the surrender of King Leopold, it could still announce that a French SCM Conference Camp for Women Students to be held in mid-July on an island off the Atlantic coast would welcome their British counterparts! It would now, however, no longer be possible even for students to meditate on the psalms on 'a fine site among pine-trees and sand-dunes on the Île d'Oléron'. Oliver, like everyone else, had to adjust almost overnight to a very different agenda but some things – including ecumenical things – would actually be made easier by that very context of war.

Leslie Hunter had only recently arrived in Sheffield himself. Far-sighted, exceptionally creative and forceful, brilliant at identifying people to carry forward his plans, he was also cold in manner and autocratically impatient with opposition of any kind. Barely five foot high and a heavy smoker, a good pianist who played Mozart to calm his nerves, and set out a game of cards even as he listened to a colleague, he was not easy to relate to. His closest colleague was his wife. They had no children but were intensely devoted to each other. 'His determination to have his own way was inflexible.'[5] Hunter's silence could be formidable. It reflected his ceaseless preoccupation with high policy and an absence of small talk. 'Leslie', his wife explained, 'is unique in that if he has nothing to say, he says nothing.'[6] Oliver found him uncannily perceptive – 'the only person I knew who could see through a brick wall' he later remarked to his son-in-law, another Sheffield priest. Though 20 years older than Oliver, Hunter had a remarkably similar background. Both their fathers had been Congregational ministers and though John Hunter, unlike Leo Tomkins, never became an Anglican, he too had felt the attraction of Anglicanism, especially of F. D. Maurice, and was happy enough when Leslie decided to become one. After graduating at Oxford, he had been for years a full-time SCM man – Theological Colleges Travelling Secretary 1913–14, Bible Study Secretary 1914–19, Literary Secretary 1919–21 – so Oliver's SCM years in the 1930s mirrored Leslie's, two decades earlier, very closely. He was consecrated Bishop of Sheffield at Michaelmas 1939. Six months later the vicar of Millhouses, Douglas Hopkins, still in his twenties, volunteered as a chaplain for the navy. He was lively, attractive, moderately Anglo-Catholic and popular. Millhouses parishioners were not pleased when Bishop Hunter insisted that Hopkins must resign his living, but he promised to find as good a successor. He found Oliver.

For the next 20 years, Sheffield would prove the very model of a modern progressive diocese, the clearest strategic expression of the ideals of SCM Christianity, and it would do so not only because of Hunter's own viewpoint and commitment both to social concern and ecumenical activism but also to a number of outstanding appointments – people who in very different ways shared his own enthusiasms: Alan Ecclestone, Ronald Preston, Ted Wickham, Pamela Keily, Alan Webster, Alfred Jowett and Robin Woods among them. Oliver was really the first of this group and he brought with him an up-to-date ecumenical *savoir faire* actually superior to that of the Bishop. But, in less specialist terms, Oliver had everything to learn. Sheffield provided his only pastoral and diocesan experience prior to his becoming Bishop of Bristol at the end of the 1950s, and it was Hunter's Sheffield model which would remain at the back of his mind as he strove to make of Bristol the most effectively ecumenical diocese of the 1960s, different as his personal style would be from that of Bishop Hunter.

Don't you know there's a war on? That question, asked so many times sarcastically of anyone who continued to expect some measure of civilized normality might, I suppose, have been put to Oliver. Could not his work in the Sheffield years almost be described without mentioning the war? While the war wholly encased it, it proved increasingly difficult to share what he felt with others or even with himself. His thought about the war can best be traced from his fairly confused pacifist start. Ursula had, for a while, been a highly committed member of the Peace Movement. Oliver was not. At least in retrospect he thought he had never quite been a pacifist, influenced in this by Temple. Yet he did appear to cling to the pacifist rhetoric which had dominated SCM circles in the mid-1930s rather longer than some of his friends. For Newbigin, for instance, the decisive moment came early in 1938 with the German occupation of Austria: 'I lay awake for hours... The outcome was that I could no longer count myself a pacifist.'[7] Oliver, on the other hand, published an article entitled 'Peace – the Day after Tomorrow' in the summer 1938 issue of *Radical Religion*, a quarterly produced by the Fellowship of Socialist Christians, and edited by Reinhold Niebuhr. It argued first for what it called the 'futility' of both pacifism and war, but ended, all the same, by still more or less committing itself to 'Christian paci-fism' as a necessary 'part of Christian faithfulness' given the character of modern war and what Oliver called rather simplistically the increasingly totalitarian nature of all states, even democratic ones. It suggests the confusion resultant from an attempt to apply Oliver's favourite 'both/and' approach in a field where it really could not work. But that simply reflects the confusion felt all around him.

The staff of SCM met immediately the war began at Annandale, 6 to 12 September, to ponder its meaning and God's guidance within it. The fruits of their discussions were summarized by Alan Richardson and others in an article entitled 'The War and Our Faith' in the October issue of *The Student Movement*. 'Read it and re-read it', advised Oliver in his editorial, and we can feel sure that he himself strove hard to remain faithful to its thrust. To summarize a dense summary is not easy, but the main points were four. First, a refusal to see things in black and white, or to claim that only one state was responsible for the war. Second, to recognize that SCM members would be divided between pacifists and those who decided to fight and that both courses must be respected. Third, to set out in a very restrained way the values of an 'open system' of society and government over and against totalitarian domi-nation. Fourth, to stress the need to prepare for an eventual 'just peace settlement', avoiding the mistakes of Versailles and opening the doors for reconciliation. There was certainly a shift here from Oliver's article of a year before. Nevertheless, SCM circles remained deeply ambiguous in their attitude to the war, at least until the summer of 1940.

In his own journal on the day the war began Oliver wrote as follows:

> Today I preached my first war-sermon. The real agony is whether we can go on being true. Tonight it was fairly easy to say certain things – remember the Catholic Church in Germany too; repent our share in bringing this horror to pass; pray daily for *our* 'enemies' – even for Hitler, who is already made the sole villain. I think they took it – but for how long will these things be possible to say? Cosmo Cantuar spoke on the air tonight, and again I felt he sold the pass. A tentative nod in the direction of penitence and the rest of it, including a soapy rebuke to pacifists, his old game of putting Christ at the service of Caesar. The myth of Hitler's sole guilt is already orthodoxy; *our* hands are clean, *our* consciences pure.

Oliver's mind remained for long – perhaps throughout the war – confused and frustrated. He wrote his worries to Robert Mackie who replied at length from Canada in January:

> What puzzles me is what has happened to your categorical, dialectic or whatnot theology. I had supper with Reinie and *his* charming Ursula the other night. He was breathing out fire and slaughter on the side of the Allies! But you have all left him there. I tried to moderate his enthusiasm… There is a war of two imperialisms, as well as a war between light and dark-ness… I don't get all hot about Hitler – he becomes a pawn: it's all he is. I don't get all hot about pacifists. They speak to me of God. But I believe – more perhaps than you suggest – in decisive and divisive action. Only the only explanation of action worth giving is Jesus Christ, not the errors and blindness and stupidity of others. The British Empire is full of the last, but I happen to be British, and I am convinced that the world would be worse for its extinction. Besides in the main its policy just now seems politically the wisest. Therefore I have no bones about the war in that sense.

In the following months Oliver published several strong pacifist contributions in *The Student Movement*. Nevertheless by May 1940 he was writing in regard to himself:

> I tried to read a pacifist pamphlet in the tube (by the Oxford neo-Thomists) and found my soul had no patience with it. God forbid I should cease to sympathise, to suffer with that part of our flock – but my own spirit knows it must be more committed. To what? Chiefly I want to preach the Gospel – but most of those to whom I talk have got to take sides more practically than I.

Faced with the hard realities of war, the progressive ecumenical world, with its strong international connections, anti-imperialism and pacifist leanings, to which Oliver had so fully belonged, found it exceedingly hard to reorientate without a sense of betraying its own past, and it hardly started to do so before Dunkirk and the Fall of France. Karl Barth's *Letter to Great Britain from Switzerland* of April 1941, accusing those who would not commit themselves whole-heartedly in the war against Hitler of having 'slept over their Bibles as well as over their newspapers', was particularly painful for SCM men to hear, precisely because they prided themselves on being people who had done neither. They now found themselves caught in the crossfire between those like Barth who called for total commitment in the struggle against Nazi totalitarianism and those, including many other continental as well as British friends, who urged the Church and its repre-sentatives to maintain some measure of detachment from the Allied cause. Could one agree with Barth without succumbing to the oily nationalism of Lang? Could one go on talking about a shared guilt without appearing blind to the scale of the evil in the Nazi system? Oliver was never a very politically-minded person and his 'both-and' syndrome made it peculiarly difficult to answer his own 'to what?' question 'practically'. He continued to see the war as 'lunacy' rather than as a struggle to which he could commit himself unconditionally. He was loyal to Churchill, dug for victory, and grieved about the fate of continental friends, but he gave up trying to formulate his own point of view. The more the Allies took the offensive, indulged in obliteration bombing and demanded 'unconditional surrender', the less he could go along with it, but he knew that a lot of things were now impossible to say, or at least to say without appearing contestatory in a way quite alien to his temperament. Unlike Bishop Bell, he was not the person publicly to advocate some alternative policy, yet he could still encourage the most open-ended of discussions among the youngsters of his parish about the war and its purposes seated together on the grass of his vicarage lawn.

Perhaps Oliver sometimes envied the single-sided clarity of his close friend and fellow Sheffield vicar, Alan Ecclestone, who was appointed to the working-class parish of Holy Trinity, Darnall in 1942. Alan, a genuinely brilliant person with a double First from Cambridge in English and History and some years of experience as a lecturer in English at Durham University was also one of the few priests to become, and remain for many years, a card-carrying member of the Communist Party!

Like Oliver, Alan at Cambridge had been deeply influenced by the high Catholic worship of Little St Mary's. They shared too an education in history and English rather than in theology. Hunter probably had little idea quite how radical Alan Ecclestone was: 'Leslie Hunter is not nearly as dangerous as he thinks he is', George MacLeod once remarked, but a conviction of his own radicality may have prevented him from realizing how far he was outflanked by Ecclestone. [8] He was certainly a little surprised to find copies of pictures by Picasso and El Greco hanging in Darnall Church. 'What strange

Stations of the Cross', he commented, but it was the copy of Padraic Pearse's poem *The Fool*, also hanging on the wall, which induced the local Roman Catholic priest to come in and pray. Cultural radicalism could break down the hardest ecclesiological barriers. Oliver believed as fervently as Alan that the Church existed to 'nurture the human soul', but Alan could express this with an uninhibited passion that Oliver could never quite show. He admired, but did otherwise. One senses instead, as the war's tentacles spread across every side of life, a pained suspension of his mind in regard to most wider issues. He concentrated desperately hard on the local job and, already with the Fall of France, developed an ulcer. When Lesslie Newbigin, who had been out of touch for quite a while, wrote from India late in 1942, 'You haven't become a bishop yet, have you?... Life is certainly not dull here: I have more jobs now – 14 village schools, a big High School, 40 village congregations, evangelistic work in umpteen others...', Oliver could only reply a trifle sadly, 'Your life sounds amazingly varied, and makes a little English parish seem very small. I have not got a single school and you seem to have fifteen in yours. As for having forty congregations, I find one a pretty full-time job.'

Oliver and Ursula's most emphatic war gesture was to invite two German Christian Jewish refugees, Ilse and Erika Friedeberg, to live with them and become full members of the family. With Ilse and Erika present at every meal, just as – in a different way – with Oliver's map of Europe on the wall with the flags showing front lines, the war did daily impinge on the Millhouses vicarage. It first impinged, particularly bitterly, just a week after their arrival when news reached them that Ursula's physiotherapist sister, Stephanie, had been killed in an air raid on St Thomas's Hospital. It impinged three months later with the Sheffield blitz. It impinged through the regular work of being an ARP Warden. Yet the impression remains that deep down Oliver did shut out this 'lunacy', so far as he could. It is noticeable how little he wrote in his journal at Millhouses: of the 200 pages of the 1939 to 1950 volume only 17 were written in the four and a half years in Sheffield and they were largely about the birth of his children, the death of his father, the death of Temple and even – a whole page – the death of his old dog, William ('William of Wykeham' was his full name). Thus there is not a single entry between 17 April 1941, recording the birth of their first child, Monica, and that a year later for her first birthday. His father's sudden death in August 1943 meant that Oliver brought his invalid mother and unemployed sister to live with them in Sheffield. It cannot have made life easier, while Ursula was often away, unwell, staying with the children at her parents in Surrey. In February 1944 Ursula wrote a sad, beseeching little poem which Oliver later kept in his private prayer book. It reflects both her repeated absences brought on by flu and anaemia and a sense that, despite his deeply felt love, he could not quite communicate or share the sense of sorrow pervading him.

> My love, you must with joy
> and strength stride forth.
> *Share* all the grief
> that being shared is halved
> And so make room for
> Glory in the Lord.

Only as the war approaches its end does Oliver's spirit start to turn noticeably outward once more to the practicalities of reconciliation and the making of a new order.

But let us start at the beginning – the basic chores of a suburban vicar in 1940. We can get the picture into focus clearly enough. Oliver was then, as always, a systematic taker of notes about small things, a writer of plans and personal assessments, all tidily preserved. There are, too, the memories of others. 'A parish priest's job is amazingly varied after a SCM secretary's,' he noted after a couple of months. It could include a bit of everything – sorting out a quarrel between a couple of 80-year olds, fixing the blackout, choosing hymns, preparing 14-year olds for Confirmation, teaching Sunday School, dropping in on Scouts and Guides, acting as an air-raid warden. He kept a pastoral card index of parishioners with comments added in New Testament Greek, always kindly but inaccessible to prying eyes. Oliver was always a believer in the value of orderliness, the drawing up of timetables, figures, lists of things achieved or unachieved, even the number of cabbages that had come up in the vicarage garden. The daily round was to begin at 7 with a cold bath and exercises and to close at 11. There was Holy Communion at 8 on a Sunday and 10 on a Wednesday as well as on feasts, Sunday Matins and Evensong, Confessions at 7 on a Saturday, private prayer morning and evening. Monday was a day off, reserved for walks and gardening – Oliver's resolute 'digging for victory' – light reading, a visit to 'the flicks', friends or the Railway Hotel in the centre of Sheffield for a cup of coffee. The other weekdays were divided between study, sermon preparation and letter writing in the morning, and visiting from 3 to 6.30 in the afternoon (extended to 8.30 on Fridays). Personal interviews would have 'right of way' over visiting and study but not over sermon preparation.

Oliver thought at first that of 7–8,000 people in the parish some 12 to 20 per cent 'go somewhere to church'. Later he realized that estimate was far too high. He soon sensed, moreover, that few of those who did so could possibly say much as to why they went. A handful 'vigorously desire a Low Church or a High Church policy' but the great majority would be happy with whatever was offered. It was the inertness of the parish community, in such contrast with the activism of the SCM world he had inhabited hitherto, which struck him. What people don't want, he quickly discovered, was to be expected to offer any sort of lead themselves. An early attempt to replace Sunday afternoon Evensong by house groups for prayer and Bible study was turned down on the grounds that Evensong was what 'was done last year' but also because house groups must mean that someone would have to give a lead. Oliver's central struggle at Millhouses was to break down this inhibition and turn a passive Church of England congregation into an active ecumenical community.

Four aspects of this campaign stand out most clearly. The first was the monthly Parish magazine *Friends*, beginning in January 1941; the second, the relationship with Millhouses Methodists; the third, the Church Meeting; the fourth, the Parish Communion. Oliver liked editing. He had given up one monthly, *The Student Movement*, in June only six months before beginning another, *Friends*. It cost 2½d a month or two shillings and sixpence a year and usually consisted of 12 pages. One page, from the second issue on, was invariably headed 'Methodist Church Notes' and was contributed by Thomas Kidd, the Millhouses Methodist Minister. There were sections of 'Parish News', gardening notes, domestic and cooking hints entitled 'Home Corner' and written by Ursula, articles on local history and Sheffield town government, advertisements and, of course, an editorial in which Oliver endeavoured to get some larger message across. Without *Friends*, one surmises, Oliver would have succeeded in doing very little in Millhouses, especially with the wartime curtailment of evening activities. With *Friends* he was able to push ahead in quite a few directions.

The first direction was ecumenical. On the night of 12 December 1940 and again on the 15th Sheffield was severely bombed. Six Anglican churches were destroyed and many others damaged, together with 40 vicarages. Holy Trinity, Millhouses, was fortunate but among the damaged buildings was Millhouses Methodist Church. The following day Oliver was round at Thomas Kidd's door, offering him free use of Holy Trinity for as long as needed. Though the Methodists were able to return to their own buildings quite shortly, this gesture transformed relationships overnight. The Methodist page in *Friends* was just one sign of it. A 'Unity Group' linking members of the two congregations in regular monthly meetings was another. But there was also an occasional sharing in services as well as many less formal ties. Even Ursula felt odd at first when present at a Methodist service in the Anglican parish church and for many local Anglicans it seemed quite amazing to have Methodists, who were seen as profoundly 'other', actually in church with them, Minister and all. *Ad hoc* and uncovenanted as these arrangements were, they constituted what may well be seen as one of the first 'Areas of Ecumenical Experiment' or 'Local Ecumenical Projects', as they came much later to be officially designated. Comparable developments were going on at much the same time in Bristol, instigated by Mervyn Stockwood, the rather brash young vicar of St Matthew's Church. Both were early anticipations, made possible by the emergencies and freedoms of war, of something only really recovered a full 20 years later.

It was in October 1942 that Oliver began an experimental weekly 'Church Meeting'. He borrowed the idea from Alan Ecclestone who had been invited to move to Sheffield in 1942 by Bishop Hunter precisely to introduce to his diocese what he had been practising in his previous parish of Frizington for years. All members of the congregation were welcome 'irrespective of age and sex' for a largely unstructured discussion which Alan saw as a tool of social revolution of a most literal kind. For Oliver it was never quite that. It began at Millhouses on a Sunday afternoon, following Evensong, in the church hall, but was soon transferred to the less formal context of Wednesday evenings in the Vicarage. Generally some 20 people came, not always the same people. An hour of Bible Study was followed by general discussion intended to clarify what it meant to be a 'member of the Church'. What was primarily political for Alan became primarily ecclesiological for Oliver, who usually sat on the floor, his favoured position for such meetings since SCM days. While this encouraged informality, Ursula wondered whether Millhouses parishioners would not find it somewhat bizarre. A year later came the start of the 'Parish Communion', first proposed by Oliver in *Friends* in December 1943 and begun on Christmas Day. It would take place at 10 a.m. on the first Sunday of each month replacing both the 8 o'clock Communion and Sung Matins. This was, of course, becoming standard fare for liturgically progressive parishes of a modern catholic sort since *The Parish Communion*, edited by Fr Hebert of Kelham, had been published in 1937. The point was to escape the formal solemnity of a sacred rite and re-imagine the Eucharist as a credible expression of the 'true family unity' of Christians in which the sacrament itself was experienced less as the culminating point of personal devotion and more as something inherently communal. Millhouses accepted it but, when a few months later Oliver proposed that it should be more frequent than once a month, the annual parish meeting responded with an emphatic no. Oliver was 'a little disappointed'!

There was one more step to come in his programme for the transformation of parish life at Millhouses away from a model of lay inertia and self-protecting insistence on retention of 'what was done last year'. It was a two-day 'Parish Conference' on 4 and 5 November 1944, intended to lead to the establishment of a number of parish 'cells' – the 1940s in-word for small groups of the committed. Canon Roger Lloyd was coming from Winchester to lead the Conference which was billed as 'A Christian Leadership Training

Course'. Oliver introduced it in the October *Friends* with a long quote from a recent address of William Temple: 'There can be no widespread evangelisation of England unless that work is undertaken by the lay people of the Church... The main duty of the ministry must be to train the lay members of the congregation in their work of witness.' Late in 1943 Oliver had been invited by Temple to serve as a member of the Archbishops' Commission for Evangelism. Here, as throughout his work at Millhouses, there was nothing startlingly personal in what he said or tried to do locally. Many of the Church Council discussions were based on questions and papers issued by Bishop Hunter, especially as preparation for his 1944 'Primary Visitation', others on the work of the Archbishop's Commission. Friends and colleagues in other Sheffield parishes, such as Alan Ecclestone and Alan Webster, were engaged in similar exercises. Leslie Hunter led a team. Oliver was one of its most reliable members, involved in various wider diocesan activities, from the development of women's ministry to the planning of a 'Church and World' exhibition in June 1944 in the Victoria Hall. His Millhouses ministry should be seen as a thoughtful and forceful local expression of what we may well call the Temple–Hunter view of how the Church needed to develop after the war.

The most notable dimension of Oliver's extra-parochial activity was involvement in the Diocesan Council for Women's Work. Although his appointment to be 'Warden' to the diocese's Women Workers was only announced in March 1941, this was almost certainly the real reason why Hunter had invited him to Sheffield and why Oliver had accepted. In no area was Hunter more of an episcopal pioneer than in his determination to put the organized ministry of women on an essentially new basis. In this he worked hand in glove with his wife. Oliver was their chosen agent to activate the revolution with a maximum of discretion.

If one reads carefully through the Minute Book of the Diocesan Council for Women's Work between 1941 and 1944[9] one sees clearly enough how this was to be done. The Bishop always chaired the Board, his wife the Executive Committee. Mrs Stannard was the Treasurer and as active as Mrs Hunter, she too being backed by her husband, Archdeacon Stannard. When Oliver began work as their warden, there were 21 stipendiary diocesan women workers – four deaconesses, ten 'licensed lay-workers', five Church Army sisters and two 'authorized workers'. Oliver's first task was to get them all together in his vicarage for a cup of tea. Next year a major step forward was taken with the appointment of a 'Head Deaconess' to be also Secretary to the Board. Her name was Helen Gunn, but she was invariably described only by her title, the 'Head Deaconess'. For some months she too lived at the vicarage in Millhouses. The Executive Committee would in future consist in practice of Mrs Hunter, Mrs Stannard, the Head Deaconess and Oliver.

The minimum salary was a frequent concern. It began as £150 but was raised in April 1943 to £175 though this too was criticized as too low for an educated trained worker. In October of that year the Bishop stressed the need 'to draw into the service of the Church educated women with a sense of vocation who were prepared to serve'. Alan Ecclestone soon found himself leading a Training Group and running a well-attended Summer School. The training, as one could expect with Ecclestone anywhere near, could be unconventional. A Mrs Aston, an RAF widow who wanted to work for the church but whose education was regarded as somewhat deficient, was sent off to attend Professor Bullough's English lectures at the university. Pamela Keily, a newly-appointed Religious Drama expert of great imaginative creativity, was awarded a series of grants. She produced a range of plays in parishes across the diocese, including Millhouses. She was capable, wrote Ecclestone, of involving 'both players and audiences in the drama of the redemption of the world far beyond their consciousness of it, yet touching at times the hidden springs of their being and bringing, if only for a moment, the whole soul into activity'.[10]

There was increasing liaison between the Council in Sheffield and the Central Council on Women's Work in London of which Hunter too became chairman. The Report of an Archbishop's Committee on the subject was published in January 1944. A resolution of the Central Council, backed by Sheffield, urged the bishops not to delay in opening Lay Readership to women and in authorizing them to conduct retreats and lead parochial groups informally in prayer. One sees here a systematic development which would almost inevitably lead on a couple of decades later to the campaign for the ordination of women. It is clear that the Hunters – in this as in much else a remarkable partnership – were fully in charge of the movement but clear too that Oliver had been chosen to pilot it through in the diocese because his sympathies were deeply involved in the advancement of women. His experience as diocesan Warden of Women Workers as much as that of Vicar of Millhouses would help shape his attitude to the ministry for the rest of his life.

Then, late in 1944, various things happened. In September a letter arrived from 10 Downing Street offering Oliver the living of St Nicholas, Nuneaton. The central parish church of an old, somewhat run-down town, it offered a bigger and more difficult job to do than Millhouses, but hardly a position of any exceptional significance. Harry Baines, the Rector of Rugby, not far from Nuneaton, was asked his opinion as an old friend and former SCM staff member. While clearly half hoping that Oliver would accept, he had to confess that 'I cannot help wondering whether you would not hurl the finely-made instrument you are against its dullness without much visible return.' Oliver eventually declined, chiefly on the grounds that the follow-up to the Parish Conference required his remaining at Millhouses. What seems surprising is that he considered it at all.

Hardly had Oliver quoted 'The Archbishop of Canterbury' at length in the October *Friends* in regard to his Parish Conference than Temple died. 'Hullo, Oliver, how's Sheffield?', Temple's friendly words at their last meeting only a few weeks before, rang in his ears. It was undoubtedly a shattering personal blow. But it also helped galvanize him into a sense that there were more important things for him to do than supervise the development of 'cells' in Millhouses. The very day after the Parish Conference he was off to represent the diocese of Sheffield at Temple's funeral. 'The choir at Canterbury', he wrote in his journal, 'was filled with an extraordinarily varied throng – but every one of us must have felt not only the loss of a beloved friend but that the lynch-pin of something we cared for had been lost – reunion, education, social witness.' Among those present was Visser't Hooft. He had come from Geneva, not only to attend Temple's funeral, but also to invite Oliver to become Assistant General Secretary of the World Council of Churches. It looks like a well-laid plot. Billy Greer, now Principal of Westcott House, wrote that very day to Bishop Hunter: 'The need is urgent and though he has certain disqualifications I think he is the only possible man for the job.'[11] It would be enlightening to know what Greer had in mind when he referred to 'certain disqualifications' but Oliver himself knew at once that this time he could not refuse: 'One thing that Temple's death means is that now hundreds of little men must just try a little harder. If I am called by God to have some small corner of his prophetic cloak fall on me – I am well content.'

In consequence, the December issue of *Friends* announced his coming departure from Millhouses in the new year and tried to explain what the World Council of Churches was all about, but it is still strange to find in it not one single mention of the Parish Conference which had seemed so central to his concerns just a few weeks earlier. How it went, how many people actually attended it, what resolutions it came to, we simply do not know. Outwardly at least it had gone clean out of Oliver's head and, perhaps, out of the heads of his parishioners as well. Even when in the following March he tried in his journal to summarize the 'credit' and 'debit' of his Millhouses years, of the Conference, so clearly intended as a culminating point of his long campaign to activate the parish, he said absolutely nothing. Given his expectations, as expressed in the response to the Nuneaton proposal, this remains somewhat inexplicable – one of those reticences in his life which one must fail to fathom. Nevertheless, one strongly suspects that the explanation lies, at least partly, in the Conference's failure to stimulate the sort of response Oliver had hoped for, a failure even he, ever the temperamentally quiet optimist, could not but recognize. There was a limit to the progress he could achieve in a tired middle-class suburb of a Northern town in war-time with most of the youth away on military service. Not only in a hypothetical Nuneaton but in an actual Millhouses was Oliver a too 'finely-made instrument' to be left indefinitely to hurl itself against a wall of 'dullness'.

In his December 'Vicar's letter' in *Friends* he set about explaining to the people of Millhouses just why he was so suddenly leaving and why the post of 'Assistant General Secretary of the World Council of Churches', a position most of them had never heard of, was so desperately important. He began with the now famous quotation from Temple's enthronement sermon about 'the great new fact of our era', a genuinely worldwide Christian fellowship, went on to explain how the World Council was developing and then remarked, as disarmingly as he could, 'I can see, having written thus far, that in my attempt to show the scope and importance of the work I have only succeeded in making it appear quite ridiculous that a person like me should have any qualifications to take part in it.' It was indeed difficult both to belittle himself so consistently and to explain why the young vicar of a very ordinary parish should suddenly be whisked off to a position of international distinction. The deaths of William Paton, William Temple and several other people during the war had, he explained, created 'the tragedy of a missing generation'. 'Archbishop Temple's sudden death was for me a weighty factor.' The 'giant in this whole field of work' had gone and 'hundreds of little men' were now needed to fill the gap. Oliver remained obstinately reluctant to admit that he might be anything more than one of the latter. Yet in his heart he knew very well that he was indeed 'a finely-made instrument' adept at functioning ecumenically not only on a national but on an international stage. Life in Sheffield had been interplayed with numerous activities elsewhere, such as the annual Theological Club Conference. He chaired that of 1943 on 'The Form of this World and its Transformation'. The following year the theme was 'Ecumenical Theology and Action'. It was chaired by Daniel Jenkins and will surely have provided an up-to-date resumé of a subject which, six months later, would become Oliver's full-time concern. Some time before, when Ursula was away at Kingswood, he actually admitted the strain within him between the budding ecumenist he actually was and the parish priest of a pedestrian suburb he was meant to be and had on the surface committed himself to being:

> Oh dear, I'm very unwilling to stop flirting with this international world,
> aren't I? Ought I to try? *I do* try and share them with the parish. Whatever
> I know of the ecumenical nature of the Church I owe to *people* from all
> lands and I more and more believe that only something of that vision and
> the sharing of a wider and deeper experience will ever shake the damned
> parochialism of English Christianity and awaken dear, staid Millhouses to
> the calling that waits on its own doorstep.

And the memory of all his friends of the thirties came flooding back. He had even written to Wim in July of that year rather nostalgically about his ecumenical past and the 'vast, invading army of all-important trivialities' that fill a parish priest's life. Beneath the surface he was itching for a change.

Oliver knew too that, faced with what he described to himself as 'the precarious and desperate cause of ecumenism today', he was almost alone within the Church of England in having the experience and the sensitivity needed. A few months later (17 July 1945), writing to John R. Mott in America, he had to admit that:

> Here, I am afraid, we sheltered too much behind the giant figure of William Temple and assumed that, because he was keen, the whole Church of England was keen too! In fact the Bishop of Chichester is now, to far too great an extent, almost the only bishop who really knows all about the ecumenical movement, though many others have a vague but kindly disposition towards it.[12]

It may seem strange that he did not include Leslie Hunter with George Bell as an exception, but he probably realized that Hunter's ecumenism was of a very diocesan and Anglican sort, with little of an international edge to it.[13] The time for keeping his own head down was over. He felt proud to regard this invitation, he could tell his parish, 'as my "calling-up papers" from the Church Militant, whose warfare enters into a new and critical phase when the European war ends'. No calling-up papers had come to him over the last five years. Now at last he could 'stride forth', sensing a form of warfare in which he could wholeheartedly participate.

Adieu to Sheffield. Oliver may, then, have been happier to leave 'dear, staid Millhouses' than anyone quite realized. He had greatly over-worked and over-worried and was in urgent need of a rest. He had learnt how to preach – his chief public acquisition in these years – 'biblically and contemporaneously' in a way that he had previously no scope to do. He himself marked that down as a credit but a choir boy who had listened to him weekly and often found him hard to understand remained 50 years later immensely impressed by his sermons – controlled, profound, never long. He had also, Oliver felt, built up a genuine sense of Christian community and he had stimulated a number of people in ways that would influence them for life. Some examples may be given. Rose and Arthur Quarrell[14] had been fairly nominal church members until their eldest child was killed at home in a domestic accident. Oliver appeared on their doorstep soon afterwards with a huge bunch of lilac from the vicarage garden. They became close friends and the Quarrells strong church members. 'One bit of my ministry which I shall never forget,' Oliver wrote to Rose before leaving, 'was the time when you told me you thought God had used little Julian's death to prepare you for Himself – I knew you said something true but it was something I could never have said to you. It had to come from you – or not at all.'

Alfred Jowett[15] had been a teacher when the war began but was dismissed as a pacifist and conscientious objector and went to work on the land. On a visit to his mother at Millhouses he told her he was thinking of offering himself for ordination and she put him in touch with Oliver who immediately arranged an interview with Bishop Hunter. As a result he was accepted at Lincoln Theological College. On a subsequent visit to Millhouses he went to the vicarage when Alan Ecclestone was speaking and that led to a life-long friendship and near discipleship.

Peter Wills was the young choir boy so impressed by Oliver's preaching and someone he used to take for walks on the Derbyshire moors. When Peter went up to Oxford his father died, quite unexpectedly, in his first term. Oliver was at once in touch with his college chaplain to give him the news personally and, when he arrived back in Sheffield, he found Oliver waiting for him at the station. His most enduring memory of Oliver was a sense of 'radiant prayer' when celebrating the Eucharist in a side-chapel of Millhouses Parish Church. After years of work in industry and as an extra-mural lecturer of Sheffield University, Peter was ordained in 1960 and later worked under Oliver in the diocese of Bristol.

In his March 1945 summing up of his ministry at Millhouses, credits and debits, Oliver noted as Debit No. 1, 'I was a poor pastor'. In the light of examples such as these, one may be inclined to disagree. He is in fact remembered in Sheffield as a very good pastor, not only because of his kindness but still more because of the depth of his quiet perception of the deeper dimensions of the heart.

# 5

# The World Council of Churches: Faith and Order

## Visser't Hooft's Assistant General Secretary

It was not the death of William Temple but that of William Paton which in point of fact wrought the decisive change in Oliver's life. It was into Paton's shoes, or some of them, that he had now to step. When still at Cambridge, Oliver had already got to know Paton while David, his son, had become a close friend and ally in the SCM. Yet of the four British 'giants' who together constructed the modern ecumenical order – Oldham, Temple, Paton and Bell – Bill Paton was the one with whom Oliver was least closely connected, probably because Paton always represented the missionary end of the ecumenical spectrum. It was an end in which Oliver's personal interest seems steadily to have decreased, despite the missionary idealism he inherited from father, mother and uncle. Bill Paton had become very much of an SCM man when still a student in Edwardian Oxford. A close friend of Leslie Hunter, he shared with Hunter a quality of forward-looking ruthlessness, backed up by hard work. With both of them, less single-minded people could feel a trifle ill at ease. Paton had returned to England in the late 1920s after some very effective years in India as secretary of its Christian Council. He willingly took over from Oldham the secretaryship of the International Missionary Council and the editing of the *International Review of Missions*, and was responsible for organizing the two highly successful meetings of the IMC in Jerusalem in 1928 and Tambaram, South India, in 1938. But his finger was in many another ecumenical pie. At the same time he produced numerous little books. Less profound and intellectual than Temple or Oldham, he was ever the forceful over-worked bureaucrat, a 'pocket battle-ship', to use an image of the age aptly applied to him. He had had a romantic streak, ardently wooing and marrying Ramsay MacDonald's secretary, Grace Mackenzie Macdonald, but her religious pilgrimage followed a rather different line from his, perhaps indeed as a necessary reaction. While Bill was always the extrovert, spearheading a new ecumenical administrative order, Grace turned inward, moving first to the Church of England and then, in 1936, to Roman Catholicism, a faith which she found best combined mysticism with practical social effectiveness.

Paton, for his part, plunged into an ever wider sea of responsibilities, combining the General Secretaryship of the International Missionary Council with that of the embryonic World Council of Churches together with numerous other government-related responsibilities once war began. It is hardly surprising that his rather overweight body gave out under the strain, but his sudden death in August 1943 at the age of 57 was a huge shock for friends and colleagues who had had little idea of how frequently he had been unwell. His responsibilities could not conceivably be taken over by a single person. Norman Goodall was persuaded to become secretary of the IMC but needed to be reassured that he would not be expected like his predecessor to possess 'omnicompetence and omnipotence'.[1] Paton's replacement as joint General Secretary of 'The World Council of Churches in process of formation' had to be sought elsewhere and it was over a year before the name of Tomkins was agreed to and he could be approached by Visser't Hooft after Temple's funeral in November 1944.

From this point Oliver's relationship with Wim Visser't Hooft would be central to his life and it is necessary to consider it with some care. They had been friends and colleagues working closely together at numerous conferences during the 1930s and had last met at Amsterdam in July 1939. Wim's international importance had grown immensely in the five intervening years, Oliver's not at all. Moreover Wim was as indefatigably determined to be at the centre of things and appear to be so, as Oliver was self-hesitantly reluctant. We must start, however, with the Visser't Hooft–Paton relationship because it helps explain a good deal.

When the standard *History of the Ecumenical Movement*[2] was published in 1954 Visser't Hooft himself contributed the crucial chapter on 'The Genesis of the World Council of Churches'. After giving an account of the first meeting of the Provisional Committee of the WCC at Utrecht in May 1938 in which Temple was elected chairman, he continued 'Dr W. A. Visser't Hooft was invited to become General Secretary, and Dr William Paton and Dr Henry Smith Leiper to become Associate General Secretaries.'[3] This corresponds to what is said in a pamphlet printed at the time entitled *World Council of Churches in Process of Formation: Interim Arrangements* for which, presumably, Wim was responsible. In his autobiography, *Memoirs*,[4] he explains further that he had already been 'invited to be the principal staff member of the new council' before the Oxford and Edinburgh Conferences even met in 1937 at a preliminary meeting, at Westfield College, London, that July. In the *Memoirs*, however, it is only 'at the end of 1938' that, in order to improve relations with the International Missionary Council, 'it was agreed that William Paton, one of the secretaries of the IMC, should give part time to the WCC as one of its Associate General Secretaries'.[5]

Despite these apparently clear (if slightly contradictory) assertions it is extremely difficult to know what the original arrangements were. When Visser't Hooft began work in Geneva in January 1939 his letterhead excluded Paton's name and read simply 'General Secretary: Dr W. A. Visser't Hooft'. However, Paton visited Geneva in March and by 21 April the original letterhead had been replaced by a new one reading:

General Secretaries:     Dr W. A. Visser't Hooft
                         The Rev. William Paton
Associate Secretary:     Dr Henry Smith Leiper

This remained the letterhead until Paton died. It is hard to see why, if Paton was only appointed an Associate General Secretary, at the same level as Leiper – as Wim later asserted – his name should have been placed on an equality with his own. In 1937–8 Visser't Hooft was a young man still in his thirties, Paton was already a senior statesman in his fifties. It seems unlikely that Paton could have been expected to take an inferior position, even though Temple and Oldham probably did place their principal trust in Visser't Hooft from the start. But it may also have seemed more uncertain then than it does to us now where the World Council's administration was actually to be chiefly based – Geneva, London or New York. A possible explanation of these somewhat contradictory pieces of evidence seems to be that under Oldham's instigation Visser't Hooft was indeed invited informally in 1937 to be 'the principal staff member' (though those who did the inviting had no real authority to do so and the nature of the post proposed was left entirely vague) but that considerable doubts were raised in some quarters as to whether it was right to confide so much to one young man.[6] Others were worried about his Barthianism. So in 1938 the Provisional Committee went slightly back on the Westfield College invitation by appointing Paton as 'Associate Secretary' alongside him. 'Associate' is an ambiguous word, and while the intention was that the two men would be 'associate' and equal, it could also be understood as making Paton simply a part-time 'assistant'. Presumably Visser't Hooft, when he produced a letterhead with only his own name, was interpreting it in the second sense but was then quickly corrected and had to accept that in principle at least he and Paton were simply two General Secretaries, even though he was full-time and Paton part-time. Eleanor Jackson, Paton's biographer, has no doubt that 'Visser't Hooft and Paton were officially appointed secretaries at the Utrecht meeting',[7] and Robert Bilheimer too agreed that the Provisional Committee appointed 'W.A. Visser't Hooft of Holland and William Paton of England as General Secretaries, and Henry Smith Leiper as Secretary in the USA'.[8] Bilheimer did so, partly at least, because in a letter to him (13 May 1987) Oliver had challenged 'the accepted version' of Wim's sole appointment. It is odd that in the long entry on the World Council in the *Dictionary of the Ecumenical Movement*,[9] Tom Stransky should revert to the incorrect 'accepted version' put out by Wim that he alone was appointed General Secretary. In this, seemingly definitive, version of the tradition Paton receives no mention at all.[10]

In practice Wim largely continued to behave as if he alone were General Secretary. Given the difficulties in wartime communication between Geneva and London this may have been next to inevitable if anything was to be done at all, but he clearly never saw the need to apologize or explain and it could reveal him at his most high-handed. Thus, for instance, in March 1943 he gave Sir Herbert Emerson, the League of Nations High Commissioner for Refugees and British Minister in Berne, an 'Aide-Memoire by the Secretariat of the World Council of Churches and the World Jewish Congress' on the subject of how to save European Jews from extermination. Paton was in no way consulted and only received it, to his embarrassment, through Emerson, yet he – no less than Visser't Hooft – officially constituted 'the Secretariat of the World Council of Churches'.[11] Wim blandly comments in his autobiography: 'What happened to this memorandum? Sir Herbert Emerson... sent copies to William Paton who made it available to several church leaders'!

When Paton died, the pattern inevitably changed. Oliver was not appointed 'Associate' but 'Assistant General Secretary (London Office)' whereas on the letterhead Visser't Hooft recovered the status he had claimed at the start 'General Secretary (Geneva Office)'. It remains hard to understand quite why in his published works Visser't Hooft effectively falsified Paton's position. But it was, in its way, characteristic of Wim's treatment of all his colleagues. For him there were great figures in the previous generation – Temple, Mott, Oldham and others. He could be generous enough in reference to them as also about his young disciples. There seems, however, to have been almost no room in his view of things for anyone but himself in the ecumenical story of his own generation. This is all the sadder given the absolutely unique contribution which Wim undoubtedly made to the World Council. No one else's contribution could diminish the primacy of his achievement, made possible by a combination of vision, energy and fluency in many languages. Yet it is striking that Oliver who was so close a colleague over many years is mentioned only twice, and in passing, in the *Memoirs*.[12] In the words of Stephen Neill, admittedly an often over-acerbic commentator on the character of his contemporaries:

One weakness of Visser't Hooft was his inability to form a team of colleagues working happily together as equals. He had worked successfully with older men than himself, such as John R. Mott and J. H. Oldham, but he did not know what it means to be *primus inter pares*. He must be *primus* and preferred to surround himself with younger men, whose gifts bore no comparison with his own.[13]

M. M. Thomas applied to Wim a favourite Indian proverb 'nothing grows under the banyan tree', and that seems true enough – not of his own immense personal achievement, but in regard to the work of his colleagues, who felt frequently frustrated by his disregard of their responsibilities and sensitivities. If Neill's judgement may be discounted as that of an embittered witness, the evidence of Francis House, one of the three 'Associate General Secretaries' in the late 1950s, cannot.[14] He has described how Visser't Hooft remained 'fully in control' of every side of the WCC organization, 'humiliating' his Associate General Secretaries by his disregard of their responsibilities as defined at the Evanston General Assembly. Where previous to Evanston no fewer than 19 small separate departments had existed, all directly related to the General Secretary, Evanston had endeavoured to improve efficiency and diminish dictatorship by grouping these into three 'divisions' each under an 'associate general secretary'. But Wim, House discovered, continued to work 'directly and secretly' with the sub-units, so that House often had the greatest difficulty in finding out what was going on within his designated 'Division of Ecumenical Action'. The 'most bitter moment' came when Wim excluded the Associate General Secretaries even from the meetings of the Staffing Committee of the Central Committee, when their own departments were being discussed! After Amsterdam, Robert Mackie joined the World Council staff with the idea that he would become Wim's right-hand man in a too rapidly growing organism but in practice that was quite impossible: 'Wim has a queer unconscious way of omitting me from conversation' he explained and, again, 'It is impossible to share Wim's burdens because I never know what he is going to do next.'[15] Robert Bilheimer, who worked very closely with Wim at the same time as House but was a much younger man and a great admirer of the General Secretary, has described his 'most unfortunate trait' – a great ability to disregard and hurt people: 'His irritation rose, his rudeness obtruded, his anger flashed.' Robert Mackie, Bilheimer continues, 'carried on a whole ministry of healing staff members who had been wounded by Wim'.[16] For Lesslie Newbigin, Wim was 'a very tough person to work with' – he relied on you to do a job well, if you didn't he came down on you like a ton of bricks.

If there was, unfortunately, a large degree of egomania in this great achiever and near icon of the ecumenical movement, Oliver was probably less affected by it than any subsequent assistant or associate general secretary. In fact they worked together, so far as one can tell, exceedingly closely and harmoniously. Apart from numerous meetings, they corresponded continually, often on quite minor matters. Ten letters could pass between them in a single month, and there is no reason to question the sincerity of Oliver's words on a card dated 22 December 1952, when leaving the employment of the World Council: 'I can't – and need not – tell you how precious these eight years have been, not least by any means for all that it has meant to be your colleague.' The success of their long collaboration was due to its grounding in their pre-war relationship and to Oliver's exceptionally cool temperament, but it owed a good deal to two further reasons: Oliver was based in London and his primary responsibility, as it turned out, for Faith and Order was one in which Wim, despite his theological training, grew relatively uninterested.

Wim, like Bill Paton, developed as he grew older into more of an organization man than a thinker. It would in many ways be awkward for Oliver that his home and family were in England, while the institution for which he worked became more and more firmly based in Geneva. But this arrangement actually gave him a freedom which he was able to utilize effectively elsewhere while avoiding marginalization in Geneva. Oliver soon came to recognize Wim's central personal weakness. Already after just a year of renewed cooperation he confided to his diary in February 1946: 'I am depressed by the thought of Wim's *isolation*. He has great gifts – organiser, thinker, prophet. But he needs someone to rub his mind against and someone who'll say No when needful...Not that he is doctrinaire, he is in some ways a great realist. But he has a certain quality of hardness.'

Wim's weaknesses were, of course, the reverse side to amazing strengths, strengths which were proved very strikingly during the war years when he carried on the work of the World Council while its Provisional Committee did not meet once between 1939 and 1946. Throughout the war he kept in touch with churches of every sort and on every side, but he also became a secret agent for the passing of information between Holland and the Dutch Government in London as well as a channel for the German Resistance seeking support in the West. He could only manage all this because of his sharpness of judgement, superb efficiency, ceaseless flow of energy and a discipline of silence which ensured that even his colleagues in the office of the World Council were quite unaware of much that he was doing. It is not for nothing that Klemens Von Klemperer has dedicated his work, *German Resistance against Hitler*,[17] to the memory of George Bell and Wim Visser't Hooft. The habit of secrecy and disregard for colleagues which was so needed for the successful achievement of Wim's extraordinary wartime mission did not, however, make it easier for him to lead a team in the conditions of peace. Of all people Oliver was the most unwilling to criticize a friend or colleague but he did admit that Wim was 'quick to fidget at tedious explanations', that he upset some people 'by his brusque way of insisting upon his own views or dismissing theirs' and that his mind preferred 'sharp, clear concepts', even slogans, to subtle distinctions.[18] But Oliver's admiration for Wim remained immense. He saw in him not only 'a broad streak of the prophet' but 'a tiger for work' and someone who was throughout life a supreme achiever.[19]

On 21 March 1945 Oliver wrote to Wim from London:

> We have at last furnished an office (temporary) for the secretary (assistant) of the committee (provisional) of the council (in the process of formation) of the Churches (in schism) of the World (in chaos). In spite of this almost completely tentative existence, there would be plenty for me to do if the Assistant General Secretary were not ill in bed. Since I wrote to you last my old tummy trouble which has haunted me for the last four or five years, suddenly got worse again.

With an active duodenal ulcer Oliver was confined to a diet of milk. By the end of April when Wim came to London for a meeting of members of the Provisional Committee he was sufficiently recovered to be allowed by his doctor to attend the meeting and to pay a visit with Wim and Marc Boegner, President of the Protestant Federation of France, to Archbishop Geoffrey Fisher at Lambeth. It was a good meeting. Fisher agreed to be a member of the Provisional Committee and, moreover, declared that his great desire was 'to follow in the footsteps of the two Williams'. For Oliver in particular that was a very encouraging declaration, all the more so as Fisher had had hitherto extremely little ecumenical experience and saw the world through a pair of exceptionally Anglican eyes.

While he never provided the sort of direction that Temple or Paton had offered the ecumenical movement and, in practice, acted more as a brake than a leader, Fisher played a considerable part in its consolidation over the next 15 years and Oliver, at least, charitable as always, came to regard 'its impulse to unity' as one of the more notable aspects of Fisher's primacy (diary, May 1961).

Even more essential than an office was a house to live in. Moving from Sheffield to London in the final months of the war was not without its difficulties but Ursula's parents still lived in Surrey, providing an initial base. It seemed sensible to be near them but a little closer to London. Her father bought a detached house near Cheam with a garden, 63 York Road, to let to them. They moved in during April, so Ursula, Oliver, their two small children, Monica and Stephen, together with Oliver's mother were soon settled there and comfortably enough. They were joined too by a succession of au pair girls – Dutch, Swiss, German, Yugoslav – to help look after the two additions to the family when they arrived, Ruth and Deborah. Old Mrs Tomkins occupied the front downstairs room until she died during the first summer there. Her room was soon taken over by old Frau Friedeberg, the mother of their Sheffield lodgers. She had spent the war in Switzerland and it was 14 months before Ilse and Erika found a flat to move her to. Later the room was occupied by Sibyl, Oliver's very simple and gentle sister. She developed cancer and was nursed by Ursula at home until the last ten days before her death in December 1948 in St Thomas's Hospital, where she had worked in the kitchen.

The first year Oliver was much at home, partly because he was often unwell, partly because his job had been initially presented as one geared to the British scene. He was with his mother when she died in August. But whether he was there or not, the house was always rather over-full with lodgers, overseas students invited for Christmas, together with Suuske, Karla, Ruza, Agnes or whoever was the au pair of the moment.

From December 1945 Oliver was increasingly away, often for many weeks at a time. When he returned, he brought presents from the countries he had visited, read books to the children, told them a saga of invented stories about 'Mr Hockalock' and bicycled with them to church on Sundays: by the later Cheam years they travelled on four bicycles – Monica and Stephen had their own, while Ruth and Deborah sat on the back of Oliver's and Ursula's. But, to a large extent, he was not there and in consequence, as in so many British upper-middle-class households, it was Ursula who had to keep things going. Oliver, for all his rather determined efforts to behave as head of the household when he was back with them, became inevitably something of a visitor. A long hug on arrival could not quite make up for the months away and, perhaps unsurprisingly, Ruth could sit up in bed and declare unhesitatingly, 'I hate daddy'. Yet when he was at home they had his almost undivided attention in a way which would seldom be the case in later years.

In the spring of 1945 it was clear enough that neither Oliver's work – whatever it turned out to be – nor most of his mind could be bounded by Cheam. The war in Europe was over, Germany defeated and ruined, Hitler dead. The execution of Dietrich Bonhoeffer on 9 April, coinciding almost to the day with the move to York Road, was a last horrid expression of the Nazi past, the release of Martin Niemöller from Dachau concentration camp by Allied troops a few days later, the first symbol of re-emergence of a different Germany. For Oliver this climacteric moment in the history of humanity was equally one within his own career, a suddenly exciting and decisive opportunity to contribute to a new world order. He felt, as we have seen, that he had at last received his 'calling-up' papers from the Church Militant – just when other people were starting to think of being demobbed – directing him to occupy one of the potentially most challenging of posts in 'a new and critical phase' of the Church's perennial warfare. If he was only too aware that within his own Church the bishops, with the sole exception of Bell, were at best 'vague but kind', almost unaware of the appeal of things to which he was himself responding, that after all is only how most bishops almost always are. For Oliver at this point, conscious that some 'corner of Temple's prophetic cloak' had fallen on him, he might at last 'stride forth' as Ursula had urged, setting behind him for a while any too humble conviction of his own insignificance.

All that was true and representative of one side of Oliver and yet that conviction of personal insignificance would not easily go away, all the more so as he had been left extremely vague as to what he was actually expected to do. Thus on Good Friday of 1945 he wrote under the heading 'Direction' another bout of self-belittlement: 'I've never been sure which of my various small gifts God meant me to develop most. By nature dilettante, I could easily dabble my days away,... I hope this job will be only temporary.' That hardly sounds like someone conscious of a prophetic cloak. It is only when he actually flies to Geneva for the first time at the beginning of December that his tone begins to change as he gets to grips with a job he can recognize as his own.

What, in fact, was Oliver's brief as 'Assistant General Secretary'? That is no easy question to answer. Wim had duly provided him with guidelines in November 1944 when he accepted the post. While these included a great many points, they almost all related to ecumenical activity within Britain, 'convincing the unconvinced, particularly in the Church of England'. Wim recognized that someone based in London might build up useful military and civilian links with occupied Germany, but he seems to have seen Oliver as essentially his PR man in Britain. It is hardly surprising that when Archie Craig, the Secretary of the British Council of Churches, saw the job description, he commented, a little warily, 'It is almost inevitable that Oliver's work and mine will have to be carefully aligned so that we do not tread on each other's toes.' Paton's role as Associate General Secretary, based in London, had effectively depended on three things. One was his own considerable network of ecumenical contacts, linked chiefly with Life and Work. Paton had never been much of a Faith and Order man. The second was the sheer importance of London in the functioning hitherto of the ecumenical movement. Temple, chairman of almost everything, had lived there; Oldham, principal architect of the great design was nearby; so was Hodgson (by then a Regius Professor in Oxford), Secretary of Faith and Order; so was Bishop Bell, the movement's chief prophet; and so, at Edinburgh House off Sloane Square, was the headquarters of the International Missionary Council. The third basis for Paton's activities lay in the IMC's connections, especially in Asia, far wider geographically than those of Faith and Order or Life and Work. Rather little of this could Oliver take over, apart from the availability of Bell to turn to when in need. His missionary expertise and connections were nil. His own experience related to Faith and Order, not Life and Work. Temple was dead. On 9 February 1945 a V2 flying bomb hit the London offices of the Presbyterian Church of England while a Faith and Order meeting was in progress. Hodgson was injured very seriously while his assistant as secretary of Faith and Order, Father Tribe, was killed.

The general importance of London in ecumenical terms would soon decline. Nevertheless in the immediate aftermath of the war London remained western Europe's capital. The London office of the World Council had so much to coordinate that 'there is little enough time left to do the things to co-ordinate' Oliver complained in his first annual report. In fact he seldom left London in 1945. Only in the following year did his job subtly change from one of 'convincing the unconvinced' in Britain to one of international leadership of a backroom sort, focused upon the coming World Assembly of the Council. It was actually the V2 more than anything else which may have determined Oliver's principal responsibility: Faith and Order. This had certainly not been central to Wim's original plan. It only appears as point four in his November 1944 memorandum with the words 'collaborate with Hodgson and Flew in organisation and study work of Faith and Order'. In January Wim agreed to Hodgson's suggestion that Oliver might give about a quarter of his time to this side of things, yet it had clearly become the central plank in a rapidly evolving range of responsibilities by 1946.

### Germany and George Bell

Point 8 of Wim's original job description was headed 'Germany'. It instructed Oliver to work on a number of things, keeping in touch with army chaplains, making contact with the civil administration and the German Confessional Church, and to distribute material about Germany to study groups in Britain. Here as elsewhere Wim clearly envisaged Oliver's role as chiefly one within Britain and, obviously enough, there was plenty to do in Britain if things in Germany were to improve though it would be difficult to do much of value without also being directly involved inside the German scene. What Wim nowhere suggests is that the Assistant General Secretary should in this or anything else participate in the World Council's central activities. His own role was in no way to be circumscribed by that of the Assistant General Secretary.

It was George Bell, with all the moral authority which the Bishop of Chichester had acquired, who was uniquely competent to take the lead in regard to Germany and it is here that Oliver first came to cooperate closely with Bell. He had met him in the SCM at Cambridge and at numerous meetings since but it was Germany which really brought them together. Bell, more than any other figure, represented the incarnation of ecumenical integrity. He had edited two standard volumes of texts on Christian unity. He had been a delegate at the first conference of Life and Work at Stockholm in 1925 and Chairman of its Council for a while in the 1930s, during which he established an unrivalled position of international Christian leadership. He was also almost the only ecumenist to pursue good relations with Catholics really seriously and to have achieved during the war a remarkable rapport with Cardinal Hinsley.[20] He had spent much of his time throughout the war years struggling to be of service to the 'other', non-Nazi, Germany. He had wanted the government to commit itself to such war aims, including the preservation of 'Germany's independence and integrity' as would actually encourage an anti-Nazi revolution in Germany, instead of calling for nothing other than 'unconditional surrender'. He had wanted to create links with the German opposition and was much strengthened in this desire by his meetings with Hans Schönfeld and Dietrich Bonhoeffer in Sweden in May 1942. He strongly opposed the saturation bombing of German towns and he did all he could to alleviate the living conditions of interned German refugees in Britain.

All this had made Bell an unpopular figure in some circles in his own country but it ensured that he was the one person of any importance in Britain to whom, in the postwar situation, German Christians could turn with an immediate sense of trust. Not, of course, that it was only Germans for whom he showed concern. Already in March 1945 he was visiting Paris and reporting afterwards about the immediate needs of Churches in France, Norway and Greece. But, once the European war ended with Germany's surrender in May, Bell was on the lookout for what could be done to support its Church leaders in the huge work of religious and national reconstruction, and Visser't Hooft was writing to him from Geneva with suggestions. Then in October he visited Germany accompanied by Gordon Rupp to attend the meeting in Stuttgart between members of the German Evangelical Church Council, including Niemöller, Lilje and Asmussen, all released from concentration camps only a few months before, and a delegation from the World Council including Pierre Maury representing France, Hendrik Kraemer representing Holland and, of course, Bell and Visser't Hooft. In the name of the Evangelical Church Niemöller handed copies to the World Council delegation of what became known as 'the Stuttgart Declaration' acknowledging 'a solidarity of guilt'. 'With great pain do we say: through us has endless suffering been brought to many peoples and countries.' Those words were Niemöller's and accepted only with difficulty by some members of the German delegation but they opened the way to a full restoration of fellowship between the European Churches. As the Swiss Dr Koechlin later remarked, 'I am still convinced that it made it very much more easy for the Germans to give the Declaration to a personality like the Bishop of Chichester whom they trusted and loved, than to any other man.'[21] The German Church was at once invited to send a delegation to the coming meeting of the Provisional Committee of the World Council.

In retrospect at least it seems strange that the Assistant General Secretary of the World Council, despite his considerable pre-war experience of Germany, was not part of its delegation to that meeting, but that was undoubtedly because the job which Visser't Hooft wanted him to do was essentially a British one. Perhaps Oliver's situation in this very betwixt and between year of his life is best symbolized by his returning to Sheffield in late September to preach at the harvest festival in his old church of Holy Trinity, Millhouses. Again it seems strange that the Assistant General Secretary of the World Council should find time to do so in that first autumn of peace but his sermon all the same sums up with great maturity both his attitude to the war and upon what his mind was now concentrating. It had been, he reminded his old parishioners, a war on two levels. On one level it was 'a war of power-politics – self-defence against aggression' in which we only fought when threatened. On that level the less we say now about 'fighting for the freedom of Poland' the better. But on another level it really was 'a war in defence of *embodied* ideals or *things built on* Christianity'. Not, he insisted, for Christianity but for things built on Christianity such as free elections, just courts, a free church. That distinction, he added, was still needed. In the war, to quote Chamberlain, 'against evil things, brute force, bad faith, injustice, oppression and persecution', we fought at times on the enemy's side, and he on ours. 'We fought on his side when we used the "brute force" of the atomic bomb' or in our treatment of deported peoples, while 'members of the enemy fought on our side in the Church opposition, in those who were imprisoned for helping Jews'. He then sketched the story of five people who really did die in the war at this deeper level, and precisely as Christians – a South Sea Islander executed by the Japanese, a Dutch minister who died in a concentration camp, a Russian Orthodox nun in Paris who substituted herself for execution in place of a much younger man, and two German pastors – Paul Schneider and Dietrich Bonhoeffer. 'These all sowed – and we have entered into their labours.' An understanding of the full meaning of the Second World War has always been reserved for those who can recognize the profound significance of the German opposition to Nazism and the many who paid for it with their lives. Very few people recognized it in 1945 but Oliver, like Bishop Bell, was one who did.

Oliver joined Bell in a very important delegation to Germany in October of the following year, a delegation given official status by the British Military Government –

rather a mixed blessing.[22] It was remarkable in being fully ecumenical, approved by Archbishop Fisher and Cardinal Griffin, and including three Catholics led by the Bishop of Nottingham, as well as representatives of the Church of Scotland and the Free Churches. Bell led the whole, being joined on the Anglican side by Bishop Hunter and Oliver. While Oliver was at first amused to find that Bell and Hunter had been accorded the rank of Major-General and he had become 'Colonel Tomkins', later on he regretted how much their close relationship with the British army inhibited free speech on the part of the German Christians they had come to meet.

In two weeks they visited Düsseldorf, Cologne, Bonn, Herford, Hamburg and Berlin and Oliver was able to meet old friends like Hanns Lilje and Martin Niemöller. Everywhere he was struck by the scale of the devastation, the misery of the inhabitants, many of them essentially homeless refugees from the east, as also the well-intentioned inadequacy of the British officers attempting to improve the situation while mired in an impossibly extensive exercise of 'denazification'. Germany, he concluded, was one large sanatorium in which, as in every sanatorium, its sick inhabitants were unable to think of anything much beyond their own sufferings and required to be treated with the utmost patience; it was no less one large prison-camp in which 'an opening of windows' was urgently needed; but then again it was 'a battle-field' in which an ideological war was already developing between Russia and the West: 'It was alarming to see how Russia is for most Germans a myth rather than a country inhabited by human beings,' he commented immediately afterwards. 'By all means let us admit that Russia is a cruel and clever despotic state but I at least believe that to shriek "Anti-Christ" is to be guilty of precisely the totalitarian error of absolutising politics. I think the German Church would be fatally wrong to regard this as 1933 all over again.' But there was also, Oliver saw, an ideological 'battle within the Church' between 'those who seek primarily Restoration and those who seek primarily Reformation'. He guessed it cut across confessional lines but confessed to 'almost complete apprehension about the dominant attitude of Catholicism', yet added, 'as for the Protestants I was almost equally discouraged'.

Beyond all this Oliver saw Germany, in terms of spiritual reality, as 'a prophecy and a sign...a reminder of the frailty of human justice when the victors in a righteous cause ...have themselves become so quickly the victims of greed, rivalry, lassitude, lack of imagination'.

Two aspects of this immensely educative fortnight require further notice. The first was relations with Catholics and Catholicism. It was certainly an extraordinary event at this period for a Church delegation to consist of both Protestants and Catholics. Probably the government would not have accepted an official Church visit which did not include the two. Both sides found it awkward, at least initially. On 19 October Oliver could note, 'Tonight at the end of three full days together, we are still *two* parties, travelling, feeding, conferring together, but always two parties. What a deep division it is -- but some comfort to know that even this represents a unique achievement of cooperation. No Catholic–Protestant group of such *formal* status has ever before left England for joint conference in a foreign country – to the best of George Bell's knowledge, and he ought to know.'

Oliver did his best to mix with the Catholics but it is clear how suspicious and critical even he could be, commenting upon them at times in a rather patronizing way. Yet some of the people he most empathized with during those two weeks turned out to be Catholics. If Cardinal Frings of Cologne gave he felt 'the same impression as Cosmo Lang of a superb barrister' (hardly a commendation!) he found Cardinal Von Preysing of Berlin 'a very great man', and became warm friends with a Monsignor Smith (who turned quickly into 'Dick') 'a very cooperative R.C.'. The two Germans he writes most warmly about were both Catholics – one, the president of the Hamburg YCW (Young Christian Workers), a young worker 'very reminiscent both in looks, manner and views of David Paton' (high commendation for Oliver!) who was extremely critical of the pressure to identify the Church with the Christian Democratic Party which he regarded as 'a bourgeois, property-bound, party, and quite incapable of accepting the inevitable *and just* economic revolution of our time'. The other, Ludwig Baum, a priest in Dresden whom he had made friends with before the war, and from whom he heard of the even more appalling conditions and regular 'disappearances' within the Russian Zone: 'Life is compounded of fear, hunger and despair at the eclipse of Christianity. Ludwig is fearless in his gentle, pacifist way and goes on doing all a Catholic priest should. I doubt if I shall see him again. I left him my gauntlet gloves – but I don't suppose he will keep them.'

Perhaps the joint conference in Berlin on the 28th represented this side of things best, both in what it actually was and in a certain surviving lack of mutual trust demonstrated by its very composition. It was surely remarkable to have Cardinal Von Preysing and the Lutheran Bishop Dibelius, the Anglican Bishop of Chichester and the Catholic Bishop of Nottingham all sitting together to discuss their problems, overleaping in each direction the frontiers of Church and nation. Yet Oliver could still comment tartly, 'A good meeting though rather disturbed in balance by RCs smuggling in four members not invited, thus collaring nearly half the membership and more than half of the time!' Nevertheless the value of the experience of being a member of a delegation of 'joint Catholic-Protestant nature' was enormous: 'a unique precedent' he concluded, 'but one that must not remain unique'. This almost certainly influenced him for life. Never before had he worked so closely or constructively with Catholics, above all with English Catholics. One can almost feel him beginning in these two weeks to overcome Anglican stereotypes about the character of English Catholicism. The printed report, *The Task of the Churches in Germany*, was written as an entirely combined operation, signed by all the delegation, published jointly by SPCK and the Sword of the Spirit. The following January Mgr Smith was able to write to Bell to tell him that he had been able to present Pius XII with a copy of the report, together with 'Karl Barth's notes' (!) and that the Pope had them all on his desk.

The other decisive aspect of this visit so far as Oliver's own development was concerned was the close relationship it helped to consolidate with Bell. The Bishop of Chichester was always something of a problem, even if you greatly admired him. Bell could lead absolutely fearlessly but he was too personal in approach to be truly a leader. And he could be a disconcertingly informal chairman. He failed to consult when he should, and his inflexible obstinacy in speaking the truth as he saw it could at times dismay even the most convinced. Perhaps if he had not had such characteristics he could not have been the prophet he was, but they did not make it easy for colleagues who shared his ideals but not his temperament. Leslie Hunter, the other Anglican bishop on the delegation, found him particularly irritating. Bell was not a leader, he commented, 'because he was very markedly a man who liked going his own way, and indeed rather enjoyed being in a minority'. But, he had to add, 'one could balance what I have said with the fact which is quite amazing that as we went round West Germany in 1946 the German churchmen, lay and clerical, regarded him with veneration. It was most remarkable.'[23] Already in August 1945 Oliver had written to Wim of Bell: 'I am constantly surprised by the things which, in his quiet and unobtrusive way, I suddenly find he has presented as *faits accom-*

*plis.*' Again, on his first visit to Geneva in December 1945, he had commented in his journal on some 'quite incredibly inept and inconsiderate action on the part of Chichester'. So, he had been warned! Now, on their shared visit to Germany, he experienced both Bell's bad chairmanship of meetings and his awkward determination to say the right thing in, arguably at least, the wrong place.

Probably the entire delegation had come to agree that the denazification process was proving disastrous: it left thousands of people imprisoned in camps, accused of they knew not what by they knew not whom, with the charges unexamined by anyone because there was no one with the time and skill to go into them. Necessary as it was at the end of the war, 18 months later it had become an obstacle to German recovery and reintegration into Europe. The final high point of the visit was an ecumenical service in the Marienkirche, situated within the Russian Zone of Berlin. Bell was the preacher to a large crowd including a Russian officer who took notes throughout what Oliver described as 'a very provocative (and many of us thought unwise) sermon' in which he declared that denazification 'should cease at once' – though he had never consulted the delegation as to whether it agreed that this be said – and then developed the theme of 'economic and industrial recovery and political unity in terms rather too concrete for a sermon and unwise for a mass of Germans not in personal *rapport* with the speaker'. They loved it, needless to say. It was, commented Oliver, 'the price of working with George Chichester – and he's worth it!' The Chancellor of the Duchy of Lancaster (ludicrously enough, responsible for the British Zone in Germany) complained to Fisher about Bell's sermon and Fisher passed the criticism on to Bell, agreeing that it was 'an error of judgement' to say such things in front of Germans. Bell sturdily rejected the criticism. It is worth noting that R. G. Laffan, the lay Catholic representative on the delegation, wrote to Bell when it was over: 'Will you permit me to say how absolutely justified were Nottingham's praises of your leadership of the delegation. It was excellent.'

Over the next few years Oliver would work with Bell very closely indeed. Already back in 1937 Bell had invited Oliver to join his new Church of England Committee of Non-Aryan Christians, but it was from 1946 that their close collaboration really dated. Oliver was very much on his own in the following years, cut off from any regular Anglican Church life. He came to see Bell as 'my bishop', someone to whom he could turn for guidance and comfort, while Bell saw him as a highly efficient auxiliary. Oliver became accustomed to notes like 'If you could come down to Chichester one day next week…it would be very useful.' Or a typed telephone message for the Bishop might read 'Mr Tomkins will pick you up at the Athenaeum Club this afternoon and go with you to Transport House.' Their temperaments were rather different: Bell was gently spoken yet almost excessively self-confident and forthright, Oliver personally diffident and glad to avoid the limelight, yet undoubtedly a better public speaker. Both were persons of great calm, who liked writing poetry as well as reading it. They grew to trust one another profoundly. After Bell died, his wife presented Oliver with his mitre – a symbol of apostolic succession. Oliver thus became the heir in diverse ways of all Britain's four major ecumenical pioneers of the previous generation – Temple, Oldham, Paton and Bell. Nobody else had so personally related to all four but if, among them, Bell came last, he may also have influenced Oliver the most.

## Preparing for Amsterdam

It was on 3 December 1945 that Oliver first crossed the Channel after the war, flying in a little plane to meet his colleagues in Geneva. He would return to Geneva the following February, going on from there to Paris, and would do the same in July. In October, as we have seen, he spent two weeks visiting Germany and in November was back in both Paris and Geneva. In 1947 he left in February for a month's tour including Rome, Athens, Istanbul, Beirut and Cairo, and in April for six weeks in America. So it went on, but the December 1945 expedition had for Oliver's own life a quite special significance. After over six years in which he had not left England, it brought him back with a jolt, and quite successfully, into a fully international world from the parochialism of Millhouses and a long stretch of ill-health in 1945 after moving to London. It gave him the experience of belonging to a team, including the German Hans Schönfeld, the Swede Nils Ehrenström, the Swiss Alphons Koechlin, the French senior ecumenical statesman Marc Boegner, as well, of course, as the Dutch Visser't Hooft, to whom Oliver had above all to relate. This quickly expanding group, hurrying in and out of 17 Route de Malagnou, the new WCC office, defined in personal terms the enterprise to which he was now committed. There were other British people in or close to it as well, notably Robert Mackie, based in Geneva as General Secretary of the World Student Christian Federation, Francis House, Bishop Bell, but, effectively, Oliver was now the linchpin in the relationship between Britain and the most exciting development under way in the Christian world at a time when British backing still remained decisively important. There was, it may be noted, no comparably significant American involved in the World Council process at that stage. Moreover, Oliver's importance was in no way limited to his being the link between Geneva and Britain, it was also a matter of providing leadership in various crucial areas, especially Faith and Order and Orthodox participation in the World Council.

Oliver himself sensed that as he flew from Croydon to Geneva he was indeed crossing a Rubicon in his own life and his description of the journey, his first in a plane, is in its way a celebration of that crossing at just the moment that the world as a whole was starting to be shaped anew by peace rather than war. It provides too an example of his journal writing at its best.

> We took off at 12 noon promptly. It took me exactly the same time to get from 63 York Road to the airport as it did to get from Croydon to Geneva, just 2½ hours. At Airways Terminal they weighed me my luggage, charged me 11/6 for surplus weight (NB a Kilo is 2.2 not 2.5 lbs!) and then I sat about in a lounge till the Croydon bus left at 10.45 and took an hour to the airport. There we had a formal customs glance and registered the amount of money we carried, and waited for a few minutes in another lounge, till we were ushered into the plane. That wait was quite exciting – looking for the first time at the monsters on the air-field – mostly still Transport Command service planes. Our silver red Swiss Air was the only civilian on the field – a smart and neutral civilian at that. Other, service, planes were bound for Norway and Germany.
>
> After our first minutes in the air, what was vastly more interesting than anything I had expected was the completely new world that lies in the clouds. Of course it was a lovely day, bright sun but a fair sprinkling of clouds. As we climbed towards them they all seemed, seen from just below their own level, to be oddly flat on the underside but all irregular shapes on

top. But soon we were through the cloud-layer, with brilliant sunshine and
a pure blue sky above. But underneath a new creation came into view which
took my breath away. The high Swiss mountains in winter is the nearest I
have seen to it. As far as you could see, a glittering white world of fantastic
peaks and valleys, soft and woolly at the edges in the foreground, though in
the distance acquiring more and more the sharp outlines of snow peaks. So
real was the resemblance to snow-mountains that it only gave me a sense of
being in fairy-land to see mountains which over-hung themselves at impossible angles, great ice-bergs which floated in complete detachment and
contours which gently and slowly changed shape under my eyes. The occasional gaps in the clouds looked exactly, in the middle-distance, like great
lakes and little tarns lying in the folds of these fantastic mountains. Since by
this time (about 12.20) we were over the channel, that illusion was the more
real because it was truly water of which one caught occasional glimpses. I do
not wonder that RAF men have peopled this strange and lovely new world
with a new mythology of Gremlins and the like!

We then climbed very high, and for an hour or more were flying in mist
whilst the inside of the windows froze over so that I could only scrape an
occasional peep-hole which soon froze over again. At about 2.15 the mountains of the Haute Savoie came in sight, which we crossed quite near their
tops and, circling Geneva, made what a hard-boiled air-traveller among the
American passengers said was a 'lovely landing' into the wind.

The specific purpose of this December visit was to attend a meeting of the 'Reconstruction
Department', but also to prepare for the long-delayed first post-war meeting of the
Provisional Committee. Ever since the beginning of the war the Provisional Committee,
the World Council's interim governing body, had been unable to meet; and ever since
Temple's death it had been headless. 'Reconstruction', most especially in regard to
Germany, but also for all the war-devastated and, until recently, 'occupied' countries of
Europe, inevitably dominated a large part of the immediate agenda. It was the reason for
the large delegation to Germany the following October. But, quite quickly, the need to get
the World Council itself fully on to its feet with an inaugural General Assembly, so that the
awkward 'Provisional' or 'in process of formation' could be dropped, would dictate the
central agenda, especially for Oliver. It was uncertain how many churches would participate or how the World Council would actually be organized. In what terms was it to see
itself *vis-à-vis* its member churches or, still more difficult, the Church universal? What
would be its ongoing purpose, once the war and its immediate aftermath were passed? His
second visit, in February 1946, when the Provisional Committee at last met, remained one
of the most memorable weeks of his life. Apart from a multitude of receptions and
committee meetings and attendance on Archbishop Fisher, the highlights were listening to
Niemöller preach in a packed cathedral and himself broadcasting an account of the service
live to both Britain and America. Already on his first visit Oliver found that the first
assembly was to meet in the summer of 1948. More precise dates -- 24 August to 4
September -- were agreed upon by the Provisional Committee in February. This left little
more than two years in which to do a huge amount of preparation. Oliver was appointed
Secretary of the first, and most theological, of the four international Commissions whose
task it was to prepare material for the assembly. He also became Secretary to the sub-
committee delegated to plan its worship.

Another large international gathering had also to be prepared – a Youth Assembly in Oslo in July 1947, successor to the Amsterdam Assembly of July 1939, Oliver's last and very memorable pre-war continental experience. After some hesitation but to everyone's relief Francis House agreed to 'organize Oslo'. Again, a WCC Conference Centre seemed essential. The February Provisional Committee meeting included a visit to the château of Bossey at Céligny, just outside Geneva, which had been offered for the purpose. Kraemer and Suzanne de Diétrich were envisaged as its first directors. By July 1946 the Preparatory Conference for the Oslo Assembly was already able to meet there, chaired by Mackie. One senses an enormous excitement in these years as the ecumenical movement hastily forged new institutions, responding not only to the pre-war decision to establish a World Council, but no less to the turmoil of the aftermath of war, the creation of the United Nations Organization, increasing realization that the world was now to be divided into communist and non-communist blocs and the coming of independence to India and Pakistan in 1947. The Church of South India, bringing together Anglicans, Methodists and Congregationalists, came into existence that same year, hailed as the morning star of a new ecumenical Christianity. Oliver's old friend, Lesslie Newbigin, was elected as one of its bishops.

On the narrower ecclesiastical front, two things struck Oliver particularly at the Preparatory Conference for Oslo. One was the almost complete absence of Orthodox representation. There was just one Greek and one Russian émigré in a gathering of 60 people. The other was the theological gap between the continentals and the Anglo-Saxons, the Americans especially. The former were overwhelmingly Barthian, the latter still preponderantly 'liberal' and somewhat suspicious of European 'neo-orthodoxy'. Much of his work in the following years would have as its underlying rationale the over-coming of this divide.

The Orthodox absence was one reason for paying so much attention to Paris and Leo Zander, who had in the past done more than anyone to help western ecumenical circles take Orthodoxy seriously, though Oliver saw Paris too as the best place for a renewal of conversation with Roman Catholics. But Paris had long been an intellectual centre for Russian Orthodoxy, though it was becoming bitterly divided into pro- and anti-Moscow groups. Zander belonged to the latter, though it was more important to improve relations with the former if there was to be any chance of drawing the Russian Orthodox Church as such into the World Council. The immediate need, however, was to make sure of the participation of the Greek and other Orthodox Churches of the eastern Mediterranean. To this end, a well-prepared tour took place in February–March 1947, whose origins lay back in 1945 in a proposal by Professor Alivisatos of Athens. Its formal leader was Yngve Brilioth, Söderblom's son-in-law and spiritual heir, the Bishop of Växjö. He had been a member of the Provisional Committee of the WCC since 1938, was about to be elected Chairman of Faith and Order (a position vacant since Temple's death) and would later become Archbishop of Uppsala. Oliver first met him in 1935, when attending a student conference at Lund where Brilioth was Dean. Throughout this tour, Oliver later wrote:

> Brilioth showed a loveable mixture of dignity and authority upon all official
> occasions with an almost childlike need to be looked after in all his personal
> arrangements… It was never advisable to let him have charge of his own
> ticket or passport! Yet everywhere we went, his regal bearing, the height and
> dignity of his spare figure in the long black coat or black gown of a Lutheran
> bishop, and the solemnity and wisdom of the utterances he made in his deep,

slow voice, impressed the Orthodox leaders that here was an envoy to be respected.

This was, perhaps, because he was so like them. With Brilioth was the Bishop of Worcester, Dr Cash, an Arabic speaker, and Edward Hardy, an American priest with expertise in Orthodoxy. The selection of the delegation's members was clearly intended to present the World Council in its most episcopal and Catholic light, it being only too obvious that a predominantly Protestant image could only alienate and frighten off the Orthodox. Oliver's was, undoubtedly, the hand which had shaped the whole expedition as the secretary of the Patriarchate in Damascus, Archimandrite Basileos, recognized to Oliver's amusement for he 'at once adopted towards me a brotherly, conspiratorial attitude – as one who knows that others may be bishops, but everything *really* depends on the arrangements *we* make behind the scenes!'

Together the delegation visited Athens, Istanbul, Cyprus, Damascus and Egypt. Everywhere they were received with a respectful enthusiasm; bishops lined up on the tarmac to greet them on landing, all the church bells in Nicosia rang for their arrival, seven-course dinners were prepared in episcopal palaces and monasteries alike. In Constantinople it was a fast day so when they sat down to lunch as guests of the Synod, there could be no meat. Instead the meal began with caviare and *hors d'œuvres variées*, stuffed cabbage came next, to be followed by a vast lobster, then a pilaf of Bosphorus mussels succeeded by a large dish of artichokes and mixed salad, before a Coupe Jacques, bananas, oranges and apples, toasts in two kinds of wine and Turkish coffee. A rather special fast day.

The high point of the tour came early on. Professor Alivisatos, the ecumenical movement's principal standard bearer in Greece, had broken his arm and was out of action but Oliver was able to call on him to discuss plans. The next day, 8 February, the Archbishop of Athens, Damaskinos, surrounded by the Greek Church's Holy Synod, announced formal acceptance of full participation in the WCC. 'Today has been historic', Oliver was able to comment, correctly enough. It ensured, in principle, that the World Council would be more than a fellowship of post-Reformation churches. In Istanbul the Oecumenical Patriarch was ill and, while the Holy Synod presided over by the Metropolitan of Chalcedon was very welcoming, the delegation did not get 'quite the clear-cut answer' they received in Athens, only a reaffirmation of willingness in principle to cooperate. Much the same was true elsewhere. The delegates returned to write the confident report that 'The Provisional Committee can count upon the reaffirmed cooperation of the Churches which we visited and their full participation in the Assembly of 1948'. That proved a little over-optimistic. The Church of Greece and the Oecumenical Patriarchate did indeed participate fully, despite some fluctuations in commitment which continued well after Amsterdam. In practice almost no one else did. At Amsterdam, of 589 official participants, only 40 represented the Orthodox and other Eastern Churches, and only 20 of those were regularly appointed delegates, the rest being 'observers', youth delegates, or WCC staff members. On the one hand, the Orthodox Churches of the eastern Mediterranean were acutely anxious to retain the support and cooperation of western Christians, especially when faced with the threat of expansion of the Soviet Communist empire. On the other hand, fears of Protestantism remained powerful. Practical cooperation was wanted, not doctrinal discussion. Moreover, the very revival in official terms of the Russian Orthodox Church, closely tied politically to the Soviet state, was inimical to ecclesiastical cooperation with the West. The Russian Church remained by far the largest within Orthodoxy and it was the Consultation called in Moscow in July 1948 with assembled representatives of almost all Orthodox Churches which ensured that the World Council's invitations would be generally declined and the aims of Oliver's delegation of 1947, for the time being, only rather imperfectly realized. It is interesting to note that while Constantinople and Athens were hesitant about any Faith and Order side to ecumenism but were anxious for social cooperation, the Russian Church was wary of the political overtones of the latter but more open to broaching doctrinal issues. While Leo Zander and Georges Florovsky were present at Amsterdam, it was as members of the delegation of the Oecumenical Patriarchate of Constantinople.

Just one month after returning from Egypt Oliver was off again, this time for America and a crucial meeting of the Provisional Committee. He travelled in the *Queen Elizabeth*, accompanied by Florovsky, Koechlin, Wim, and several other members of the Committee. The *Queen Elizabeth* itself impressed him greatly, perhaps unduly: 'If, in our day, we put into an inevitably short-lived ship the beauty which once went into Versailles and the Sistine Chapel and Hampton Court – it's not we but posterity that should grumble!' America was full of interest but generated chiefly foreboding, an impression of 'impending doom': 'America is blinded by her possession of material power without any real convictions about how to use it. Even her Christianity moves mostly on the level of Pharisaism...in all this she is little or no worse than the rest of us, but a rich proud man can do so much more harm than a poor proud man...'

Oliver, however, had come to America not to meditate on the nature of American Christianity but for a crucial meeting at Buck Hill Falls, Pennsylvania, at which arrangements for the coming Assembly had to be settled and a 'Call' addressed to the world's Churches announcing and explaining what it was all about. There were to be 450 voting delegates, 600 official 'visitors' (including the wives of delegates), 100 youth group delegates, 150 staff, as well, of course, as plenty of pressmen – 'some zoo to look after' Oliver observed.

> It is a formidable prospect: This Assembly will have to do as much as Edinbro', Oxford and Madras rolled into one, and then some. There is the whole study-process to bring to a head in something which the Assembly will bite onto; there is the whole question to put to the Constituent Churches (now 106 of them) as to the kind of Council they want, in view of the manifold activities which the Council has developed before it even exists; then there is the need to embody it all in some kind of a really workable constitution.

How much was the press to be allowed in? To everything, thought the Americans; to as little as possible, thought the Europeans; to some things, but not others, concluded the Anglican *via media*.

Oliver stayed in America nearly two months. Important as the Provisional Committee meeting was, experiencing the American theological scene at a time of considerable creativity may have mattered for him still more: New York and Union Theological Seminary in the age of Niebuhr and Tillich, Washington, Yale, Harvard and Chicago, preaching when asked but, still more, listening, best of all 'grand long arguments with Reinhold and Ursula Niebuhr' at Union, and much else. These two months initiated him decisively into the complexities of American Protestantism. He found the parish clergy 'exactly as ignorant as their counterparts at home' with regard to the principles of ecumenism. Thus, 1947 was proving one ceaseless learning process as he hurried from place to place, the meditative but ever attentive bureaucrat pigeon-holing in his tidy mind every detail helpful to ensure success for the coming 'zoo'.

After America, Oslo. The Assembly of Christian Youth held there in July was the first major world Christian conference after the war, just as its predecessor in Amsterdam in July 1939 had been the last in pre-war days. In Amsterdam Oliver had been very much of a participant, at Oslo he could be more of an observer, though he had found time to write its official preparatory study *Youth in the World-Church*. Organized by Francis House, its great success lay in the presence among the thousand delegates of more than two hundred from Asia, Africa and South America, a vast advance in globalism on any previous conference. Oliver was struck – perhaps unexpectedly, when seen retrospectively – by how similar the world of 1947 seemed to that of 1939 with threats nearly as great hanging over it. 'In 1939 we knew we were heading for war; in 1947 we are not sure... only the stakes are higher.' He did detect, however, a changed bearing on the part of Americans and remarked to Niebuhr on the quietness of the American delegates – 'none of the robust optimism and vigorous denunciation of other people's iniquities'. He wondered whether it was due to moral embarrassment at representing a power which had turned to the imperialism which in the past they had always loved to denounce in others. Niebuhr agreed. But his most forcible impression was of the quality of the representatives of the younger churches like D. T. Niles of Ceylon, M. M. Thomas of India, Philip Potter of Dominica and many others. They felt themselves, he judged, 'heirs of the new age' enjoying 'a splendour of new birth' where Europe was tired and America an adolescent suddenly sobered by responsibility. It was a characteristic of Oliver's mind to move back and forth between such vast, shrewd, if slightly facile, generalizations and the cautious, nuanced evaluation of small particulars. Oslo was a good preparation for the atmosphere of Amsterdam. Ursula for once was with him, having left the children with her parents, and the conference was followed by a holiday and voyage home from Bergen to Newcastle.

An intensely busy year followed as Amsterdam approached. Journeys to and from Geneva, conferences, sermons, lectures, radio interviews – his children were becoming quite blasé about hearing their father's voice 'on the wireless'. Once Oslo was over, Francis House took up his new post as the BBC's Director of Religious Broadcasting so the World Council was sure to get at least its fair share of radio time. Everything in Oliver's life was now to be focused on preparing for the Assembly but, above all, there had to be ever closer concentration on his special responsibility, the primary 'Faith and Order' section of the Assembly's agenda. An account of 'The Universal Church in God's Design', it needed to provide some kind of agreed theological basis upon which to build the existence of the World Council. The Commission charged to work on this theme was in place before the end of 1947. Theoretically Leonard Hodgson was still Secretary of Faith and Order yet he seems to have taken no part in the preparation of this section. Instead, Michael Ramsey was the principal English theological voice. It is again noteworthy that three years later it was Michael Ramsey, not Hodgson, who provided most of the basic draft for the pre-Lund report of Faith and Order on *The Church*.[24] Oliver certainly admired Hodgson, 'my friend and mentor'. They shared a common liberalism. However, it seems clear that Hodgson had effectively withdrawn from any very directive role in Faith and Order well before Amsterdam.[25] The veteran Swedish theologian Gustaf Aulén, the Bishop of Strängnäs, was chairman of the pre-Amsterdam theological commission, 'Section I', with Oliver as secretary and editor. They were backed by a team of theological heavyweights and produced a volume of papers to be submitted to the Assembly and published immediately afterwards. Besides the more traditionally theological pieces it included chapters by Visser't Hooft and Oliver focusing precisely upon the notion of the Church in the new context of the ecumenical movement and the World Council.

When the Assembly arrived, the Commission was reconstituted with Hanns Lilje as chairman, Oliver as secretary and a partially new, much enlarged, membership. However, most of the work seems to have been done within a small drafting committee. Anders Nygren replaced Aulén as the Swedish Lutheran voice, joined from Germany by Edmund Schlink. However, the hard core remained the same throughout – Karl Barth, Georges Florovsky of St Vladimir's, Paris, and Michael Ramsey, now Professor of Theology in Durham. Barth was the greatest theologian of the age and unflinching representative of the full Protestant tradition, while Florovsky was the leading theologian of Eastern Orthodoxy and Ramsey of Anglo-Catholicism. Effectively Florovsky and Ramsey represented a Catholicism with which Barth's Protestantism, and most ecumenical movement ecclesiology hitherto, was unable to cohere. If the prime tension lay between Catholic and Protestant understandings, a second tension which mattered hardly less concerned the relationship between the WCC and the Church or the Churches. People like Archbishop Fisher, one of the World Council's new presidents and a prominent figure at Amsterdam, were exceedingly anxious to insist that the World Council was not the Church and could in no way speak for the Church. Was the World Council not already subscribing to a certain ecclesiology by even describing its members as 'churches'? Were the Greek Orthodox and the minute Greek Evangelical Churches equally 'churches'? Was not the World Council, despite its formal position of not being a Church and not possessing an ecclesiology of its own, in fact by its very existence imposing a kind of theology upon its participants? Such questions would haunt the World Council for years, but the theological wrestling between Catholic and Protestant conceptions of what it means to be church was never sharper or more titanic than in Section I of the Amsterdam Assembly. Listening to and recording its debates Oliver graduated as ecclesiologist.

'Barth, Ramsey, Florovsky and Nygren were the four points of the square,' he wrote in his journal but the sharpest confrontation lay between Barth, on the one hand, Ramsey and Florovsky, on the other. 'They excommunicate one another and denounce each other as heretics from adjacent chairs or with hands on each other's shoulders.' The disagreement between the two sides within the small drafting committee proved indeed extremely intense and 40 years later Oliver remembered 'the sense of sheer despair I felt as secretary after the first two or three sessions... nothing was clear except the depth of our disagreement. I remember sitting up until 3 a.m. working at a draft for our report in which I tried to articulate where our disagreement lay, and I recollect the relief with which I heard Karl Barth say next morning after reading it: "I think you have succeeded in squaring the circle!" '[26]

From Barth that was praise indeed. This would not be the last time that Oliver quietly engineered a formula to shape the evolution of ecumenical theology and practice. The agreed text of Section I surely did just that. Instead of pretending to agree as to what the Church really is, it insisted instead on stressing dialectically in a section entitled 'Our Deepest Difference' the 'irreconcilable' within existing beliefs: 'There remains a hard core of disagreement between different total ways of apprehending the Church of Christ... As so often in the past, we have not been able to present to each other the wholeness of our belief in ways that are mutually acceptable.' Many more Protestant-minded delegates felt disappointed that this intrusion of Catholicism, as they saw it, championed by Florovsky and Ramsey, threw a spanner in the works of a neat theological grounding for the World Council upon which all could agree. But in reality their formulation made it possible for the Orthodox to enter and the whole ecclesiological debate of subsequent decades (Vatican II included) could well be read as a commentary upon its seven pages.

Meanwhile in another room a committee chaired by George Bell was endeavouring to produce a brief and ringing Assembly 'Message' to offer to the world. It included Kraemer and Niebuhr, Niemöller and Stephen Neill, Kathleen Bliss and Lesslie Newbigin. Draft after draft were rejected. Bliss provided Amsterdam's most memorable line 'we intend to stay together' but in the end it was Newbigin more than anyone else who formulated the full final version and typed it out on Niemöller's machine, having none of his own. It is noteworthy that Amsterdam's two most important texts were largely drafted by Tomkins and Newbigin.

On 23 August Geoffrey Fisher as Chairman called upon Marc Boegner to move a resolution which began: 'That the first Assembly of the World Council of Churches be declared to be and is hereby constituted.' For Oliver that could be regarded, in ecclesiastical terms, as the central moment of his career. He had been present at Edinburgh eleven years earlier when the decision was taken to establish the Council. Now it existed and in one way or another most of his subsequent creative work would be done in its service.

> Is there a murmur of a mounting Kyrie?
> It is evening.
>   Is this lifting of hands a sacrifice
> Or only the votes of a democratic assembly?
>   You come from the ends of the earth
> Do you come to sit down at the feast of my kingdom
> Or only at another Conference-Table?[27]

Appointed by the Assembly to be Secretary of Faith and Order, something he already virtually was, he also remained Assistant General Secretary of the World Council. Henceforth he would have two letterheads, but his most productive work would relate to the former. Faith and Order was now his full responsibility under its chairman, Bishop Brilioth. Oddly enough he agreed to serve for only two years. It is hard to understand how he could have thought this sensible, given the nature of the job in the immediate aftermath of the World Council's inauguration and the fact that already a conference of Faith and Order was proposed for 1952. Perhaps it was just one more sign of diffidence and the somewhat nostalgic desire to get back to a more traditional pastoral ministry in England, the 'mirage' of a wonderfully ecumenical parish, as he later admitted it to be. In fact he stayed for almost five very full years, devoted to working out the theological implications of the World Council's existence, building up a relationship with Roman Catholics, and fitting in a tour of Ceylon and India into which he had been inveigled at Amsterdam by D. T. Niles. All would culminate with the Lund Conference of August 1952.

The organizational shape of the World Council changed with Amsterdam. Various, largely honorary, 'Presidents' were elected, including Marc Boegner and the Archbishops of Canterbury and Uppsala. Far more important in practical terms, George Bell was chosen to be chairman of the Central Committee. It was certainly helpful for Oliver in London to be so close to Bell in Chichester, especially as Bell was a good friend. He was also a very presidential chairman, often imposing his own point of view with a firmness that neither Americans nor Europeans expected of a chairman. Bell behaved more as a bishop controlling his diocesan conference but he was so sincere and impressive a person, so deeply revered, so experienced in the history of the ecumenical movement, that he could get away with it to everyone's gain. The very large Central Committee with over 80 members, most of whom had had no previous experience of the international side of ecumenism, really needed forceful leadership of this sort, especially at the start. It was helpful for Oliver to have the personal trust of the Central Committee's chairman.

There were now to be no fewer than five 'Associate General Secretaries': two in Geneva (Stephen Neill and Robert Mackie), two in New York (Henry Leiper and Frederick Nolde) and Oliver in London. Mackie had taken over the Department of Inter-Church Aid and Service to Refugees while Neill was responsible for the study programme. Undoubtedly this narrowed the range of Oliver's responsibilities, enabling him to concentrate more closely on the specifically Faith and Order side of his work. However, the fact that his secretaryship of Faith and Order was an independent appointment ensured his continued special standing and undoubted primacy among the Associate General Secretaries.

In the months of preparation for Amsterdam Oliver had found time to write most of his first book, *The Wholeness of the Church*. He completed it on All Saints Day, 1 November, and it was published in January 1949, an attempt to explain to the common man the motivation which lay behind this flurry of international ecumenical activity, the meaning of Amsterdam. More than anything else he wrote before or after, it expressed his gospel. He had wanted to call it *The Nature of Ecumenicity* but he also wanted it to sell and, as everyone pointed out, 'Ecumenicity' was too unfamiliar a word to help that. But ecumenicity is what it is all about as he makes clear in the opening sentence. It is a good book, brief, clear, thoughtful, a book for the young, for the laity, for the people of Millhouses. 'If the ecumenical movement comes to be thought of chiefly as the gathering together of ecclesiastical leaders, usually in a foreign country, it may gain an occasional notice in the papers, but it will not become something to which the ordinary Christian feels that he belongs' (p. 11). It was Oliver's desperate, justified, worry that the gap was growing, not diminishing, between the advances achieved together by ecumaniacs and the consciousness of 'the ordinary Christian', which explains why he attempted to impose a two-year limit on his secretaryship of Faith and Order. What is most special about *The Wholeness* is its consistent concern for the local Church. Oliver was continually hankering to get back to the parish, or wherever, to convert 'the ordinary Christian' to ecumenicity. Yet there is an odd slip in the book which may be painfully revealing. He explains the existence of three concentric circles. The innermost circle is ecumenicity itself, 'something which happens in the souls of Christians'; the second is the ecumenical movement, 'the conscious manifestation of ecumenicity'; the third, the outer circle, is the area of organized activity, most notably the World Council of Churches. The circle of ecumenicity is, he explains, like a camp-fire circle. In the inner circle the blaze is most warmly felt, while further away (presumably in the third circle) only 'a flicker illumines and dies again' but then, forgetting his model, he declares that in the formal organization of the World Council 'the facts are more easily ascertained than in the two outer circles' (p. 17). Without realizing it, with an almost Freudian slip, he has reversed his whole image and put the World Council back as the inner circle! This in its way neatly reveals Oliver's own problem throughout. What he longed for was to fan a central glow of parochial ecumenicity upon which everything else could draw, but the reality, even of his own experience, was rather the opposite. It was within the World Council and comparable bodies that the people 'near the centre' were able to 'feed the blaze and are warmed and lit by it'. If he had personally felt the blaze most strongly in his SCM days, it was now the case that

– in the words of one quip – the World Council was simply 'the SCM in long trousers'.

*The Wholeness of the Church* proved, all the same, an influential book, encapsulating in a readable way Christianity's latest priority. It was used as a study-book by the Annandale staff that winter and one of them, Philip Potter, recalled its impact on him more than 25 years later when General Secretary of the World Council, especially that emphasized sentence 'Ecumenicity is something which happens in the souls of Christians'. William Nicholls, writing his impressive *Ecumenism and Catholicity* a couple of years after Oliver's book, recorded his debt to it. In 1950 Oliver went to stay with Princess Wilhelmina of the Netherlands, the former queen who had retired after 58 years while the World Council was actually assembled in her country. She met him carrying a well-worn copy of *The Wholeness* which she appeared to have read 'very thoroughly'. His gospel was being heard.

## Catholic relations and the Toronto Statement

In the busy years of 1949 and 1950 the new Secretary of Faith and Order had numerous different fronts to develop and coordinate but none was more significant, though hitherto we have heard little of it, than that of Roman Catholic relations, and none much closer to Oliver's heart.[28] In this Oliver represented a rather English point of view. The English, Anglicans chiefly, had long been far more anxious to keep in view a vista of reunion with Rome in a way that European and American Protestants had not. Both Paton and Bell had experienced disagreement with Wim over Catholic relations. It was not that Wim was anti-Catholic, Barthian as he was, but he was less willing to stick out his neck in their regard; he tended to pick on Catholic weaknesses whereas the English stressed their strengths, insisting on the supreme importance of doing whatever could be done, given the inherent significance of Rome. There was thus a rather interesting correspondence between Paton and Visser't Hooft in the summer of 1939. Archbishop Lang had associated himself with the Pope's appeal for prayers for peace. Wim criticized this, Paton firmly rejected the criticism. While Wim agreed (25 May) that 'I am all for cooperation with Rome when there is reality in it', Paton replied that 'I am afraid that you and I must agree to differ' on this subject. A little later, however, Wim wrote that he had attended an 'ecumenical retreat' in Paris which included Maritain, Congar and Gabriel Marcel, adding, 'I have come away from this meeting with the feeling that in the Life and Work part of our movement we need to pay far more attention to the live movements in the Roman Catholic Church.' Paton replied at once:

> I think that you and I are really in more agreement than sometimes appears
> in regard to this business of the RCs. I am wholly convinced that no official
> approval of ecumenical activity can be expected from the Roman hierarchy
> at the moment...at the same time, we should be fools to ignore the power
> of Rome, her scholarship and her saintliness, and we ought to take every
> chance that we get of keeping in touch with her scholars and of collabo-
> rating in practical matters, where collaboration is possible.

That is really where matters still stood on the WCC side ten years later. What proved important in Oliver's initiative was a determination not to let it remain an aspiration in regard to 'practical matters' but, instead, to push forward on the theological front quietly but with determination.

No Catholic was formally present at Amsterdam (other than journalists). Hundreds had asked to attend as observers but Rome at the last moment had forbidden anyone to do so by a Holy Office *monitum* of 5 June. However, the Jesuit Fr Charles Boyer of the Gregorian University, who had founded a centre and journal entitled *Unitas* in 1945 and become Rome's semi-official expert on the subject, was conveniently present in Amsterdam throughout the conference and had private interviews with various participants arranged for him by Wim and Oliver, most notably Bishop Bell. Bell was already in regular correspondence with another churchman in Rome, the Englishman Mgr Duchemin, the Rector of the Beda College, where English 'late vocations' were trained for the priesthood on a shortened theological course. Duchemin had written to Bell the previous January to tell him about a small study circle on unity they had started at the Beda led by the English Jesuit scholar, Joseph Gill. Duchemin met Bell in England shortly after Amsterdam and in December Boyer wrote to the bishop, saying that he had been talking with Duchemin and they suggested that someone 'authorised by your Lordship' be sent to visit Rome unofficially. A very great deal followed from that suggestion but it is worth noting that it was in origin a Roman, not an Anglican, initiative. As a result of this Bishop Neill visited Rome in June, unofficially of course, but effectively an emissary both of the WCC and of the Church of England. Bell, after all, was now both Chairman of the World Council's Central Committee and of the Church of England's 'Council for Foreign Relations'. Neill, moreover, was both a WCC Associate General Secretary and an assistant bishop of the Archbishop of Canterbury. Perhaps because Neill seemed, all the same, in reality more a representative of the World Council, Canon Prestige of St Paul's was sent by Archbishop Fisher on a further Roman inspection in November. While Neill had met only Boyer, Duchemin and Gill, Prestige also met Mgr Montini and Cardinal Tisserant. Everyone was immensely affable. Everyone agreed that conversations, held discreetly and without undue expectations, could only be useful in dissipating false impressions of the other side.

It is thus clear that 1949 was a time of considerable ecumenical activity involving Rome despite the lack of any publicity and Oliver's own very considerable exertions need to be placed within this wider context. He had himself attended a conference at Bièvres with Catholic theologians, including Yves Congar, back in 1937. It had deeply affected him. He had since read a certain amount of French Catholic theology – Congar, de Lubac, Mersch, Villain. He had even managed to include a few pages by Maurice Villain in the Amsterdam volume for section I, *The Universal Church in God's Design*. Villain confidently concluded that 'between the Ecumenical Movement and the Roman Catholic Church a convergence is not only possible, but is gradually taking place'.[29] That chapter was the sole public participation by a Catholic in the Amsterdam process. In the official history of the ecumenical movement put together in these years, edited by Ruth Rouse and Stephen Neill, Oliver wrote the chapter on 'The Roman Catholic Church and the Ecumenical Movement'. One of the best in an uneven book, it is significant that this was the topic allotted to him but, in point of fact, no one else in World Council circles was so well informed in this regard. Undoubtedly what he wrote here owed a good deal to Villain's chapter, if he is rather less optimistic than Villain. The care with which he had prepared it is evidence of how truly the relationship between the World Council and Catholicism became for him a primary preoccupation immediately Amsterdam was over.

Anyone wishing to enter into dialogue with the Catholic Church in 1949 was faced with a dilemma: Paris or Rome? France, Belgium and, to some extent, Germany were home to a lively Catholic theological revival which included some outstanding biblical and patristic scholarship as well as creative reinterpretations of a rather stale scholastic or Thomist tradition. It was also notably ecumenical. A little of this had even crossed the Channel to influence the English Dominicans in Oxford or appear in articles in the *Downside Review*. From 1946 Blackfriars, led by Henry St John, was already involved in a regular series of conferences with the Anglican Community of the Resurrection at Mirfield. The key figure in these developments was undoubtedly Yves Congar, a lively mind, a formidable scholar, a prodigious writer, and an active, almost mischievous strategist of ecclesiastical renewal. Behind him stood the more enigmatic figure of Père Chenu, a Dominican even more feared by conservatives for the way he was historicizing the work of Aquinas. Together they were the leaders of the Paris school of Dominican theology based at the Saulchoir, but they were paralleled by an equally lively, more patristic, group of Jesuits at their school at Lyons Fourvière. Cardinals Liènart of Paris and Gerlier of Lyons were both quietly sympathetic to these developments which were beginning to be called, in some quarters, the 'nouvelle théologie'. On the ecumenical side much of this had been inspired by the Belgian Benedictine monastery 'of Union' at Chevetogne, and its founder Dom Lambert Beauduin. If you took the road to Rome you encountered Fr Boyer together with the official mind of the Catholic Church but also some rather second-rate theology. If you took the road to Paris you encountered one of the most exciting theological milieux in the world, but a milieu already under deep suspicion in Rome, and one shortly to be largely, if temporarily, silenced. One further difference: the French tended to reinforce the habitual Anglican disregard for English Catholics – a disregard Oliver certainly shared to some extent – while in Rome it was gently suggested that Anglicans would be wiser to contact English Catholics than French ones. 'It is worth recording a hint thrown out at the Vatican,' noted Prestige, 'that a certain degree of caution might usefully be observed in dealings between Anglicans and French Roman Catholics.' None the less the first conference Prestige set up was in Paris, at Istina, a Catholic ecumenical institute. Held in April 1950 it included some of the most influential French and Belgian theologians: Fr Dumont, the Dominican Director of Istina, Frs Beauduin, Congar, Louis Bouyer and others. After that, however, Prestige followed an emphatically Boyer line with five-a-side teams led by the two of them. The first took place in the episcopal palace at Strasbourg in September 1950 with Owen Chadwick and Ian Ramsey joining the Anglican team while the English Jesuit, Maurice Bevenot (who had been an observer at Faith and Order in Edinburgh in 1937) and one remarkable Dominican from Paris, Jean de Menasce, a convert Jew who had studied at Balliol and was an Iranian expert, joined the Catholic team. Brilliantly versatile as he was, de Menasce was not primarily a theologian. But he was joined by his friend Mgr Journet, from Fribourg, who undoubtedly was. The next meeting in the series, and the last before Prestige died, was held in England and included George Patrick Dwyer, later Archbishop of Birmingham, and Mgr George Smith of St Edmund's College, Ware. Good as it was to bring in English Catholics, the decline in theological terms from the Istina meeting is obvious, a near inevitable consequence of following Roman advice.

Oliver followed the alternative road, not Rome but Paris. He seems never to have been in touch with Boyer but already in January 1949 he was in Paris visiting Istina and holding conversations not only with Dumont but also with Dom Clement Lialine of Chevetogne, editor of their journal *Irénikon*. Lialine was decidedly critical of the way the World Council seemed to be developing. He felt that the Faith and Order dimension was losing out to Life and Work concerns. While Oliver did not accept this criticism, the fact that it was made, and by someone as ecumenically well informed as Lialine, contributed considerably to what he thought and did over the next 18 months. It would have to be demonstrated more convincingly, he realized, that the WCC was not just an expression of pan-Protestantism with a shallow ecclesiology preoccupied with putting the world to rights in political and social terms. In March Oliver spent ten days in Germany, renewing contacts throughout the country, explaining the meaning of Faith and Order to numerous Protestant clergy gatherings, with Hans Schönfeld as interpreter, but also finding time to meet ecumenically engaged Catholics in both Cologne and Paderborn. He was impressed to discover that there were regular Catholic–Lutheran theological discussions taking place with the approval of the Archbishop of Paderborn. Technically the Catholic participants all belonged to a Catholic 'Ecumenical Circle' while the Lutherans belonged to a Lutheran 'Ecumenical Circle', but the two circles never met separately. In this way, it was held, the Catholics were not taking part in 'combined study'! In Germany as in France it was generally maintained that the 5 June *monitum* did not really signify a Roman veto on any sort of dialogue with the World Council but, rather, a fear of being stampeded by the number of Catholics interested and, very probably, the objections of the Archbishop of Utrecht, Cardinal de Jong, to the descent on Amsterdam with a good deal of publicity of a group of radical French and German ecumaniacs.

The most exciting and fruitful of Oliver's Roman Catholic contacts were, however, the four days he spent in Lyons over Easter. He arrived by train from Geneva to be met by the Abbé Paul Couturier, the great apostle within Catholicism of spiritual ecumenism, an 'invisible monastery' of shared prayer: the recovery through prayer of Christian unity 'such as Christ willed and by the means which he wills', Couturier's formula which everyone could be happy with and on the basis of which was developed worldwide observance of the 'week of prayer for Christian Unity' (18–25 January) each year. In 1937 and 1938 he had visited England, going particularly to Anglican religious communities like Nashdom, Mirfield, and Malling Abbey where he had been presented with a set of mass vestments. In 1946 he had written a circular letter to hundreds of priests in France asking them to celebrate mass on the coming feast of St Bartholomew, 24 August, praying God's pardon for the crimes committed by Catholics against Protestants on that and other days. There had been a warm response. In 1949 Couturier was 67 and universally revered – 'One of the very few absolutely disinterested people who ever came to visit me,' Archbishop Lang called him. Early on Easter morning Oliver attended Couturier's mass; he wore his Malling vestments, 'entirely enwrapped in Anglicanism' as he described himself. 'It was necessary' Maurice Villain wrote after his death, 'to be a witness of his Mass – in which he saturated himself with all the liturgical words, pronouncing them slowly and intently in an impassioned dialogue, accompanying them with gestures of sovereign majesty – in order to perceive the tragic side of his existence, which was apparently so peaceful yet so profoundly torn.'[30]

They then went together to the cathedral, occupying reserved seats by the sanctuary, for the great pontifical Easter mass celebrated by Cardinal Gerlier with all the specialities of the ancient 'rite lyonnais', including six concelebrants and the quaint rite in which the wine was first tasted by a deacon to ensure that it was not poisoned. As the Cardinal processed out he gave a special bow and smile to Oliver. It did not, however, occur to Oliver that this could be intended for him – there must be someone else of importance behind him, he imagined. Next day at an hour long and very friendly audience with Gérlier, the Cardinal ragged him for not returning his salutation, and Oliver had to confess the reason. He was still someone temperamentally unable to recognize that he was of some importance. When Oliver raised the issue of the *monitum*, Gerlier insisted that it was directed against 'irresponsible' participants and that the Pope could have no objection to 'responsible' discussions. The important thing, Oliver concluded, was to multiply personal contacts even in Rome itself and Couturier remarked to Gerlier that what was needed was an 'atomic bombardment' of personal contacts with Rome. The Cardinal smiled tolerantly.

Lengthy discussions with numerous theologians including de Lubac and Congar filled these days and Oliver found himself expounding the total programme of the WCC in French with a fluency which amazed him. Congar committed himself to the confident prophecy that 'Rome will come into the ecumenical movement, but the time is not ripe.' They agreed nevertheless to try and set up an initial meeting between Catholic ecumenists and WCC staff for the autumn, a meeting focused on the theological issues relating to the establishment of the World Council and the reform of the Church. When, however, Oliver asked if Père Boyer of *Unitas* in Rome might not be included, Congar was adamant: 'Certainly not, it would be like inviting the Gestapo and the "maquis" to the same dinner'! (Boyer cautioned Neill in Rome a couple of months later about Congar, if in more restrained tones.) Oliver learnt a good deal in Lyons about the ability of Catholics to criticize their Church in a way wholly consonant with a fundamental loyalty. Even more important, he met in Couturier an ecumenist whom he could recognize as a saint. More down to earth, he went with Couturier to buy a 'real French beret', the characteristic headgear of a French Catholic priest. Ever after he wore his Couturier beret on less formal outings. Oliver went on to Taizé to establish contact with its highly ecumenical Protestant monks and its leading theologian, Max Thurian. This was his first visit to Taizé, a place which would with time become more and more central to his inspirations, bonded together with that of Couturier. Villain, Couturier's eventual biographer, was there at the same time and celebrated mass in the chapel immediately before the community eucharist. Again and again Oliver was struck on the Continent by how close Catholics and Protestants could already be in committedly ecumenical circles.

As soon as he returned to England he wrote a long letter to Wim with copies to Bell and Brilioth reporting on all that had happened and proposing a bilateral conference to be held at Istina in Paris that September. He also listed most of those who should (and did) take part on both sides: Congar, Daniélou, Dumont, Lialine, Villain, Jérôme Hamer, and the lay philosopher Jean Guitton, on the Catholic side, with Wim, Suzanne de Diétrich, Stephen Neill, Nils Ehrenström, Leonard Hodgson and himself on the World Council's. It is worth noting that this meeting took place six months before that of Prestige but brought together many of the same people, including three Anglicans. It was only after it had taken place that Prestige visited Rome in November. Oliver's conference was also quickly followed by a much-discussed correspondence in the columns of *The Times*.[31] It began with a special article, unsigned, on 31 October reviewing the state of Roman Catholicism highly sympathetically, while making certain criticisms and suggesting that the time was ripe for Rome to think anew about the 'ways and means' needed 'to bring into being a revivified Christendom'. Most people presumed that the article had been written by some ecumenically minded Anglican. In fact, the author was a Catholic priest, Dom Aelred Graham of Ampleforth. While the extensive correspondence which followed revealed deep differences of attitude upon both sides, it did suggest that many English Catholics were in sympathy with the article's main theme. Particularly striking was an appeal from Dom Columba Cary-Elwes of Ampleforth to recognize that 'the time had indeed come for a *rapprochement*'. In December an official *Instruction* was published in Rome, *Ecclesia Catholica*, which for the first time publicly approved ecumenical theological discussions while laying down rather rigid rules about them. Moreover the Lord's Prayer and other approved prayers could be said together, something which more intransigent Catholics had rejected in *The Times* correspondence only a few weeks before. If in some ways this *Instruction* looked to non-Catholics as highly restrictive (as it was meant to be!), it opened the door in principle to a long road: 'Patience, patience, patience', pleaded Fr Dumont.[32]

The difficulty in following this up was that in Rome itself a powerful reaction against anything new in theology was setting in, evident in the encyclical *Humani Generis* (August 1950) and even in the definition of the Assumption of Mary the same year. Prestige found 'the Romans quite unaccountably friendly' in June. Two months later his fury at the news that the Assumption was to be defined was vitriolic but it did not stop him going forward with the Strasbourg meeting the following month. Whether you took the Paris road or the Roman one, the difficulties were huge but Oliver, like Prestige, refused to draw back. Nor were the roads entirely distinct: indeed in September 1950 just before the first Boyer–Prestige conference at Strasbourg, Congar told Oliver that Boyer had just summoned a gathering of Catholic 'Ecumenists' in Rome and had asked him for advice. It did not, however, prove a viable alliance. Oliver's second conference took place at the monastery of Présinge in the diocese of Lausanne in September 1951. In the increasingly repressive atmosphere Lausanne was a good place to meet because its Catholic bishop, Mgr Charrière, was exceptionally friendly. Congar, Dumont and Hamer were able to come as well as one Englishman, Columba Cary-Elwes. Journet was also included, the only overlap with Prestige's Strasbourg conference of the previous year. The World Council's team included Kraemer and Max Thurian, but it was Oliver's own paper, delivered in French, that matters to us most. Entitled 'The Council, the Churches of the Council and the Church of Rome',[33] it set out his own understanding of their relationship, including the moving conclusion:

> The Council is in debt to Rome. It is a debt which some of us gladly acknowledge, others are unconscious of and some would deny. But Rome stands today as a perpetual commentary upon our work which we cannot ignore…every emotion from deep revulsion and even hatred to almost unbearable longing and love is to be found amongst us… All that we ask of you, I think, is that you share our pain. I for one do not ask that you should share it from within the formal organisation of the Council. There are many practical reasons against it, but of deeper ones the most cogent for me is that so long as you are outside, there can be no serious danger of mistaking our Council for the Church.

At Lyons two and a half years earlier he had concluded that 'Rome is moving towards ecumenical cooperation, but very slowly'. A more open move will come, but 'not in my lifetime'. If that proved a mistaken judgement,[34] it was partly because of the ecumenical conversation already actually achieved in those years in the teeth of difficulties. For that no one did more than Oliver and the presence of official Catholic observers at Lund in 1952, something for which he had worked very hard, was a tiny presage of a better future.

While Prestige's conferences were informative, Oliver's were also creative. The Istina meeting of September 1949 proved climacteric for the World Council's own self-interpretation. What, if anything, the Catholic theologians had insisted on asking, did membership of the World Council imply in regard to an understanding of the nature of the Church? Did it see itself as, in embryo, a World Church? Did it represent or presup-

pose a specific ecclesiology? If many Catholic critics suspected that it did, and a pretty
Protestant ecclesiology at that, so too did many Orthodox. Thus, 1949 was filled with
fears that the Greek Church might actually withdraw from the Council, persuaded so to
do by Michael, the Metropolitan of Corinth, among others. It was in response to these
pressures, both Catholic and Orthodox, that Wim and Oliver immediately after the Istina
meeting began a process which led in due course to what came to be known as the
Toronto Statement, for long a defining document for the World Council. Already in
October a discussion paper was circulated, above Wim's name, headed 'The
Ecclesiological Significance of the World Council of Churches'.[35] It was to go through a
number of editions and some very intense discussion before the Central Committee
approved it in Toronto in July 1950.

The Toronto Statement entitled 'The Church, the Churches and the World Council of
Churches' proved so important a document in ecumenical history that Oliver's relationship to its writing needs further examination. The original 11-page draft has Wim's name
at the bottom and in one brief section it uses the first person singular in characteristic
style. Much of its matter seems redolent of the Istina discussion. While being an expansion of 12 'theses' Wim propounded at that meeting, it would have been strange at any
time for the General Secretary of the WCC to produce a paper in this field without the
cooperation of the Secretary of Faith and Order. While Oliver always speaks of it simply
as Wim's, the latter in his *Memoirs* explicitly says that he wrote it 'with the help of my
colleague, Oliver Tomkins'. Given Wim's marked reluctance to refer to Oliver's contribution in general, it seems necessary to conclude that in this case it was very considerable.
The entry on the Toronto Statement in the *Dictionary of the Ecumenical Movement* goes
so far as to reverse the relationship and claim that it was Oliver who 'together with W. A.
Visser't Hooft drafted a statement on the ecclesiological significance of the WCC'. This
is incorrect. The original text was surely Wim's but it went through several editions and
it would be impossible to distinguish between the work of the two and pointless. They
cooperated very closely, had attended the Istina meeting together for the shaping of which
Oliver was responsible. Their draft stressed a number of crucial points – that 'The World
Council exists in order to deal in a provisional way with an abnormal situation', that it is
not based on any one ecclesiology, that no Church need alter its own ecclesiology in order
to enter the Council and hence that it is acceptable for members of the Council not to
recognize one another as 'true and pure churches' so long as they share a common belief
in the Lordship of Christ and in the need, through the Council or otherwise, to seek the
unity of Christians within and without their own Church.

When this document, having been through numerous revisions and considerable short-
ening, was discussed at Toronto, there was a great deal of tension. In the words of Visser't
Hooft, 'the debate became one of the most heated we have ever had in the Central
Committee'. For many American Protestants in particular, whose strongest theological
voice was Henry Van Dusen, President of Union Theological Seminary, the World
Council had no reason to think of itself as provisional. It already represented a near ideal
model, roughly the degree of unity and practical cooperation which separate churches
need. Its membership should imply that every member church accepts every other as a
full and proper church. If that is so, then the Eastern Orthodox Churches, Georges
Florovsky declared in a passionate speech, could be forced to leave. They were having a
Protestant type of ecclesiology imposed upon them. 'There was nothing for it but to let
everybody blow off steam', commented Oliver in his journal, but 'if feelings ran very high
the final result was to leave the fellowship more securely grounded than before'. He

himself was secretary of the sub-committee to which it was referred. 'In the end altering two sentences made everyone happy' and the Central Committee approved the basic principle of the Toronto Statement: 'There is a place in the World Council both for those Churches which recognise other Churches as Churches in the full and true sense, and for those which do not.' For the Orthodox, it has been said, this was the great charter of the WCC. Without it their presence would always have been precarious. It provided, more-over, a ground on which to continue the ecclesiological dialogue with Roman Catholicism. Had it not been for Oliver's visit to Lyons and its immediate fruit, the Istina meeting, it is questionable whether any of this would have happened.

It seems appropriate at this point to reflect a little further on Oliver's personal attitude to Catholicism. Clearly it became steadily more positive as he moved away from the rather simple Evangelicalism of his youth. The almost innate Protestant distrust of Rome faded with the years, perhaps even too generously. People like Congar, Villain and, most especially, Couturier had converted him through personal contact and the recognition of sound learning, perhaps even a more sophisticated theological scholarship than he had expected, but above all holiness. The reactionary message of the encyclical *Humani Generis* and the papal declaration of Mary's Assumption undoubtedly distressed him but not to the extent that they upset, for instance, Pierre Maury who exploded that year in the Faith and Order executive asking why on earth they wanted Roman Catholic observers at Lund, when what they ought to be doing is witness against Rome and its corruption of the Gospel. Oliver did not entirely disagree yet he did not see it quite like that himself. He was, as ever, a 'both-and' person but he was also drawn profoundly in his own soul towards Catholicism. On the Continent when he could, he went to mass. On Good Friday of 1951 he attended the service in Westminster Cathedral – the lessons, the adoration of the cross, the Mass of the Presanctified – and envied its dramatic and moving quality, spending 'a good part of my meditation trying to give God a convincing reason – to me if not to him – why I am not a Papist'. He had, of course, many cogent reasons but probably for him, unlike for many other people, none was wholly convincing. He once wrote that if he lived in America he thought he would become 'a Roman'. Yet he also found much in Catholicism to be in poor taste or morally perplexing. Thus, on the voyage to Ceylon the previous October he had encountered a Mill Hill priest returning to his mission.

> Fr W of Borneo is overjoyed at the price of whisky on board. He was slightly giggly by the time he got back from Port Said and when I met him later at the bar on board, he told me that he had tried to buy brandy on shore and split a drink with the pious Muslim store-keeper, who refused saying that his God didn't allow him to drink. 'I've got a better one than you' said Fr W. He gets heavily thomistic about closing time. One night, he slowly unrolled S. Thomas Aquinas' argument from Design, but even at the uncharitable risk of leaving him to drink alone, I couldn't see it through. Yet he spent most of his convalescent leave, after Jap. prison camp, working for three years voluntarily in the slums of Paddington before he could get permission to come back to his beloved Dyaks. Graham Greene didn't alto-gether invent him, but he is certainly one of the paradoxes of his queer church.

Too many Catholic priests were not quite gentlemen as B. K. at Westcott had taught one to be. They lacked sobriety. For Oliver, Catholicism was both powerfully attractive and uncomfortably 'queer'. Deep down in his own personality he was very much an élitist; a certain down-to-earth coarseness in the ordinary Catholic clerical character kept him at a distance yet a sense of harmony with the Catholicism of liturgy and spirituality had come no less to underlie his ecumenical endeavours more than almost anyone was allowed to know.

## On the road to Lund

Most surprising in Oliver's activities in 1949, an intensely busy year, was a quite considerable foray into politics.[36] It began in January with a meeting at the House of Commons between the Parliamentary Socialist Christian Group, which had been founded after the 1945 General Election, and the Socialist Christian League, an older, more clerical group. Faced with the growing tensions of the Cold War and the sense that the world was being disastrously divided between communist and capitalist camps, but faced also with the prospect of a General Election in 1950, Christian Socialists wanted to work out a fresh position from which they could influence the country and the Labour Party policy. Stafford Cripps, the most prominent Christian Socialist, was Chancellor of the Exchequer and could therefore not be a member of the group, but a number of MPs were, notably Sir Richard Acland, Tom Driberg, Woodrow Wyatt and Henry Brinton. On the non-parliamentary side were various clerics including Fr John Groser, a veteran Christian Socialist, Joseph McCulloch, the Rector of Clapham, Eric Fenn, Mervyn Stockwood, Alec Vidler and John Collins of Christian Action, also Kathleen Bliss, who had taken over from Oldham the editorship of the *Christian News-letter*. Also Oliver. He was present at the January meeting contributing vigorously to the discussion, after which he produced the first draft of a pamphlet setting out the group's position. He was present at a two-day conference in February at Church House and again at a still larger conference, again at Church House, in June, when he actually opened the proceedings with 'a diagnosis of the world situation, stressing the duty of Christians to see its revolutionary qualities as the working out of a purpose in history'. This meeting formally set up the '1950 Group' with Driberg as chairman, Acland as treasurer and McCulloch as research officer. Oliver was once more a speaker at a research conference of the Group chaired by Charles Raven in September. This time his title was 'The True Objective of Immediate Politics', a subject he was given, not one he chose as he modestly made clear. He stressed that Christians needed to approach politics dialectically, as both participants within and critics of the political process. This conference set up a number of working parties to explore various themes, among them that of 'world solidarity and living standards' to be led by Acland, Oliver and Groser. The following March Acland had to inform the Group that none of the members of this working party had been able to do any work, which would be taken over by another working party at the London School of Economics. In Oliver's case at least, given his other commitments, this hardly seems surprising but it appears to have brought his active involvement in the 1950 Group to a close. The Group itself soon faded away, as did the Labour Government. In 1951 the Conservatives returned to power. This was the only time in his life that Oliver became seriously and publicly involved with political circles. It is remarkable to find him labelling himself unambiguously a 'Socialist Christian' and fascinating to hear him declare 'Dick Crossman remarked to me lately that the struggle in the Labour Party is no longer between Christians and near-Marxists but between different understandings of *Christian categories*.' But it did not last. His ecumenical activities were at the time far too demanding, while his temperament was inimical to what could appear a partisan taking up of positions within the political field. What remains interesting is that in 1949, in the full flush of post-Amsterdam exuberance, he was willing to go so far.

Thus, 1950 was a year of journeys. Numerous European meetings in its first months were followed by June and July spent almost entirely in North America, with weeks of engagements up and down Arkansas, Missouri, North Carolina and Washington before the Toronto meeting and a further week in Canada. Hardly had he returned to Britain than he was off for a week in Germany from which he got back for a single night in a hotel with Ursula before leaving for a conference in Switzerland on one of the preparatory volumes for Lund. In September he was back in France for a Faith and Order Executive meeting while early in October he left for the three-month Asian tour which D. T. Niles had pressed on him at Amsterdam over two years previously. He arrived back in January 1951 in time for another round of WCC and Faith and Order meetings, spent part of April in Geneva, Paris and elsewhere, was in Sweden in May and Salonika, Crete, Athens and Belgrade in June. The ten days in Sweden in May, preparing the ground for the conference, proved a particularly pleasant time. After three days in Lund he went on, via Stockholm, to stay with Brilioth, now Archbishop of Uppsala. That Sunday he participated in Brilioth's consecration of two new bishops, one of them a brother-in-law. He also visited Brilioth's mother-in-law, old Fru Söderblom, now 81, delighted that no fewer than three of her sons-in-law were bishops. She had turned her home and especially Söderblom's library into a shrine filled with his books, desk, personal mementoes of all sorts. Oliver saw it first by candlelight and thought it 'as nearly haunted as anything I have ever sensed'. These days spent with Brilioth were foundations, not only for the conference, but for the harmony of their personal relationship. A long and tense Central Committee meeting at Rolle near Lausanne took up the first 11 days of August followed by a Faith and Order Commission at Clarens where he in fact announced that he would be leaving the Secretaryship to return to work in England the following year. While it would be pointless to follow all this activity step by step, it is much to the point to be reminded of the extraordinarily peripatetic quality of life in this period, the range of people he encountered and the wealth of experience that went with it.

The most weighty of these journeys was undoubtedly the three-month visit to the Indian sub-continent, moving from south to north. It was the longest time in his working life that Oliver spent outside the western world. Appropriately it was to that area which was at the time the ecumenical front-runner. The Church of South India, revered by ecumaniacs as a huge breakthrough but reviled by Anglo-Catholics, had been in existence for three years. Elsewhere there were union schemes in preparation in every part – Ceylon, North India, Pakistan. Oliver's purpose was gently to appraise what had happened hitherto, to spread the message of Faith and Order persuading people to send delegates to Lund, and to knit the two processes better together, that is to say the theo-logical dialogue on the nature of the Church sponsored by the World Council with local schemes of organic union. The danger in the whole World Council approach was that it did in a way necessarily consecrate denominations – Orthodox, Lutheran, Anglican, Baptist, Methodist. Local organic unity, on the other hand, involved the disappearance of denominational traditions as such within a new shared identity which of necessity claimed to transcend each and every denominational identity. The ecumenist's dilemma was whether to regard 'denominationalism' as a sinful adherence to outmoded schismatic traditions blocking the arrival of a truly united and Catholic Church or whether, like

Geoffrey Fisher, to hold that this was unrealistic, impoverishing and unnecessary. The denominations had merely to stop unchurching one another. The Church of South India was the principal witness to the need for an organic unity which went much further than that.

Oliver arrived at Colombo to be met by D. T. Niles, Ceylon's principal ecumenist. Ten days in the country were spread between Colombo, Kandy and Jaffna, preaching, listening and discussing with Anglicans, Methodists, the 'Negotiating Committee' for Church Union and whoever. From there on to India. A week in Madura with Lesslie Newbigin, its bishop, was followed by ten days in Travancore, India's most Christian area, endeavouring to understand the schisms that rent the Syrian Orthodox Church and finding hope, like so many Anglicans, in the 'Reformed Orthodoxy' of Mar Thoma. Then on to Calcutta, Bangalore, Benares, Allahabad, Delhi, Lahore, Bombay and Cairo. Inevitably his impression of the Church of South India derived largely from his days in Madura. He perceived in Lesslie a model for apostolic episcopacy. This was all the more heartening given that Lesslie, by background a stubborn Presbyterian, had been helped by his own correspondence and recommendation of Michael Ramsey's *The Gospel and the Catholic Church* to see that the episcopate was something biblically based. But Oliver noted too that many 'local churches have allowed the fact of union to make no difference at all to their spiritual life'. That could, however, be excused on the ground that these were early days. Probably the most memorable two days of the whole tour were those accompanying Lesslie on a pastoral visit through the villages, 'a terrific revelation of the depths of poverty and near-famine as a chronic condition' and also of the minute resources of the tiny Christian communities they met. He watched Lesslie baptize half a dozen converts in one village and confirm four in another, after sitting cross-legged on the floor for an hour or two examining the candidates in Tamil. Oliver roamed meanwhile through the village streets. Just one man managed a little English: 'Ask the Americans who had us some food.' Lesslie was one of the last ecumenical leaders of the West who had also been a missionary. While Oliver's father and uncle had been, for him the days in Madura were his only face-to-face encounter with 'grass roots' (he liked the phrase) Christian experience in the non-Western world. It meant a lot to him but it was very limited.

What Oliver did not explore at all in his tour was the Catholic Church. He knew that nine-tenths of Christians in Ceylon, for instance, were Catholics, while the one-tenth was divided between Anglicans, Methodists, Baptists, Presbyterians and others. It was sensible enough to hope for a united church joining these mostly tiny groups together, but he seems not to have reflected on the wider reality that Christian mission in most parts of Asia must mean a largely Catholic mission. Even the Church of South India, significant as it was, included only a small minority of South Indian Christians. In the following half century Catholic leadership would become ever more obvious as the advantages brought to Protestantism by the British Raj receded. But the Catholic clergy in Asia in 1950 was not ecumenically cooperative as it would become a generation later. Oliver did not stay long enough or look ahead imaginatively enough quite to see how objectively inadequate, even though intrinsically sensible, the current ecumenical agenda was in regard to Asia. It is a pity that his sympathies with French Catholicism did not carry him through to discovering people like Jules Monchanin or Henri Le Saux (later Abhishiktananda). His perception of the prospects of Christianity in India remained confined rather closely within the ecumenical orthodoxy of the moment.

He did achieve one thing of considerable importance during his week in Madura. He astonished Lesslie by informing him that the Central Committee of the World Council had included him among 25 people chosen to prepare a theological draft for the theme of the second Assembly in 1954, 'Christ the Hope of the World'. Lesslie did not want to agree but, as so often happened, 'Oliver's patient reasoning prevailed' and he agreed to go.[37] He would, in fact, become the committee's chairman and principal spokesman, one of the leading figures of the Assembly at Evanston.

Oliver's dominant concern throughout the years of his secretaryship of Faith and Order was its third world conference held at Lund in August 1952 and this became all the more intense in the final 18 months after his return from Asia. It would be possible to read the Lund volumes and, still more, subsequent comment on Lund and hardly notice Oliver at all and yet, in reality, it was supremely, if unobtrusively, his conference.[38] Archbishop Brilioth in his presidential address was certainly not over-stating things when he paid tribute to 'our indefatigable general secretary, Mr Oliver Tomkins, who has brought into the movement a new eagerness' and also a new efficiency. The Continuation Committee of the Second Conference at Edinburgh had decided to pursue three themes – the Nature of the Church, Intercommunion and Ways of Worship. Naturally enough little was done during the war years except in America. Almost everything in the three volumes dedicated to these themes published in 1951 was in fact put together in the previous couple of years under the stimulus of this 'new eagerness'. Oliver did not edit any of them himself, though he contributed the longest chapter with that on Intercommunion, but he made sure that they were actually done, bullying theologians here and there to get on with it, though occasionally they did turn round and say 'No', like Michael Ramsey, who was in fact preparing a good deal of material for him but, when begged for still more, replied, 'I simply cannot face *any* further commitment – not even if you had got the Pope to begin reunion with the Man in the Moon' (27 March 1950). These three volumes provided an invaluable collection of material on which to base the Lund discussions and subsequent thought. It was Leonard Hodgson, still Faith and Order's official Theological Secretary, who wrote their brief general preface, but it was Oliver who wrote in his own name a further short book entitled *The Church in the Purpose of God* (1950) as introduction for the conference, summarizing the issues with superb clarity. Besides this and his 32-page chapter on 'Intercommunion in the Ecumenical Movement' he delivered to the conference itself a lecture of remarkable maturity on 'Implications of the Ecumenical Movement'.[39]

Oliver's two most enduring contributions at Lund, however, went well beyond all of this. The first was to bring to the fore the issue of 'non-theological factors' in the separation of churches. In 1937 an American commission had submitted a pamphlet at Edinburgh on *The Non-Theological Factors in the Making and Unmaking of Church Union*. Little notice seems to have been taken of it, however, and the subject was not included in the post-Edinburgh agenda. However, at the first meeting of the new Faith and Order Commission held at Chichester in July 1949 a long letter from C. H. Dodd on this subject was read out by Oliver. In point of fact it was the result of his going to see Dodd in Cambridge and persuading him to put the gist of their conversation in this form. It was included in the minutes of the meeting, as also in *The Church in the Purpose of God* (pp. 79-82), and provoked so much attention that there were study conferences on the subject in 1951 both in America and at Bossey. It became a sort of fourth theme for Lund. It should be obvious that what divides churches in reality is often politics, culture, language, class and the sheer weight of history rather than the theology which ecumenical conferences tended to concentrate upon. Ever since Lund it has constituted a major theme within ecumenical thinking. The fact that this is the case owes a great deal to Oliver.

His final contribution reflects that ability to find the right phrase at the right moment which characterized him all his life. In his lecture to the conference he declared towards the end that 'The implication of our confessed unity in Christ, beneath and above our divisions, is that we should do together everything except what irreconcilable difference of sincere conviction compels us to do separately. Our present structure of Christian cooperation is too often based upon the assumption that we do everything we can separately, and only when we have reached the end of our resources there do we act in unity.' D. T. Niles picked on the first sentence and persuaded the Message Committee to incorporate it in the brief text released for publication immediately after adoption by the conference: 'Should not our Churches ask themselves whether... they should not act together in all matters except those in which deep differences of conviction compel them to act separately?' The principle of 'doing together everything except what deep differences of conviction compel us to do separately' became famous as 'The Lund Principle',[10] but few remembered that it was, essentially, a formulation of Oliver's.[11] His final contribution was to edit the conference volume the following year.

At this point Oliver stood with Wim *sans pareil* in the sheer professionalism of his ecumenical ministry, combining theological acuteness, a remarkable grip on all the relevant information, and practical efficiency. And yet he had resolved to leave the World Council and return to work within the Church of England. While longing for a parish he had in fact been offered the principalship of a theological college – Lincoln. After considerable hesitation and the consulting of ever so many friends and advisers, he accepted the offer in February 1952 on condition that he could continue a certain amount of work for Faith and Order. In writing his acceptance letter to the Bishop of Lincoln he emphasized his 'desire to continue to serve the ecumenical movement from a job within my own church'. He sent a copy of this to Wim with a hand-written covering note:

> I must confess that I was strongly tempted in my heart during the days at Lambeth to say that I would like to stay with the World Council! It is such a grand fellowship and the friendships it has brought mean a lot to me. But I am sure, deep down, that it was *only* a temptation! I have reached the end of what I feel it in me to do for the beloved ecumenical movement at the *committee* [his emphasis] level. And I grow more convinced that in this country at least...the next stage lies in fighting hard to make ecumenism come alive within the churches nominally committed to it, and that there is my place.

But even at Lund he found himself 'wondering why I am leaving WCC'. In point of fact he was very far from escaping 'committees'. Indeed, he had just agreed to fill a newly created post – chairman of the working committee of Faith and Order. His successor as secretary, Bob Nelson, lacked his authority and experience, while Brilioth, venerable as he was as chairman of Faith and Order, was not much good at bearing the burden of the regular running of the commission. So Oliver was appointed chairman of its working committee, leaving Brilioth to appear only for state occasions. Immediately Lund was over, he chaired the first meeting: 'I tremble before the Bishops and Moderators over whom I shall have to preside.'

# 6

# Lincoln Theological College

In January 1953 Oliver and Ursula together with their four children moved into the Warden's house in Lincoln Theological College, the Bishop's Hostel as it was also called, and Oliver began a new career. Why did he do so? The basic reason is simple enough. He had for years been anxious to return to pastoral work in England so that he could better spread the ecumenical message, being only too well aware of the gap between the ideals and practice of the World Council, on the one hand, the weakness of ecumenical awareness or resolution within the Church of England, on the other. Having resolved not to stay in full-time World Council service once the work of the Lund Conference was finished, he had to do something else, but nothing was suggested to him other than this. He had no independent financial resources and four children. His old friend and colleague from SCM days Dick Milford had been Chancellor of Lincoln Cathedral since 1947. The theological college was nominally the 'Chancellor's School' (Scholae Cancellarii) and remained subject to his general supervision. It was Milford who invited him to visit Lincoln in mid-December 1951 and see how he felt about it. 'Nothing about the prospect makes me *glow* as the thought of a parish does,' Oliver commented in his journal. 'It would be very hard if I discovered that this vision of "being ecumenical locally" when I leave WCC has only been a mirage and not a call of the Lord. Told them all that I should take a lot of convincing!'

In fact, it did not take a great deal. Within a very few days he was writing that 'Lincoln looks more solid and the parish more mirage-like'. Fisher, Bell, and almost everyone else he consulted encouraged him to take it. 'I should need the sort of prophetic certainty I've never had about anything to put my parish-dream above all that.' Actually the pressure, apart at least from the people at Lincoln, was far from overwhelming. David Paton pleaded almost desperately, but in vain: 'Harden your hearts against pressure... Don't you dare take Lincoln unless you are sure, and don't be overborne by weighty urgings. The weighty too often have no conscience for they are horribly aware of the needs they have to fill and proportionately too often neglectful of the needs of the individual they bully.' Oliver, he insisted, was anyway too similar to Milford to be the right person – they needed something different. Indeed, Dick had admitted as much:

> I should love to have you here and cannot think of anything more delightful. But that is part of the difficulty. Our training, background, strengths and weaknesses are too much alike. I too have a nodding acquaintance with reputable theology, even less than yours... Whoever was here, I could, I think, ensure that the college does not entirely forget the world wide church, the Ecumenical Movement and the breezes from outer space. But for that very reason, I suspect that we ought to have as a Warden someone who will give confidence to the staff, students, and the Bishops that our

scholarship is sound and accurate. It doesn't matter so much at Westcott, because of the University lectures.

Milford wrote this in November when hoping for an alternative candidate. It is strange that he should so entirely have abandoned such considerations a few weeks later. If he declined he would be left, Oliver feared, with 'only a hypothetical alternative', but as he still had a full year to work for the WCC (and, in fact, it could have been longer as his successor at Faith and Order, Bob Nelson, intimated that he could not take up the job until June 1953) that hardly seems decisive. For a few short weeks he agonized, mistrusting his 'lack of desire', belly-aching over 'that mythical parish which I hate to relinquish for the reality of Lincoln' with its 'cold' weather (!), 'horrid house' and 'dim schooling'. All the same, on 9 February he wrote to Milford to say he would accept, provided he could do it in combination with chairing Faith and Order's new working committee. The delight of Eric Abbott, who had been Warden of the college some years before, 'removed his last doubts' and he set about thinking how he could follow in the footsteps of his old guru, B. K.

It remains a strange decision, indicative, perhaps, of a continuing lack not only of self-confidence but also of self-knowledge. Here he was, a man of 44 who had been extraordinarily successful in a very special job of the highest importance, involving for an Anglican priest a unique degree of international and inter-denominational experience, allowing himself to be persuaded over a very few weeks into taking on a job for which he was quite unprepared, was not greatly suited and did not want.

The principal of a small theological college far from any university needs to do a lot of teaching. Oliver was not a trained theologian, his expertise lay within a very special field which hardly entered the normal curriculum, nor was he a natural teacher. Just two years earlier he had spent the Lent term of 1950 on sabbatical at Westcott House and had given a series of lectures on the ecumenical movement both there and in the Divinity School. They had not been a great success, as Robert Runcie, on the Westcott staff at the time, still remembered 50 years later. There was far less interest in ecumenism in the theological colleges of the 1950s than in those of 20 years earlier. As a teacher Oliver failed to enthuse and he had himself been fully aware of this: 'I am not much good at making all this sound really exciting and convincing. Most of my colleagues could have done it far better.' He felt an 'inability to *grip*'. His conclusion was that 'there is an apathy in the Theological Colleges for "ecumenics" except among a handful – but I'm not much good at curing it!' Yet that is what less than two years later he had committed himself to doing. It is not that the imagined return to a parish ministry would have made any great sense (though to become, say, Vicar of St Mary's, Oxford, the university church, a post he was actually offered in 1947 when Milford left it, would have been a different matter). Lacking prophetic power, as he knew he did, he could have had little success in converting the Church of England to ecumenitis from no better vantage point than some single parish pump. His strengths lay in working, not through charismatic personal authority but by quietly ensuring from within that a system functioned effectively and creatively for the ends he had in mind.

It is surprising that no one saw what should have been obvious enough – that Oliver was ripe for a bishopric. By 1952 he was far more expert than anyone else other than Bishop Bell in what Temple had called 'the great new fact of our era', the worldwide ecumenical movement. He knew the WCC and its related movements inside out; he had been immensely successful and effective in holding down one of the top international ecumenical positions;

Cartoon of Oliver by Alistair Cooke.

Leo and Oliver in China.

An international group of Ecumaniacs (1949). From left to right, D. T. Niles, H.-L. Henriod, Oliver, Hendrik Kraemer, Suzanne de Dietrich.

Engagement: Oliver and Ursula,
May 1939.

Oliver and Ursula
– wedding day.

Leo Tomkins in his study at Paddington, 1938.

Katey Tomkins, 1939.

The family in 1948. This was the photograph the Abbé Couturier placed daily on his altar at mass.

A confidential word with Archbishop Fisher at Amsterdam, 1948. John R. Mott on the right.

The family at Lincoln, 1958

An exploratory visit to Bristol, August 1958: Oliver and Ursula with Dr and Mrs Cockin.

The Bishop in full pontificals.

Oliver Tomkins and Martin Niemöller.

Oliver hated wearing gaiters but they had their uses: a centenary episcopal kick-off in Bristol.

Oliver Tomkins and
Wim Visser't Hooft, 1964.

Meeting Pope Paul VI in 1965.

Oliver's final meeting of Faith and Order, Bristol 1967. Left to right, Paul Minear, Gene Carson Blake, Oliver Tomkins, Lukas Vischer.

Leaving Stavanger, Norway, 1985, after celebrating the 75th anniversary of the founding of Faith and Order – Oliver's last overseas ecumenical trip. He was still wearing the Abbé Couturier's beret.

Headstone of Oliver's grave beside Bristol Cathedral.

MAY
THEY
ALL
BE
ONE

JOHN 17²¹

Both near to retirement: Oliver Tomkins and Michael Ramsey, 1973.

he was familiar with half the leading figures in world Protestantism and quite a number in Catholicism and Orthodoxy as well – in comparison almost all his Anglican contemporaries looked distinctly provincial; he had written at length and with great clarity on the theology and practice of ecumenism. He had also proved himself pastorally mature in the handling of people, and he had even had as much parish experience as many bishops. He was the right age. Kenneth Riches, three months younger, became a bishop that year. Donald Coggan, 15 months younger, was made one in 1955; Gerald Ellison, two years younger, became Bishop of Willesden already in 1950 and of Chester in 1955. Mervyn Stockwood, five years younger, became one at the same time as Oliver. Why was Oliver not considered, especially as Fisher had seen him at work and knew his effectiveness? The answer would seem to be that his career had not been a normal one: work abroad or outside the regular Church of England network did not count. One can compare Francis House who, when he left his position as Head of Religious Broadcasting, went to talk about his future with Fisher and was steered back to Geneva. Francis had already had exceptional overseas experience as well as that at the BBC. He would have made a refreshingly creative bishop. When Michael Hollis, former Bishop of Madras and first Moderator of the Church of South India returned to England in 1961, aged 62, all he could find was a parish in Sheffield offered by Leslie Hunter. Yet 62 was not a great age and Hollis had the most impressive pastoral and ecumenical experience behind him. Similarly Ambrose Reeves, Bishop of Johannesburg, deported from South Africa after the Sharpeville massacre, failed to be given a diocese in England. Fisher did indeed include his name on a list of possibles for the diocese of Blackburn but ensured that he would not be chosen by suggesting that the Prime Minister must decide 'whether it is politic at such a moment to put in an English diocese a Bishop around whom so many storms had arisen through his championing the cause of the indigenous African population'.[1] That sort of consideration could apply to almost any creative person. It is not as if there were a plethora of able candidates – at least not in Fisher's eyes. While Attlee had begged for younger nominations and disliked Fisher's proneness to suggest translations from one diocese to another, Fisher was inclined to lament that 'we have drained the reservoir dry at the moment'. Thus in January 1956 it was announced that Montgomery Campbell, Bishop of Guildford and nearly 70, was to be moved to the supremely difficult and important see of London, at which Campbell himself remarked that they had 'scraped the barrel bare'.[2] According to Michael Ramsey, Fisher's judgement of character was 'superb'.[3] Given that Fisher had had ample opportunity to get to know Oliver personally, one may question whether his failure to suggest his appointment to a bishopric until 1958 showed superb judgement. There can be no doubt that Oliver's talents were eminently episcopal.[4] If he had been appointed in 1952 or, even, two or three years later, say, to London in 1956, the subsequent leadership of the Church of England might well have been different. Consecrated only in 1959 and not for one of the top dioceses he was too junior a member of the bench to be considered for promotion when Fisher retired in 1961.

Late in his time at Lambeth, Fisher appointed a senior 'Lay Secretary', the first lay person to hold major responsibility inside the tiny Lambeth curia. It was Robert Beloe, Chief Education Officer for Surrey and one of the most imaginative educationalists of his time. Many years later when Oliver was retiring Beloe wrote to him (19 August 1975), 'I don't think I've told you what I have said to some – that, with hindsight, I wish we'd got you at Lambeth in 1961. You'd have hated it, but you'd have done the C of E and the country so much good.' Coming from Ramsey's lay chief of staff, someone who knew the inner workings of the Church of England better than almost anyone, and who also knew both Ramsey and Tomkins extremely well, this, surely, is a remarkable commendation. It was the lack of imagination of Fisher and, indeed, everyone else including Oliver himself in the early 1950s in regard to his capabilities – proven as they already were – which ensured that he would not enter the episcopate until a little too late to approach its apex. Alan Webster, the Dean of Norwich (and later of St Paul's) who had succeeded Oliver at Lincoln in 1959 and knew him well, lamented, at much the same time as Beloe's letter, that Oliver had 'not been allowed to move to the forefront of leadership'. Instead he was left at a crucial period to struggle with a job for which he was not suited and did not want. Yet, probably, no one ever noticed!

Publicly Oliver's *persona* changed in 1953. The University of Edinburgh gave him a doctorate *honoris causa* and the Bishop of Lincoln made him a canon. Where, hitherto, he had been simple 'Mr Tomkins' he was now 'Dr Tomkins' or 'Canon Tomkins', seemingly more appropriate titles for a moderately senior ecclesiastical figure. Privately his lifestyle changed still more. For years his principal workplace was Europe or still further afield, his home Cheam. Now the two were under a single roof, the warden's house being attached to the college and separated off by a single, rather awesome, door through which in termtime the warden departed early in the morning hardly to return until well after supper. Monica was now eleven, Stephen nine, Ruth almost seven and Deborah four. The house was not too 'horrid', at least it was more spacious than that in Cheam, and the college gardens were huge, but everything was regulated, in theory at least. In termtime Oliver had all his meals in college except tea, several times a week two students arrived punctually at eight for coffee with him in his study but on Sundays a larger number joined with Ursula in the sitting-room. With her temperamentally free, unregimented soul, this new kind of monastic existence, so formal, so regulated, was harder to bear than that of Cheam. Her husband was mostly now so close and yet also so distant, so conscientiously committed to the other side of the college door.

For the children little of this mattered. They were at school most of the time. When at home they found some of the more extrovert students good fun; in the holidays, when the students were away, they could take over the college, playing murder in the bedrooms, roller-skating along the corridors, hiding in the coal cellars or climbing on to the college roofs. Oliver had spent childhood holidays in Norfolk with his cousins and cherished the dream of owning a boat and sailing with his children. A heavy old rowing boat, named *Boadicea*, once acquired, was endlessly worked on – Oliver loved to work with his hands – but when taken down to the canal for rowing or sailing it did not prove a great success. 'An undignified little tub' with no keel, it was much loved (at least by Oliver) but little used. At Christmas there were parties in the college with Scottish dancing and charades. Oliver would act the wicked uncle, Monica the captive princess, Ursula the prince who rescued her. In summer there were holidays in the Milford caravan.

For their children, all in all, this was a good time but for Ursula and Oliver it was not. After 15 months Ursula suffered a breakdown, due in part to an enlarged thyroid. Given her temperament and the narrowly institutional and clerical world now surrounding her, it should perhaps not surprise one. She made no significant friends in Lincoln outside the college, while inside it the rigidity of life on both sides of the door was deeply uncongenial, yet it did surprise Oliver and he could not fathom it. They took a week's holiday on their own in the Cotswolds in July to help matters, actually staying in a small hotel, 'a splash' he called it, but that could hardly cure her, especially as he was off almost immediately afterwards for two months of ecumenical activity centred around the Evanston Conference. He does not seem to have sensed what lay beneath it all. Even a return of his own ulcers he would have been unwilling to admit was a sign of the strains of being in the wrong place.

Years before, in 1947, when visiting the Episcopalian General Theological Seminary in New York, he had been very critical:

> I spent one enjoyable and profitable evening with a couple of veterans and their wives. Both had served in the Marines... As I expected, they felt suffocated by the seminary and its sheltered ecclesiastical atmosphere. I incited them to take advantage of being the veteran generation, of whom their teachers are scared stiff as being mainly much more experienced men than themselves, to bust wide open the sacred confines for the sake of their less dominant successors. I hate this seminary-smell... There is no excuse for it in the middle of New York.

The trouble was there was still all too much excuse for it ten years later in Lincoln. Oliver altered almost nothing at Lincoln. The 1950s were a conservative decade and many a 1950s seminary could give one the impression of returning to a prep school. Oliver, it seems, had quite forgotten his hatred of 'this seminary-smell'. He frequently spoke of the students as his 'boys', the annual pantomime was a major event prepared months in advance. A sense of confinement was extreme. Everyone had his appointed place in chapel so that the staff could see if anyone was absent (with the help of a chart in front of them of names for each place!). It was still an intensely male institution with no woman on the staff. Oliver did increase the number of married students and tried hard to be helpful to their wives, whom Ursula gathered together on Thursday afternoons for a 'College Wives' Group'. If in terms of the practice of later decades the openness of college life to women in Oliver's day must look decidedly skimpy, in terms of what was customary elsewhere at the time it was definitely on the generous side. But Oliver's underlying presuppositions were traditional enough. Jill Sargent was a wife who much appreciated the support she found in the college. She was also a social worker. 'Shortly before we left Lincoln (1957), Oliver summoned me to his study in order to say two things. First, he thought I should join the Mothers' Union and secondly, he did not think I should continue my career in social work... Oliver and I agreed to differ.'[5] She never joined the MU while eventually qualifying as a psychiatric social worker.[6] At the time almost any bishop or college principal would have given the same advice to a young priest's wife. While Oliver failed to escape the conventional viewpoint, he expressed it very politely. And in his notes for what to say to wives, after referring to the career woman's need to adjust to becoming subordinate to someone else's work, he added a corollary 'therefore great importance of wife's sexual satisfaction'.

While Oliver was Principal at Lincoln, Edward Knapp-Fisher was Principal at Cuddesdon. Every year Knapp-Fisher gave a talk on the value of celibacy. B. K. and Eric Abbott were celibates, so was Cyril Garbett, the Archbishop of York when Oliver went to Lincoln. So had been Archbishop Lang and Bishop Gore, fiercest of Anglo-Catholic prophets. While Davidson, Temple and Ramsey, three other great archbishops of the twentieth century, were married, not one had children. Fisher, on the other hand, had six sons. From this point of view Oliver was of the Fisher school. The advance of Anglo-Catholicism had certainly been accompanied by a distancing from the Protestant image of a bishop or priest as a married family man. Fisher was quintessentially Protestant and establishmentarian. The theological colleges had grown up in the Church of England in the late nineteenth century parallel to the march of Anglo-Catholicism. Largely modelled on Roman Catholic seminaries, they offered a celibate, semi-monastic training for men who would later, it was accepted, mostly marry. It was natural that their principals and staff had tended to be unmarried too. Lincoln was fully part of this tradition. But Oliver's marriage was central to his life, 'a very sheet-anchor' he called it in the retreat notes he made before moving to Lincoln. He fully accepted the discipline laid upon his students of chapel, common meals and the rest 'yet it was obvious', remarks John Yates, the college's tutor and chaplain, 'how irksome, to put it mildly, this was in term-time for both Oliver and Ursula'. Oliver never contemplated any major change, soon as that would actually follow him in time. He did, however, endeavour to increase the available accommodation for married students and made their wives welcome to a degree unusual at that time. Even the existence of girl-friends could be admitted. Oliver had at one time contemplated becoming a monk but he recognized the reality that the normal priest is and should be a married man and that it is therefore unhelpful to celibatize his training unnecessarily. Lincoln became as a result the first theological college quite to recognize that married men are married. 'He departed,' continues Yates, 'and with him in some respects a whole era in the ethos and spirit of ordination training in the Church of England.' That is put too strongly. Robert Runcie became Principal of Cuddesdon a year after Oliver left Lincoln. He found a regime in force even more monastic than the latter's and he did not greatly alter it. Women remained extraordinarily excluded from the life of Cuddesdon, apart from the Sunday eucharist. That was the condition of things in many places all through the progressive 1960s, so we should not judge Oliver too hard for failing to alter them entirely in the conservative 1950s.

When things appeared to be going badly, as was the case a number of times, Oliver tended to blame his own failures in prayer or his inability to be an Eric Abbott. 'Part of my trouble,' he wrote in a mood of self-examination in October 1954, 'has been an immense inferiority-complex' with regard to Eric. B. K. Cunningham represented perfection in a theological college principal according to the standard view of Oliver's generation. Eric Abbott was his unrivalled successor and imitator. Homosexual in temperament, intensely lonely, profoundly spiritual and sensitive to the feelings of others, the almost tortured bearer of a gospel of love, Eric published little and was never a man of causes or campaigns. Instead he was almost ceaselessly preoccupied with the pastoral care of young males. Oliver's near contemporary and friend at Cambridge, he was appointed Warden of Lincoln Theological College in 1936 when only 30, became Dean of King's, London, nine years later and then Warden of Keble College, Oxford. In 1959 he returned to London as Dean of Westminster Abbey. Thousands of clergy all their lives felt they owed him an incalculable debt. When he died in 1983 Westminster Abbey was packed for his memorial service. Even when on holiday Eric spent most of the morning and other times as well writing letters and postcards of greeting, encouragement and advice. Oliver was simply different. He entirely lacked the kind of psyche which activated Eric. He did indeed imitate Eric in developing the 'ministry of the postcard' but on holiday, as all the rest of the time, he also read countless detective stories (34 books of 'light fiction' in 1950 alone!), messed around with *Boadicea*, went for walks with the children, or hastened away to yet another ecumenical meeting. Where Eric had given his professional heart to guiding the young, Oliver had offered his to ecumenism. Both were needed. The trouble was that having succumbed to becoming a theological college principal, Oliver felt guilty because he was not Eric. As Paul Oestreicher, a Lincoln student in the 1950s, has written: 'Eric Abbott had produced disciples, "Abbott men". There were not to be "Tomkins men".' It is not obvious that this was a disadvantage.

Oliver, like Eric, believed in the central importance of a life of prayer, especially in the seminary. Eric liked to quote William Temple's remark when he preached the Cambridge University mission in 1926: 'Most people think that conduct is what matters and prayer helps it. The truth is that prayer is what matters and conduct tests it.' Oliver, like Eric, often turned to Von Hügel to learn about prayer. He tended to feel – like many other active priests – that he did not pray enough, that he had made too little progress in prayer and that there was nothing he admired more in Catholicism than its praying – both liturgical and mystical. In the retreat he made at Alton Abbey in December 1952 in preparation for Lincoln the first defect he detected in himself was in regard to 'meditation and contemplation: I realize bitterly how little progress I have made in twenty years in these aspects of prayer... this retreat has left me painfully aware of how infantile, nay carnal, my mind is still when it comes to seek God for his own sake in quietness and contemplation.' Nearly five years later he was writing again, 'Please God, these years of Lincoln will teach me, long overdue, a depth and steadiness of prayer, in which I am still so weak. I long for more mystical prayer, but so often have to fall back upon "intellectual" and "institutional" forms, to use Von Hügel's illuminating distinctions' (June 1957). The daily eucharist in college meant more and more to him as did the round of the office. That may well have been the main contribution Lincoln made to his own life. Severe in self-judgement, he was almost desperately determined to communicate a rounded sense of prayer to the students and in this, one feels, he did not fail. In the words of one student, Reggie Askew:

> Above all things, from him I learned prayer; long, late and silent prayer; not by what he said, which was curiously tentative (something which it took me a long while to recognise as a very good sign), but by his example with its unstated assumption that the life of prayer was not described, but entered...we did not watch him praying. He was behind us, watching and praying. We learned that prayer was wearisome and arduous, a terrible intercessory toil, and that it needed fidelity and stamina. But for all it was undiscussable it was essentially collaborative, ecclesial, and not a private world. There was no competition, but we usually left the Chapel before him. One passed him in the silence, his head lowered, his face intent, lined with resignation, and a patient look of mountainous sadness, grave, fatherly and dependable. It was very encouraging.

Askew's retrospective testimony is valuable, not just because he was decidedly critical at the time of other sides of Oliver's work, especially his teaching, but because he went on himself to train ordinands over many years at Wells and Salisbury Theological Colleges and as Dean of King's, London. Yet the phrases he chooses are remarkable: 'a terrible intercessory toil', 'lined with resignation', 'a patient look of mountainous sadness', suggest the strain, even anguish, prayer involved for Oliver at Lincoln.

Oliver was by no means an outstanding teacher of theology, as he himself had already discovered. He had always lacked 'an absorbing interest' in the subject as John Yates divined. For the most part his lectures were dull, if judicious, being rather closely based on a few recent books, such as J. G. Davies's *The Spirit, the Church and the Sacraments* or the Jesuit Bernard Leeming's *Principles of Sacramental Theology*, both of which he read to turn into notes for lectures. They seldom inspired, even when he spoke about his favourite theme of unity as he did a great deal. A principal purpose of the Christmas pantomime was to take off the Warden, playing back to him his idiosyncrasies. The central stanza of 'The Warden's Song' at the end of his first year went as follows. It tells one a good deal.

> W:  I do my best to educate you all,
> Ch:  Which we quite appreciate,
> W:  And to make it your concern
>     Ecumenicity to learn
>     And koinonia radiate.
> Ch:  We will make it our concern
>     Ecumenicity to learn
>     And koinonia radiate.

Yet later he would tell himself that he had done too little to teach about ecumenicity and hence had failed to get it across. Temperamental reluctance to press a point emotionally could make him appear almost uninterested. He could even be accused by students of not appearing to believe in the Holy Spirit! The self-confessed preference for 'Both-And' hardly makes, at least in the eyes of fairly commonplace listeners, for a sharply focused message. The notes for his lectures on the Holy Spirit survive, neatly set out, thoughtful, honest, a little tentative but drawing in a whole range of issues. One could learn a lot from the approach but it was not, at least on the surface, at all dogmatic. The criticism seems rather hard. Years later, only a little before he died, Oliver looked at them again and then wrote at the end, 'These are the notes of the lectures of which Reggie Askew said "You lectured to us on the Holy Spirit in a way which made it clear that you did not believe in him." I wonder if I could do any better today. I don't think He likes being "lectured" about.' The criticism had cut him very deep.

Dick Milford later published a little volume of poems,[8] including one entitled 'Partners in Dialogue' about three positions 'Yes-But', 'Both-And' and 'Either-Or'. The lines on 'Both-And' run as follows:

> Both-And takes part in the debate with all-embracing charity,
> Assents to all conflicting views, nor seeks excessive clarity.
> 'There must be truth in all opinions men have held sincerely,
> Trust to your heart to guide you right, and not to reason merely.
> The Light that lighteth every man has everywhere a witness,
> Any belief that long survives gives evidence of fitness.'

Doubtless that would be a caricature of Oliver's views, but Milford knew him very well and his proneness on all occasions to appeal to 'Both-And'. This poem can hardly fail to reflect, tongue in cheek, the impression Oliver made. Lincoln had a good teaching staff in his years there: Tom Baker, John Yates, Robert Symonds, John Fenton, Basil Moss and Dick Milford were probably all more lively and academically up to date than Oliver and the students appreciated their teaching, but a small theological college in the 1950s far from a university was immensely dependent on its principal: 'colleges then were run as benevolent dictatorships' (John Yates), and nothing could quite make up for any perceived weakness in the principal, however much at heart he was loved and admired.

A certain remoteness, an 'inscrutable smile', 'a beaming enigma', a willingness to stand back and watch for grace to work rather than to be constantly intervening, might all be appreciated afterwards more than at the time. At the time students again and again expressed a certain dissatisfaction with a remoteness in their principal which they could, of course, link, if perhaps unfairly, with his rather lengthy absences on international ecumenical business. It became something of a college joke that they had to pray so often for the success of a conference in some remote and hitherto unheard-of place because the Warden was attending it.

How did Oliver evaluate his Lincoln years? The best clue, albeit still a partial one, is to be found in his journal though it is noteworthy how little he wrote in this period, except when well away on World Council business. In his preparatory retreat at Alton Abbey, 16–19 December 1952, he went over things as was his wont at the hinge moments of his life quite extensively, evaluating, confessing failures, thanking God for so much, resolving to improve. As regards Lincoln itself, he decided, 'the initial fear and mistrust is, thank God, a good deal abated'. He chided himself on failures to advance in prayer, on 'poor self-discipline' – smoking too much, reading 'voraciously but undiscriminatingly'. He thought that college life with its 'countless bells' would be 'very good for me'. He prayed for joy in this work, reread B. K.'s life and believed that 'from what I have seen of the boys already, they will quickly kindle my sympathy', but admitted 'so far I have seen little enough evidence of any "enthusiasm" for the job. It has been my hesitation all along… Unless God gives me joy in this work I fear that something essential will be lacking.' After adding up all the 'gifts and lacks' – the former, he believed, owed 'wholly' to God's grace, the latter 'wholly' to his own faithlessness – he finally concluded that it stirred:

> some flutter of joyful anticipation! It all depends upon the grace of God – but then he *is* very, very gracious. If only the end of it all may be a few generations of men genuinely matured in Christ – 'full men first', as B.K. would say, with priesthood coming to crown a rich humanity, each being completely the unique self he was meant to be, living out the secret name which God has written on his forehead. To share in a work like that! What more *could* I ask? Don't be a faint-hearted fool!

Did he protest too much? Could it really be true that failure could only be his fault? His habit of moralizing left little room for other explanation. Nine months later, having been ill three times the previous term, he was persuaded to cancel various engagements and take 'a clear fortnight' of holiday with Ursula in Dorset in early October: 'Perfect sunny weather, long walks, lazy reads – I working through *The Man on a Donkey* and Ursula discovering Charles Williams. Such holidays together should be more frequent!' The following July they were away together for another week, this time in the Cotswolds, but now in a hasty attempt to deal with 'Ursula's mystery illness'. After that he was off for most of the rest of the summer in America.

Settling back in Lincoln in October 1954 proved exceptionally painful. It should have been so good. For the first time, as he noted, the college was full of men who had known no other warden. Instead it was, he felt, 'the nadir of my misery about this job'. He knew he was failing to 'get' them, he was aware that his long absence at Evanston had been much resented (with him away some new students had been interviewed by Ursula, ill and in bed!). But worse was to come. 'A few days ago a bitter letter from a recent ordinand, one of my best-loved lads, full of pent-up disappointment – speaking of "four generations, now, of spiritually under-nourished ordinands", of my treating them as "items on my in-tray to be dispatched as rapidly as possible into the out-tray" '. It was, Oliver admitted, 'very difficult to take'. Eric Abbott comforted him by saying that he too had his disappointments and rebuffs. 'I shan't get this right until my resentment at being a "failure" at a new job is drowned in fresh floods of love for God and for these lads for His sake.' He blamed himself for a lack of facility in small talk and ended this passage pathetically, 'Is it in their final term that I fail them most?'

He kept the letter marked 're being a *hopeless* Warden'. Only a very tidy, or conscientious, person would have done so. But it is hard to dismiss it as a matter of 'pent-up disappointment'. The writer was Michael Paton, youngest son of William Paton, master ecumenist of the previous generation, and brother of Oliver's old friend David. That made it all the more difficult to take, as did Paton's insistence that he was speaking in the name of many. He stressed how much Oliver's Compline addresses were appreciated, but reiterated that most of the men found him distant, his heart too obviously elsewhere. Two things had persuaded Paton to write:

> The first was hearing you speak in your drawing-room about Evanston, when it was forthcoming; you lit up with interest and affection in a way that we had never seen; and it was quite clear to me that you are in love with the Oecumenical Movement and are in no danger of venturing to commit bigamy with the Bishop's Hostel! Secondly, I realised that you proposed to go on as before, maintaining extensive contacts with the World Council, doing as much work (tho' no doubt less than they would like you to) for them as you feel can be fitted in without letting the Hostel down too badly. Well, it won't work.

Paton dismissed the idea that Oliver was 'simply treating the hostel as an interesting stepping-stone on the way to a bishopric'. That, in Oliver's mind, was quite untrue though possibly not in the mind of the bishops who had encouraged him to go there. It was because Paton, helped by his own family background, had actually seen deep into the dilemma at Oliver's heart – deeper than Oliver dared admit – that this letter hurt so much. It was futile to turn away from the central problem to focus instead on his weakness in small talk.

That was October 1954. Dick Milford was in India throughout this period. Oliver wrote to him about college business in October and November: 'There is not a great deal of news from here'. He said nothing of his misery or Paton's letter, though he did refer somewhat dismissively to the 'legend' that he was away too much on ecumenical matters. Given Milford's close friendship and special responsibility for the college, this does suggest how private a person Oliver was in coping with real problems, indeed how little he could admit them even to himself. There is no further entry in the journal for eight months. The next one (5 June 1955) is far more cheerful: 'This has been a *happy* term – now it is able to be my first charge and I have more idea of what I'm after, I feel much freer and happy with them. The particularly difficult element has left.'

Six months after that, December 1955, he seems less sure: 'This year's end sees us complete a cycle of three years at Lincoln... I sense that at last I am beginning to be accepted by the men and to be developing my own way with them. My lecturing is still painfully scrappy and inadequate, but I feel freer and happier with them than I have ever done before.' The next relevant note was penned 18 months later, in June 1957, sailing west across the Atlantic once more:

> At last I begin to feel that I 'fit' Lincoln and belong through and through to its concerns – though it remains a lonely job in that I continue to have *very* few clues as to the kind of impact I have on others...unsure whether my 'boys' find me rather forbidding or softly lenient – I suspect a sort of 'kind

heart under a stiff front' kind of myth – and it's probably true, tho' the stiff front is largely shyness and the kind heart is partly sheer vacillation! More distressing, if true, is the discovery through some remarks of R.A. that my anxiety not to bully the boys into positions not *genuinely* their own has appeared as a bored detachment from any real convictions at all!... R. was obviously very disappointed in my failure really to kindle him about Christian unity – is this the only fruit of my scrupulous desire not to present the Ecumenical Movement as though it were only the Warden's hobby-horse?

A month later, sailing back again, his Faith and Order meeting over, he returned to musing about himself and his job: 'In spite of temptations to extreme sloth, my mind is beginning to look home and look forward. A note from Ursula that the *Church Times* rang up to enquire about Frank Woods

> 'because he may be in the news soon' gave me a twinge of jealousy in case it should be Chichester! The evil seed of constant hints that I'm 'sure to be a bishop soon' I have always tried to prevent from sprouting! But, at the end of nearly five years at Lincoln, I find myself sometimes wondering what next – for I now know that young men, much as I have learned to love them, will never be an entirely satisfying métier... I now realise that I owe it to the young to give them a *firmer* lead, not least in everything to do with the Ecumenical Movement. If I can really learn to be an infectious teacher, I can probably serve the Church better in the great cause of Church Unity than I could anywhere else. I mustn't be afraid of being labelled 'ecumaniac' among them.

On 7 January 1958 Bishop 'George' Cockin of Bristol wrote to Archbishop Fisher to say that it was time for him to resign, he gave his reasons, added that it should happen in the autumn, and then continued, 'I have a clear idea of the man who would make an admirable successor... That is Oliver Tomkins. When one thinks of the needs of this diocese and city, with its strong ecumenical traditions, its great educational opportunities, and its excellent civic and industrial relations, he strikes me as ideally suited to meet the demands.'[9] Fisher was not at first over-enthusiastic. 'Oliver Tomkins is among the people who gets serious consideration from time to time,' he admitted, but continued 'His health was at one time not good. If I remember right he had to take a day off a week in bed in order to keep going. As you will realise no Bishop can guarantee to do that.' To which Cockin responded, 'I am almost sure that you must have confused him with another Principal.' It was extremely unusual for a bishop to attempt to select his successor in this way but in due course Fisher was convinced and in June wrote to the Prime Minister proposing Oliver:

> The Archbishop of York and I both agree that the time has certainly come when he ought to become a Bishop and that he is specially qualified for this Diocese. He has taken a leading part in all the most lively and creative issues confronting the Church: his work on Faith and Order in the World Council of Churches has been outstanding; as Warden of Lincoln Theological College since 1953 he has won the complete trust and confidence of Bishops and clergy.

Macmillan accepted the suggestion on 4 July though with the slight complaint that he had not been offered more than one name. He did, however, admit that this could be appropriate when 'there is one outstanding candidate'.

So it was that later that month Oliver was offered the diocese of Bristol. As so often in his life at crucial moments, he was away from home. Ursula forwarded the Prime Minister's letter together with one of her own 'Can one say No?' One feels she was desperate not to, but knew that Oliver would hesitate anxiously, both because it went against his ingrained humility to accept, at last, so big a step up, and because the very mixed record at Lincoln was actually something more difficult to terminate than a more obviously successful work would have been. 'I must try' he wrote into his journal in Geneva,

> to get light upon whether I am now, at last, doing a job at Lincoln which is qualitatively good enough to insist upon a few more years to do it in, in view of the long time it took me to get into my stride. I feel that I have been effective for only the last two or three years... Indeed my illness last Lent was a further crisis. I think that duodenal spasm taught me new lessons in letting-go... I think I must admit that I don't see myself as being used to develop any *new* insights in theological training *at Lincoln*. Its very circumstances – of isolation, two years limit, distance from university facilities etc – preclude the development of those very aspects which modern training may require... So it's merely a question of whether I ought to go on in the job as inherited in the 'Lincoln Tradition': the conventional, post-Tractarian conception at its best.

Everyone advised him to accept and, of course, he did. The 'boys' cheered and clapped their hands enthusiastically when he broke the news. So everyone, for one reason or another, was happy.

It would be hard to avoid strain in a small in-turned community of young men, high ideals, rigid rules and a sensitive principal who, nevertheless, gave a sense of aloofness. Successful as the bishops judged his work at Lincoln, the impression remains that Oliver was in the wrong place. It really should not take an intelligent person three years or more to settle into a job. It is doubtful whether he was really at ease with it even after five years, though he could hardly admit that to himself, and it was absurd to imagine that he could somehow still 'learn to be an infectious teacher'. He should have known, and indeed probably did know, that much from the start. Without the slightest doubt numerous Lincoln students felt at the time, and still more, in retrospect, that they owed Oliver a very great deal. But he was in reality too senior for the job. He was not a natural teacher. There was, moreover, something about his slow speech, his enigmatic smile, his refusal to appear 'charismatic' or evangelistic in approach, which distanced him from most of his 'boys' in ways that neither side quite understood. Perhaps such qualities actually made him a better principal, enabling the students to mature more without any over-dependence on himself. Yet he might well have seen from the start that to continue a 'conventional, post-Tractarian' seminary was not his métier while he had not the radical temperament to pioneer something different. While he would conscientiously have continued the struggle if required, one can only be grateful that at what was to prove a crucial moment in ecclesiastical, and especially ecumenical, history he was removed to a far more open and congenial position.

By the time Oliver had personally answered 260 letters of congratulation, many of them ecstatic, he must have lost any worry as to whether it was right to go to Bristol. Some, especially among the bishops, had been hoping and expecting it for a while. For his old bishop at Sheffield, Leslie Hunter, 'it will be good to have you in the episcopate'. The Bishop of Peterborough thought 'you will have one of the most attractive dioceses and the perfect predecessor'. Billy Greer at Manchester insisted that Cockin 'had wanted you all along'. Donald Coggan at Bradford commented, 'I only wish it were in the Northern Province!' George Simms, Archbishop of Dublin, thought Oliver 'so wonderfully well equipped', while the Bishop of Leicester declared to a friend 'Now the C of E will be alright'. A fellow canon of Lincoln presumed to say that 'from the little I have seen of you in the last five years, I am quite sure that you will be one of our really great bishops'. While for another correspondent it showed that 'we are not doomed for ever to mild-mannered mediocrity'. Messages poured in as well from old Lincoln students. Reggie Askew declared that since hearing the news 'we have been going round feeling definitely impressed with the Church of England', while another wrote 'This is an event which we, and several generations of Lincoln men, feared might take place in their time at the Hostel and thus remove you. We are selfishly grateful this Hostel calamity was postponed until after our departure... Bristol is so very fortunate.' From the academic world there were letters from Leonard Hodgson and Charles Raven, Donald MacKinnon, John Robinson and Henry Chadwick among others as on the Catholic side from Abbot Butler of Downside and Dom Columba Cary-Elwes, Dom Bede Winslow, Fr Gordon Albion and Jérôme Hamer.

'How much it will extend your scope in the oecumenical field,' wrote Leslie Paul, while for Robin Woods 'This is splendid for the whole Church – a positive replacement for George Bell when such was needed on the bench.' A correspondent from the continent remarked drily, 'The good Brilioth will now rest content that Faith and Order is in the hands of a Bishop once more again' and Wim Visser't Hooft declared it 'remarkable that one of the very oldest descriptions of what is a bishop, namely the expression of St Ignatius, "a man wholly consecrated to unity" applies to you in a special way!' A group of nine men who had been fellow-students of his father at Cheshunt College before 1905 sent their good wishes but, perhaps most moving of all, an old and almost blind man put pen to paper 'because your uncle Oliver was my Sunday School teacher... He was tall, his legs ate up the ground. I am afraid we were not too good but I loved him and I think the others did... No doubt you have heard much about his ordination. It was the most solemn service' – exactly 60 years before the episcopal ordination of the second, no less long-legged, Oliver. All in all they surely confirmed Geoffrey Fisher's remarkable insistence in a letter of 21 July that 'The invitation which comes from the P.M. comes equally, and I think I may say more insistently still, from the Church: that is to say, not only from me but from other wise persons through me.' That admission, surely, said a great deal.

Edward Woods, Bishop of Lichfield, Oliver's patron and mentor in Cambridge days, died in January 1953. His sons, Frank and Robin, both of whom became bishops, were among Oliver's most steady friends. He had remained very much part of the large Woods circle, surrounding an extensive family (Edward had six children and ever so many grandchildren), so it was natural that Frank and Robin should turn to him to write a memoir of their father, and difficult for him to say no, yet still more difficult to do it well. He set about it in 1954 and it was published in 1957, the only significant literary product of his Lincoln years. Oliver certainly realized at this time that he was likely to be a bishop soon and the depiction of his former hero will have helped him imagine the sort of bishop he wanted to be. He was not uncritical. 'It mattered little, as years went by,' he wrote in the preface, 'that in many ways one disagreed with him. His great gift was neither intellectual originality nor balanced statesmanship (so uniquely blended in his great colleague, William Temple). Edward's gift was that he made things lovable.' A liberal Evangelical, an enthusiast of the First World War 'Life and Liberty' movement, in which he succeeded Temple as chairman, and in the ecumenical movement, especially of Faith and Order whose conferences he had attended both at Lausanne in 1927 and in Edinburgh ten years later, he conquered hearts by the sincerity of his charm and simple religious commitment. He was the most regular of religious broadcasters, and it seemed to matter little that what he said was platitudinous. 'A stupid saint' some called him, but his judgement generally came down on the right side and, in many ways, Oliver shared his attitudes, not least his fondness for G. K. Chesterton's saying 'If you want to make a thing live, make it local'. He quoted it twice in the book.

Perhaps it was the matter of class that Oliver found most difficult to handle. Part of the charm of the Woods family for the young Oliver was its sense of social security, grounded on considerable wealth. They were related to Frys, Barclays and Gurneys, all wealthy, devoutly Protestant families, bankers and brewers. High Leigh, Edward's wife's home, now a large conference centre, was a spacious 'Gothic' mansion in Hertfordshire. The Woods and their numerous relatives took for granted a Victorian upper-class bonding of prayer, prosperity and play: tennis, shooting and missionary activities. Edward Woods devoted himself unstintingly to the service of God and mankind, but he did so in a way that even by the mid-1950s was coming to appear archaic to most ordinary people. In one of the book's illustrations the bishop appears 'on a day off', gun in hand. Oliver had no interest in shooting, but he could hardly criticize, and only very gently draw attention to, behaviour which was coming to appear inappropriate in a religious leader. The book does, however, succeed in depicting a man who in a very genuine, if somewhat old-fashioned, way managed to combine the spiritual and the secular quite unaffectedly, with great serenity and charm, an optimistic conviction that grace and humanity really do go properly together, a conviction that Oliver absolutely shared. Oliver, particularly perhaps the later Bishop Oliver, will often have had Edward Woods at the back of his mind, not so much in his ecumenical activity, which he had far surpassed, but rather in the way he managed family and household, especially at occasions of socializing. From that point of view Edward Woods and the challenge of writing his biography mattered rather more in the shaping of the mature Oliver than might at first be apparent.

During his first eight months at Lincoln Oliver had remained not only chairman of the working committee of Faith and Order, but also the commission's secretary. Only after completing the report of the Lund meeting, which he dated August 1953, was his successor, Bob Nelson, finally available to replace him. This quite heavy ecumenical commitment at the start undoubtedly affected his ongoing relationship with the college, setting up an enduring impression that half of his attention was somewhere else than Lincoln. All the more was this the case because the second Assembly of the World Council, held at Evanston, near Chicago, in August 1954 came only a year later and took Oliver to America for a considerable time. Faith and Order had to prepare a 'report' to present there, the first of the Assembly's section reports. It was essentially a rehash of what was said at Lund, where it had been agreed that it would help the study of the Church, its unity and disunity, to place it more emphatically in relation to a theology of Christ. The Evanston submission 'Our Oneness in Christ and our disunity as churches' reflects this. It was hardly a revolutionary insight. Furthermore, it reaffirmed the 'Lund Principle' urging the Churches to act together in all matters except those in which deep differences of conviction compelled them to act separately; again, reflecting Lund, it invited the Churches 'to consider frankly the influence of social and cultural differences' upon matters of faith and order; finally, in regard to intercommunion, it stressed that 'for some but not for all' being conformed to Christ should mean renouncing 'eucharistic separateness'. This report had, of course, been produced by Faith and Order's working committee and its final wording was largely Oliver's work. Archbishop Brilioth was not a member of the Working Committee and actually needed some persuasion to go to Evanston at all, but it was he who as chairman of the Commission on Faith and Order presented the report to the assembly with Henry Van Dusen in the chair. The Orthodox delegates led by Archbishop Michael at once read out a statement declaring that 'the whole approach to the problem of reunion is entirely unacceptable from the standpoint of the Orthodox Church'. Van Dusen politely commented that 'suitable use' would be made of Archbishop Michael's 'important declaration' while Georges Florovsky, backing Michael, admitted that in the context of Evanston the Orthodox were defending an unpopular cause. There had in fact been only a very small Orthodox presence at Lund, and none at all from the Church of Greece. It was not much better at Evanston where also, once more, there were no Roman Catholic observers – the Archbishop of Chicago had forbidden their attendance.

The World Council's problem was that it was desperately anxious to retain and enlarge Orthodox membership, without which its credibility could only be severely undermined, and yet that the ecclesiology of most of its members, which was bound to be visible in World Council statements in one way or another, remained profoundly unacceptable to Orthodox theologians. While the Toronto Statement had been an attempt to head off this conflict, the tension kept recurring. It is interesting to note that Oliver himself was losing patience. As he wrote in his journal when the Assembly was over:

> The Orthodox continue to be a problem!... Archbishops Michael and Athenagoras made intransigent speeches wherever possible. This naturally provoked other groups who felt that they too would like to say just what they thought without being inhibited by accommodation to other views. And of course the mass of the Assembly had no inkling of the bitter interior controversy which makes it the more essential for the Orthodox to preserve a facade of unity. With obscurantist bishops, German-liberal professors and evangelical lay-movements, they have a tricky team to drive! But some day soon they have to be told, in love, the truth that they can't indefinitely trade upon their minority privileges.

But why not? Why shouldn't they go on protesting against what so easily looked like the dominance of a Protestant consensus?

The reality was that the international ecumenical movement in the 1950s was already in danger of running out of spiritual steam. Evanston was not a distinguished assembly. It was also too American in its culture to please the Europeans. 'All this mania for photography,' lamented Oliver, 'recording, televising, and broadcasting destroys any chance of spontaneity, at least for us who are unused to it.' The atmosphere of the Assembly itself was subtly affected, he felt, by 'American Protestant vitality'. The whole process of 'deciding truth by democratic vote', when most of the delegates had hardly even read the texts in question, was plainly fatuous. Michael Ramsey, now Bishop of Durham, hated

Evanston: 'the vulgarity of showing off the delegates as though they were exhibits, and the insincerity of pretending that platitudes were pronouncements of world-shaking import'.[10] 'There were times at Lund,' Oliver had to admit, 'when we were just as ridiculous'. Yet Oliver's heart was too committed to organized ecumenism for him to leave with the disgust that Ramsey felt. 'Surely the time has come for the WCC to stop growing as an organisation in view of its specific and limited job, lest it create an impression that it is aiming at a type of power to which it has no right and makes no claim.' Yet he could still feel that 'All in all, it was a great occasion.' Forty years later he summed Evanston up as follows in a lecture to the Focolare Movement: It was 'chiefly notable for getting the WCC on to the map in terms of publicity because there we lived under a blaze of public lighting in order to be televised in order to let people know that we existed in order that they might produce the money to enable us to go on existing!'

The British age of the World Council might be said to end with Evanston, the American age to begin. Bishop Bell retired as chairman of the Central Committee to be replaced by Franklin Clark Fry, hitherto its vice-chairman. There was certainly an increase in senior Americans on the staff in Geneva. Nevertheless the British presence remained exceptional and would do so for at least another dozen years. There were still two or more British Associate General Secretaries: Leslie Cooke, a Congregationalist, replaced Mackie in charge of Interchurch Aid, while Francis House returned to Geneva, filling what was effectively the Anglican slot, held previously by Stephen Neill. They would be joined by Norman Goodall. Plenty of Oliver's British friends also remained on the Central Committee – Ernest Payne, its new vice-chairman, Kathleen Bliss, Ambrose Reeves, now Bishop of Johannesburg, Lesslie Newbigin, representing the Church of South India. Britain was anything but under-represented after Evanston, that would only change in the late 1960s. Nor would it be replaced by a comparable American dominance but by greater internationalization. Given the extent to which the World Council had been financed by Americans from the start, their restraint in the early years might seem remarkable. However their impatience, such as it was, was less with the British than with the dominance at Geneva of European Barthians.

Robert Mackie's departure in 1955 was, all the same, the end of an era. He had been General Secretary of the World Student Christian Federation (in succession to Visser't Hooft) from 1939 and the senior Assistant General Secretary of the World Council in residence at Geneva since Amsterdam. He had built up the Department of Interchurch Aid and Service to Refugees from the shambles it was in when he took it over, reorientating it to long-term purposes. At the same time he had mitigated with a ministry of personal care the damage done within staff ranks by Wim's abrasiveness. It is extraordinary that the World Council's Dictionary of the Ecumenical Movement (1991) has completely excluded him from the record, even in regard to Interchurch Aid, yet it well reflects his own quality of selflessness. He at least would not have taken it amiss. When he left to return to his native Scotland, however, the tributes were overwhelming: 'You have served as a kind of ecumenical cement to hold together the galaxy of primates and prima donnas' or, again, 'We shall still have a World Council, of a sort, after you depart, but it will no longer be the one we have known.'[11]

Despite Oliver's wish that the World Council would 'stop growing as an organization' in point of fact its organization grew ever more complicated after Evanston with a multiplication of committees and departments. Faith and Order too established no fewer than eight distinct theological commissions in which, Nelson reported, more than 'eighty prominent Christian thinkers from thirty-seven churches in seventeen countries'[12] were at work. They were programmed to deal with a vast range of subjects including, fittingly enough, 'institutionalism': 'How is our inevitable and seemingly inextricable involvement in ecclesiastical institutions, with all the temptations of bureaucracy and denominational aggrandisement – how is that involvement really militating against the manifestation of the oneness of the Church of Him whom men crucified in order to defend their institutions?' It seemingly did not occur to Faith and Order in the 1950s that this question might well be asked of the World Council itself. While Robert Nelson was the efficient organizing secretary of this extensive programme, Oliver remained its leader, but in the complex new institutionalism of the WCC decreed at Evanston the Working Committee of the Commission on Faith and Order had become just one of a plethora of 'working committees' within the 'Division of Studies' chaired by Walter Freytag. The Division of Studies had, of course, its own committee on which Faith and Order was represented by Oliver and Georges Florovsky. In 1948 Faith and Order was one of the two founding bodies of the World Council. Six years later it had been reduced to one of four departments within one of three divisions. It is difficult not to feel that, despite the grandiose plans, Faith and Order had greatly declined in relative importance within the World Council – exactly, of course, as critics like Dom Lialine had suspected already in 1948. In fact in 1957 a special committee was set up to consider the very 'Future of Faith and Order'. When in 1960 Oliver presented to the Central Committee plans to ensure the significance of that future within the World Council Professor Hromadka, remarking that 'Faith and Order had apparently become invisible for some time', welcomed its revival. So much for Nelson's eight theological commissions! While there were numerous reasons for this decline, the standing of Faith and Order cannot have been helped by Brilioth's detachment, Wim's pragmatism in relation to the mood of the moment, and Oliver's fairly lowly status and personal sense of unease with regard to his international activities. But more important may have been a wider lack of ecumenical vitality in the 1950s, even stagnation. No Assembly was less lastingly significant than Evanston in the first 50 years of the World Council. The 1950s were not a creative decade for theology and they were in general an age of conservatism, not innovation. Much delicate effort too had to be put into trying to ensure that international Christianity was not identified with American politics within the Cold War.

For Oliver this was a time when his own public involvement in anything at all was at its lowest level for many years. Yet the withdrawal that Lincoln entailed may actually have worked to his advantage. There was little to be achieved in the post-Evanston years and therefore little lost by doing little. He would find his second wind on becoming Bishop of Bristol at exactly the same time that Cardinal Roncalli became Pope and had, within months, breathed new life into the entire ecumenical process. Harold Macmillan's letter of July 1958, offering him the diocese of Bristol, reached Oliver in Geneva, where he was chairing the annual working committee of Faith and Order. It seems somewhat symbolic that it was so. Going to Bristol, did, of course, mean leaving Lincoln but it certainly did not mean leaving Faith and Order. On the contrary. It could only strengthen his position ecumenically and internationally. He hummed and hawed in his usual way, consulted others, thought he felt a '*deep* uncertainty' and would like to have called it a 'struggle' but Ursula sensibly remarked that that was too strong a word. On 14 August his appointment was in the papers. He felt a real sadness at leaving Lincoln but everyone else was delighted. It was so obviously right. The December pantomime in the college that year was *Robinson Crusoe or Oliver's Travels*. With the New Year of 1959 he was preparing himself in retreat for a job for which he was absolutely fitted and at

Westminster Abbey, on Epiphany, that most mysterious celebration of some wise ecumenical travellers, he was consecrated bishop. His two episcopal 'presenters' were George Cockin and Billy Greer. He had been the preacher at Greer's consecration 12 years earlier. All three were SCM veterans. When the liturgy was over Oliver and Ursula, accompanied by family and friends, having changed to evening dress, watched *The Nutcracker* in the Festival Hall, passing from one sort of ballet to another. The relaxed ability to enjoy *The Nutcracker* on the night of his episcopal consecration expressed the confidence of a priest who felt he had arrived, able to mix the sacred and the secular with a quietly amused relief, able also to spend money a little frivolously. Hitherto he had never even owned a car. Financially too he had moved into a new world.

# 7

# Bishop of Bristol

**Being a bishop**

Bristol suited Oliver. The city, the university, the diocese, cathedral, bishop's house, the dignified and comfortable mix of town and country, the middling scale of it all, neither too grand nor too humble, neither too rich nor too poor, neither too Anglo-Catholic nor too Evangelical. His predecessor, George Cockin, was known for his ecumenical attitudes. In youth he had been vigorously SCM. He had arranged the services throughout the Oxford Life and Work Conference in 1937 and had been a representative of the Church of England 11 years later at Amsterdam. So Oliver could feel that he too suited Bristol. Indeed, he had, he admitted to himself, long had a hunch that this might be the diocese for him. Bishop's House was conveniently situated within the city, an attractive and capacious Queen Anne house with a fine walled garden, but not too grand. Any sort of a palace or castle he would have found embarrassing. Here there was comfort but nothing for which a bishop needed to feel guilty. He always enjoyed a certain amount of patrician comfort, so long as he had not sought it, and he could do so now. He did feel guilty about the pension he would receive in retirement, so much greater than that of his clergy, but when he raised the disparity at a bishops' meeting, he found painfully little support.

In 1959 the family was half grown-up: Monica 18, Stephen 16, Ruth 13, Deborah 11. They would all marry in the Bristol years. And Ursula blossomed, the strains of Lincoln little by little fading away. Oliver remembered his personal life with the World Council as 'scatty and unregulated'; at Lincoln, on the contrary, everything was excessively orderly; Bristol fell between the two but undoubtedly remained closer to the Lincoln model. He might still blame himself for a lack of regularity. What others observed was a personal self-discipline and a certain austerity in household management. A normal day began with Oliver praying alone in the chapel before breakfast at 8.30 followed by house-hold prayers at 9. If he was away, Ursula led them. His children sensed a remarkable regularity and smoothness in his relations with them. 'In your household you can't do anything without a bell', his most secular son-in-law-to-be commented. There was too a firm sense in regard to detail of what was right: 'that's our society' he would say, if his children questioned the rather upper-class atmosphere they now lived in, but he wanted them to be able to relate to everyone. You visited old ladies in the city, but you had your riding lessons too. You must certainly not swear. When once he broke a sherry glass and said 'damn' in a daughter's presence, they were both very embarrassed: it was so out of character. He made sure that all the children had the chance to attend special occasions from time to time – a Lord Mayor's dinner or a garden party; just as he invited old Mrs Friedeberg to birthday lunch in the House of Lords. Episcopal perks and personal relations were interwoven.

There seemed to be more holidays than previously, at first on Exmoor and then after 1965 on the north Pembrokeshire coast, near Newport, when they bought Bryn Cottage close to another owned by Robin Woods. The purchase was made possible by a legacy from Ursula's grandfather. On holiday Oliver was the boy scout, always equipped with the necessary, whether string, compass, map or binoculars. He loved dogs. They had not had one since Millhouses but acquired a handsome Welsh collie at Bristol. Alas, it bit the President of the Mothers' Union and had to be put down. Unlike many an upper-class clerical home Oliver's witnessed no accumulation of valuable possessions – pictures, china or furniture. Only books to read, and papers. Oliver loved reading, it was recreation as well as work. He loved especially to read aloud to the family on their holidays and he read very well. In earlier days it could be the *Six O'Clock Saints*, later on Exmoor *Lorna Doone* or, on a family holiday in county Cork, Somerville and Ross, *Reminiscences of an Irish R.M.* Otherwise he was quite a silent father, saying little unless asked something quite directly, especially when on a walk, in this treating his children much as he treated young clergy. He still found it hard to give up smoking. While he had convinced himself that it was a moral weakness not to do so, his pipe was only abandoned in the mid-1960s and cigars, finally, some years later.

The structures of family life were firm, with a certain formality, but the content of life in Bishop's House was very fluid, with the comings and goings of diocesan staff, student lodgers, ordinands on retreat at Petertide and Michaelmas, when everyone else had briefly to vacate their rooms, the clergy themselves when they needed advice. One Archdeacon was very critical that they took in 'lodgers' (often students in distress from a university women's hostel over the road, at the request of its warden). He felt it gave a bad example to clergy wives! But they had taken in lodgers all their married life. In the family the Beatles were popular and Deborah was very proud when her father asked her to write down for him the words of 'Eleanor Rigby'. Games were played uncompetitively. Oliver was keen on word games and excellent at chess; at Christmas parties for clergy children there was a game of 'Hunt the Bishop', eventually discovering him, maybe, in a cupboard or the cellars. At table visitors could obtain the impression of everyone talking incessantly without waiting for anyone else, except for Oliver who just listened. If the argument was over a fact, he might steal away to his study and return with a book to settle the matter. He did not obtrude himself intellectually on his family but would gently put a book into their hands at a suitable moment – Graham Greene's *The Power and the Glory* for a teenage daughter or the latest published work of Teilhard de Chardin for Ursula. Little by little Teilhard became for her the best guide to a vision of life encompassing both science and mystery. There were no rows, no sense of tension, no insistences on this or that point of doctrine, and each of his children, despite at times the embarrassment of the label 'the bishop's daughter' (or son), took to his beliefs and kept to them. It was a real, if quiet, satisfaction for Oliver to see Monica and Stephen active in the SCM. Again, money was never talked about, despite his own long shortage of spare cash and an early nervousness which went with the continued habit of very careful accounting.

Oliver's sustained efficiency as a bishop depended not only on his own orderliness, ceaseless calm activity and a certain steely quality but also on his staff. Here he was exceptionally fortunate. His secretary he inherited from George Cockin and after 17 years with Tomkins she continued in the job throughout the episcopate of his successor, John Tinsley. Alice Brindle was a model of confidentiality and commitment and hardly less of a workaholic than Oliver, but their styles did not always agree and her filing system upset him. When he spoke of 'my files' she would reply firmly 'they are not your files, Bishop'.

In administrative matters she had at times to push him to get decisions and he could be capricious. He was not expected to enter her office but she did enter his bedroom. When ill, he would sit up in bed wrapped in a shawl dictating letters. He took Alice and her new assistant, Jean Gray, up to London to Freddie Temple's consecration as Bishop of Malmesbury in 1973 and then on to tea in the House of Lords. For his retirement service in Bristol Cathedral he personally wrote out the cards for both of them. The underlying bond of affection was profound. On occasions late in the evening Alice was still at work when Oliver had left for some engagement, a lull descended on the house and Ursula would tiptoe across the stone-flagged hall to the office to persuade its occupant that enough was enough. Together she and Alice would roll up the hall carpet, wind up the old gramophone and embark on a country dance. Ursula's love for informality and the unconventional, for sitting on a vicarage hearth in a housing estate with her feet tucked under her, physically and emotionally relaxed, was as important in the Tomkins mix as Oliver's passion for precision and decorum, even if some people were startled by her informality and even unpredictability. Hardly less important were the Sintons, the couple who 'lived-in' and ensured that the more material side of things was also under control. Gordon and Sinty came from Yorkshire in response to a *Church Times* advertisement for a couple to 'assist in the running of Bishop's House'. He took care of garden and car, she worked with Ursula on the shopping and the cooking, as well as keeping an eye on the younger children in the early years if Oliver and Ursula were both out.

Oliver remained as ever a fast reader, his table covered with books and journals, the field wide and never singly focused. In his annual reading list he only includes 18 titles for 1959. It was, he concluded, 'a lean year', usually there were 30 or more. But the mix was much as ever. It included 'eight theology' but mostly of a fairly slight, contemporary sort. Only George Tavard's *Holy Writ or Holy Church* was more substantial. It included two Anglican biographies: Eric Kemp's life of Bishop Kirk, and Charles Smyth's of Archbishop Garbett. There were various novels but, unusually, no thrillers; there were two books of 'history' – one of Bristol, the other Geoffrey Ashe's *Arthur's Avalon*, and the novels included T. H. White's *The Once and Future King*. Arthurian interest seemed a necessity for a West Country bishop. In general, the annual reading list included ecumenical tracts, Anglican biography, some special holiday reading, retreat reading, background works for particular conferences or visits abroad. Whatever seemed of contemporary concern found a place – *Lady Chatterley's Lover* or *The Lord of the Rings*, neither of which he much liked. Anything by Michael Ramsey was read and praised as also anything by or about Teilhard de Chardin, though he found *The Phenomenon of Man* distinctly hard going. A few books he read to review. Never, even at Lincoln, was there much academic theology. He liked the books of old friends – Leslie Hunter and Daniel Jenkins, Alan Booth and Alec Vidler – and he much enjoyed a light novel – P. G. Wodehouse, Margery Allingham, Ngaio Marsh, Agatha Christie. He was always well informed but not, and he would not have dreamt of considering himself, a learned or scholarly bishop.

In public life he admired Hugh Gaitskell and felt that nothing went quite right after Gaitskell's death, but at Bristol he steered very clear of any trace of party political engagement. There was little here to remind one of the man who had been so active a member of the 1950 Group. Africa was at the forefront of the news in the early years of his episcopate and at the 1959 General Election he felt it his duty in the *Diocesan Gazette* to make a few points – mostly, it must be said, rather obvious ones. They included the assertion that 'our relation to the awakening nations of Asia and Africa is the most enduring issue'.

Oliver was well aware of the overseas churches in general and Africa in particular, but he was by no means an expert in such subjects. In theory he liked a rebellious spirit, like Canon Collins who was an expert in African affairs and the anti-apartheid struggle, but he preferred him to remain at a distance; imitation there was none. Where he was responsible, he believed emphatically in order and a political impartiality which remained respectful of the status quo. He had the deepest respect for the royal family and particularly admired the Duke of Edinburgh. Royal visits to Bristol mattered enormously as did his own visit to Sandringham to preach in January 1963, though respect did not diminish an ability to see the humorous sides of that weekend. Again, he enjoyed a chat with Bristol's best-known MP, Tony Benn. Oliver spoke up forcefully in the House of Lords for the abolition of capital punishment but it may be his maiden speech in the House, early in December 1963, which expresses his approach best. It was on prison after-care. He did not attempt to comment in regard to differences in opinion as to the form it should take but concentrated on the underlying principles. 'Rehabilitation at its best is the social working out of forgiveness.' It was characteristic of Oliver that he illustrated his argument with a quotation from a recent novel, John Braine's *Room at the Top*.

Oliver's priority at Bristol had obviously to be diocesan ministry, but what did that chiefly mean? He thought and prayed about it regularly, evolving a pattern which was personal and innovative, rather than radical. The suffragan see of Bristol was Malmesbury and its incumbent in 1958 was Ted Roberts who had moved there not long before from a long and happy period as Archdeacon in Portsmouth. In Bristol he had been less happy and he wrote at once to Oliver, to congratulate him, to offer to retire if Oliver so wished ('there can hardly be anything more daunting for an incoming diocesan than to find a set of firmly entrenched staff officers...') and to add a rather devastating judgement: 'Bristol's besetting sin is in fact smooth bureaucracy just as her crying desperate need is for love.' Bishop Roberts's predecessor was Ivor Watkins who had been translated to Guildford. He had had 32 years of Bristol experience, including ten as suffragan to Cockin. He said much the same: 'Bristol is without doubt the most efficient diocese in the country but in gaining that it has almost lost its soul!' Cockin had been a layman's bishop and very few of the clergy, it seems, had seen him as a Father in God. The two archdeacons, of Bristol and Swindon, had run the diocese most effectively but lacked the ability to substitute on the pastoral side for what was missing in Cockin, despite his high intelligence, interest in industry and ecumenical commitment. The late 1950s were a time of church growth and this was particularly noticeable in a well-run diocese like Bristol. In the first three years of episcopate Oliver was able to consecrate no fewer than six new churches in different parts of the diocese, and he was able to report too that the number of men ordained in the Church of England in 1960 was the highest for any year since 1914. At the end of Geoffrey Fisher's archiepiscopate it was still very much the established Church of the nation, riding distinctly high.

In his retreat before Consecration Oliver listed 'the chief ways in which I can best serve the Catholic Church in my own diocese'. First of all he placed 'Evidence of the Love of God. Men need to know that God loves them. Everything else starts from that. And they only know it when God quite evidently loves them through one of his servants. It is only on this basis that teaching, reproof, social witness etc will have any force. And I suspect that love will often be suspect as patronage or sentiment.' It is noticeable that he started at once by demonstrating 'kindness and affection' especially to his archdeacons! While his strategy changed with the years that first point did not. 'I wonder' he speculated in that retreat 'if I can be *both* a parson's and a layman's bishop?' Few, he thought, succeeded in being so. Understandably he resolved at first to concentrate on 'specifically Christian works' – the celebration of the sacraments. Even in a relatively small diocese with only 155 parochial livings this involved a continual rush, a round especially of confirmations which left him, six months later, 'a little breathless'. He preached no fewer than 99 sermons in 1960, most of them within the diocese.¹ Its very smallness initially encouraged the delusion that the bishop could be everywhere but he soon realized this would not work. Instead, he needed 'to block out say two days a week as free from all committees and so forth and reserve them for personal visitation and writing and reading'. He also had to be absent increasingly on ecumenical and other extra-diocesan work. He soon decided he needed more guidance from the diocese itself on what his priorities should be. Almost certainly he became with time more a parson's, than a layman's, bishop – *pastor pastorum* and 'Father in God' were the phrases which kept coming back: ever available to talk with a priest in trouble whether in his study or on a long walk. It was something he had seen and admired in George Bell. He could be firmly authoritative, insisting a little fiercely on the observance of liturgical rules, but always appreciative too of what his priests did or hoped to do; he worried about their loneliness, entertained their children with lively Christmas parties and sought any possible way of making the diocese rather more obviously a team, even a family, and less of a hierarchy. The ceaseless flow of post-cards to his clergy, remembering anniversaries of every sort, became famous. He felt profoundly fatherly. Oliver astonished his staff some three years after coming to Bristol by saying that he found the way he was exercising his role as bishop unsatisfactory. The world was indeed visibly changing in the early 1960s, and the Church with it. When Ramsey replaced Fisher at Lambeth, gaiters were no longer required and Oliver was more than happy to relinquish his to the clothes box of a drama company. But changes needed to go deeper than that. He wanted to be more accountable to those he served. The half-yearly Diocesan Conference was too large a body to plan or advise the bishop. So he proposed in 1964 that its Standing Committee be transformed into a largely elected body of some 20 people, lay and clerical, to become 'The Bishop's Council'. An idea of his own, it was soon taken up in other dioceses. Important as this was, in the long run it may well have been awareness that Oliver was, above all, a bishop of prayer that mattered still more – to his ordinands and priests, first, but later to many others too. The posthumously published collection of his prayers reflects above all his Bristol years. As with Basil Hume, prayerfulness, when not divorced from humour or an admission of continued amateurishness, could be very appealing, much more so than theological acumen or administrative efficiency – though Oliver failed in neither.

Two texts may sum up the way he perceived his ministry as a bishop, one from the start of his work in Bristol, the other from near its end. 'I am among you as he that serveth' was the theme for his enthronement sermon in the cathedral and he applied it not only to himself but to everyone. All alike were called to be 'servants of God's Love' within a vision of the diocese so 'honeycombed by companies of Servants of the Love of God' that it would present an 'irresistible witness to the love of God' through the corporate life of a local community. That was how he wanted it to be and, however idealistic it might appear, his own leadership would be consistently carried out with that ideal in mind. Late in his episcopate, in 1973, Freddie Temple became Bishop of Malmesbury and the address Oliver gave to the Diocesan Synod when licensing him may be used to complement the thinking of his enthronement sermon after 15 years of episcopal experience:

When all has been said about universally valid principles, it is a fact that episcopacy has had a variety of dress – from the purple-edged toga to gaiters... No one wants the autocratic prelate any more – if ever they did. Barchester is being submerged in Metropolis, and Dr Proudie is dead, and Mrs Proudie even deader. But has synodical government made of him only a principal chairman of committees? I believe not – and I believe that a new and fruitful role is emerging. I think that I can best describe it as a *listening leadership*.

At Bristol, as throughout his life, it was as a listener that he excelled, and it was because he listened so well both to individuals and to groups that he actually could then lead them with authority. When Oliver reflected on the role of a bishop, this was not for him a merely Anglican side of his ministry, something detached from his ecumenical preoccupations. Getting episcopacy right in practice was essential to commending it to the wider ecumene.

But a bishop has also to be a pastor of souls. In December 1963 a young man of very limited intelligence, Russell Pascoe, was hanged in Bristol Prison. It was the first execution there for ten years and the last. He had taken part in the unpremeditated but brutal murder of an elderly farmer. The chaplain informed Oliver that Pascoe wished to be baptized. On Sunday, 15 December, in the prison chapel Oliver gave him baptism, confirmation and first communion. He behaved like a child, the Governor sitting beside him and finding the places in the prayer-book. On the next day it was clear there would be no reprieve and Oliver visited him again. He read the story of the penitent thief and left a marker in a Bible. On the 17th was the execution. Oliver was in his cell early in the morning when Pascoe repeated after him a general confession and received absolution and communion. With 20 minutes to go they chatted about the Church across the world and down the ages: 'I wanted him to feel that he belonged to something big and significant.' There was even a twinkle in his eye. They shook hands and Oliver said they should meet again some day in God's company. The chaplain accompanied Pascoe to execution. Oliver did not. The actual end, the chaplain told him afterwards, 'is too sickening and nauseating to describe; and it *must* go'. Oliver's support for the abolition of capital punishment was reinforced, something he felt would come, 'certainly if there is a Labour Government', but the assurance of his personal care for the neediest of all in his diocese is what comes most clearly across, an essentially pastoral, not political, response to a horrible event. He would support abolition in the Lords if he could but his primary responsibility, like that of millions of other priests, was to proclaim the gospel as effectively as he could within the world as it is.


## A wind of change

In late October 1958, midway between the announcement of Oliver's appointment to Bristol and his consecration as bishop, John XXIII was elected Pope. Three months later, this time between Oliver's consecration in Westminster Abbey and his enthronement in Bristol Cathedral, Pope John announced the calling of an ecumenical council. And he announced it on a date particularly significant for Oliver, 25 January, the final day of the Week of Prayer for Christian Unity. In Pope John's mind his council was always intended somehow to further Christian Unity, though just how was not at first clear. Oliver thus began his episcopate precisely at a moment when the ecumenical world, as he had known it, was about to undergo an extraordinary change. Where, up to then, the leadership of the Catholic Church was immensely reluctant to have much to do, at least publicly, with any other Church or with the World Council, so that every little thing – such as obtaining Catholic observers for a major conference – could become a bruising struggle, suddenly all would seem different. Already in October 1959 there was a meeting at Assisi between a World Council group and Catholic theologians held with full papal approval.

Early in 1960 the German Jesuit biblical scholar, Cardinal Augustin Bea, suggested to the Pope the creation of a special commission within the curia for ecumenical affairs.[2] This became the Secretariat for Promoting Christian Unity established in June of that year with Bea as its President and Mgr Jan Willebrands as Secretary. Willebrands, a Dutchman, had founded in 1952 the Catholic Conference for Ecumenical Questions, a somewhat informal gathering of theologians concerned with ecumenical issues and, in particular, to keep in touch with the development of the World Council. Willebrands had become a good friend of Visser't Hooft and for the next few years the close rapport between these two Dutchmen would be a considerable asset for ecumenical progress. The foundation of the Secretariat, however, by no means signified a sudden curial conversion to the cause of ecumenism. On the contrary. Cardinal Bea's influence was fought at every point by Rome's entrenched theological conservatives led by Cardinal Ottaviani, Prefect of the Holy Office. It did mean all the same that Rome no longer spoke monolithically or, even, predictably.

It took some time for Oliver, settling into Bristol, to realize quite how much was changing but by the August 1960 meeting of the Faith and Order Commission and the World Council's Central Committee in St Andrews, it was becoming clear that the whole geography of the ecumenical movement was beginning to shift. Though it was only two months since the Secretariat of Unity had been founded, it was already represented here by Willebrands and the English Jesuit, Bernard Leeming. Officially, it was necessary to play down exaggerated hopes, to insist that all the changes meant no more than that 'a dialogue with the Roman Catholic Church becomes possible'. Visser't Hooft at St Andrews stressed that the World Council must not now come to be seen as an entity somehow comparable to the Roman Catholic Church, just as he insisted that they could in no way 'give up convictions and principles which belong to the very essence of our movement' in order to facilitate contacts with Rome. In 1960 it was still difficult to believe, for instance, that the issue of religious liberty might soon cease to be divisive. But there was the private side, including the gossip, as well as the public. Thus at St Andrews Reinhold von Thadden gave Oliver 'a most interesting account of a private audience with the Pope, his dislike for his "Romans" in the Curia, his affirmation that the Church *is* one in all Christians in the Lord Jesus, his insistence that the Vatican belongs to us all, and not just to Catholics'.

Even Geoffrey Fisher, an old-fashioned Protestant as he was, realized that something had changed and one of the last things he did as Archbishop was to meet Pope John in December 1960 following a visit to Jerusalem and Istanbul. The meeting took a good deal of arranging, it was done largely through Willebrands who had met Fisher at St Andrews, but in curial Rome there was much misgiving and apparent insistence that this could only be a private visit. In London too it needed to be stressed that there were no doctrinal implications. When Fisher felt he needed to explain to the Queen what he had in mind she replied cheerfully enough, 'I hope you won't get as many angry, pleading, hurt, or merely how *could* you do such a thing, letters as I got last year before I went to the Vatican!'[3]

When Fisher eventually arrived in Rome, he encountered truly extraordinary efforts on the part of Cardinal Tardini, the Secretary of State, to play down the significance of the event as being simply a visit by one 'Dr Fisher'. These attempts failed. Pope and Archbishop sat together amicably for an hour. Fisher's assistants, John Satterthwaite and Freddie Temple, were also called in and, though Tardini did manage to prevent a photograph, he failed to stop a long further meeting between Fisher and Bea.

Fisher's retirement followed almost at once. He was succeeded by Michael Ramsey, moved from York – the Prime Minister's choice, not Fisher's. This meant that for the next 15 years Oliver had at Lambeth a man with whom he had worked closely in the past and enormously admired. Oliver was never one to criticize and his determination to appreciate Fisher was considerable, but there can be no doubt that cooperating with Ramsey would be more congenial. As an increasingly ecumenical Anglo-Catholic and a theologian of eminence, but someone without any Romanizing tendency – rather the opposite – Ramsey could seem the right man to head the Church of England at a moment when ecumenicity was bursting forth in all directions and Pope John had opened the gates for a deep readjustment of relationships. Yet a certain unpredictability and the lack of a naturally collaborative touch could undermine the effectiveness of his leadership, especially as he was a notoriously incompetent chairman. Moreover, while Oliver had greater experience than any other Anglican bishop of dialogue with the Catholic Church, he would not become Ramsey's principal representative in this field. His involvement with the World Council made it impossible. Just as around 1950 the theological colloquia he set up on behalf of the WCC with Catholic theologians were quite distinct from the specifically Anglican-Catholic ones happening at much the same time, so now, the two relationships needed to be kept distinct – hard as that was in practice, given the position he now held in the Church of England.

Oliver became a key figure in the Joint Working Group between the World Council and the Secretariat of Unity. For the task of heading the specifically Anglican–Roman Catholic dialogue Ramsey chose John Moorman who had become Bishop of Ripon five months after Oliver went to Bristol. Three years older, Moorman was a distinguished historian and Franciscan scholar, vastly more learned than Oliver, he was all the same less of a theologian. He had been Principal of the decidedly Anglo-Catholic Theological College at Chichester, appointed by George Bell who influenced him greatly. He had undoubtedly been Ramsey's personal choice for Ripon. Ramsey believed that learned bishops were needed and, for appointments in the northern province, Canterbury deferred to the judgement of York. Moorman was more unambiguously an Anglo-Catholic than Ramsey, a man who loved medieval religion and longed for reunion with Rome, but was a little lukewarm about reunion with anyone else. Moorman and Tomkins had much in common, sharing a special devotion to B. K. Cunningham as well as to Temple and Bell. Both had been close to pacifism at the start of the Second World War, but their temperaments sharply contrasted. Moorman tended to relish outspoken commitment to unpopular positions while Tomkins ceaselessly pursued the achievement of consensus on a middle ground. The former had flung up his parish and become a land worker during the war. Evidence of clerical bellicosity produced in him such comments on the Church of England as 'Nothing you can say can ever express one tenth of its badness'[4] – Oliver could never have written quite like that.

Already in May 1961 in the Convocation discussions on the Ceylon Unity scheme their contrasting approaches were manifest: Ripon attacked it, Bristol defended it. Later on, in an unguarded moment, and somewhat unfairly, Oliver would call Moorman 'The

C of E Ottaviani'.[5] When the Vatican Council began, Ramsey appointed Moorman leader of the Anglican observers and, when it was over, chairman of the new joint Anglican–Roman Catholic International Commission which first met in January 1967. Moorman's role was thus central to the most significant development in Anglican ecumenical relations at that time. If Oliver received Bishop Bell's mitre, Moorman received his ring and wore it every day of his life. For Moorman Rome was the natural nodal point of any larger ecumenical geography, while Geneva filled that role for Oliver. It is striking that he never once visited Rome until 1965 when he was 56, while Geneva was almost a second home. The tension between the two models was palpable. The larger history of Anglican ecumenism in this period may be seen in terms of a triangle, defined by its three corners, Ramsey, Tomkins and Moorman, each deeply committed to the pursuit of unity but in rather different ways. Their differences could, however, never quite be spelt out in public. No other bishop had a comparable significance.

Bristol did not appear a hopeful place for the local development of a new relationship with the Catholic Church. Bishop Rudderham of Clifton was well known as one of the least ecumenical of English bishops[6] but even here change was possible and even remarkably early. On 14 December 1961 Rudderham wrote to Oliver to inform him that he had changed his policy of not allowing Catholics to take part in 'public meetings in connection with the work for Christian Unity'. He had come to realize, he told Oliver, that his own views were 'not those of the majority of the Catholic Bishops of this country' and had therefore put aside his own judgement. What is still more remarkable is that, instead of choosing someone of exceptionally cautious temperament to represent Catholics publicly, he assigned Fr Joe Buckley to this role. Buckley was, like Oliver, a great Francophile. He had studied theology at Saint Sulpice in Paris and for him the French clergy were the best in the world. For years he ran a superb Gilbert and Sullivan Society in his Westbury-on-Trym parish and Oliver and Ursula became annual attenders at his operas. They also became close friends. Oliver loved French Catholicism but suffered from a typically Anglican distrust of English Catholicism. Buckley helped him overcome that.

Important for the invigoration of Oliver's own ecumenical ministry within Britain at this time was a somewhat informal body which came to be called the Inter-Church Group.[7] Its establishment was suggested by Daniel Jenkins, Oliver's old Congregationalist friend, a popular and prolific writer, who had conceived the idea 20 years previously of the Theological Club which Oliver chaired in the 1940s. Here again Oliver was to take the chair. The Group's first meeting was in October 1960, the autumn when in so many ways ecumenical activity was hotting up. It met twice yearly, generally over a couple of days and in quite a number of places from the Athenaeum to Cumberland Lodge and Farnham Castle. The aim was to bring together Anglican and Free Church leaders to steer the course ahead in what was quickly being recognized as an exciting new period of Church life. David Paton, now Secretary of the Missionary and Ecumenical Council at Church House, wrote up the minutes. The core of membership consisted of old SCM hands like Jenkins, Paton, Kenneth Slack, Eric Fenn, Billy Greer and Oliver himself, to whom were joined younger men like John Robinson, the Bishop of Woolwich and John Weller, a Congregationalist. Ideas were exchanged on how to ensure that local ecumenical initiatives could be built into parish structures so that they did not simply fizzle out when an ecumenically-minded priest moved elsewhere. Intercommunion too inevitably came up for repeated discussion and already early in 1962 plans were being laid for the 1964 Nottingham Conference of Faith and Order with John Weller as its organizer. It proved, all in all, a valuable think-tank for Oliver on how to advance the ecumenical cause nationally as well as internationally and within his own diocese. It is striking how Oliver's role of leadership in ecumenical matters seems to have been taken for granted within the Church of England almost from the moment he became a bishop. Thus by early 1961, before Fisher's resignation as archbishop, he had already been appointed to chair a new round of Anglican–Presbyterian discussions and a Bishops' Committee on Intercommunion. This was much assisted by his very close relationship with David Paton, who would combine the work of bureaucrat and lobbyist. David fought, Oliver presided. They worked particularly closely in the Presbyterian conversations, where David was once more the secretary. 'More than thirty years affection makes me hope that you and I will continue this work together,' David remarked to Oliver.[8] Here as elsewhere Oliver's presidency was effective because it was grounded in a very sure network of personal relations and loyalty, while David's own effectiveness was enhanced by a special personal rapport with Ramsey deriving from their shared experience of being schoolboys at Repton under Fisher.

Much the same was true in regard to the Faith and Order team in Geneva which was being revamped and enlarged. Robert Nelson had been replaced as Commission Secretary in 1957 by Keith Bridston and he, in 1961, by Patrick Rodger, a very able young Scottish Episcopalian priest. A friend of Dick Milford, he had ferried Oliver around Edinburgh on the occasion of his honorary D.D. At the same time they head-hunted Professor Paul Minear, a distinguished New Testament scholar from Yale, to take up a new post as Director while a young Swiss theologian, Dr Lukas Vischer, was appointed Research Secretary – a truly formidable team with which Oliver would work for his last six years as Chairman of Faith and Order's Working Committee. Vischer would be appointed one of the two WCC Observers at the Vatican Council the following year, providing some of the most outstanding of outsider reports on its proceedings. With the Inter-Church Group, David Paton at Church House, Rodger, Minear and Vischer in Geneva, Oliver had in the following years a highly effective and congenial network of ecumenical collaborators. He would need them.

### All in each place: the road to New Delhi

'I am sorry you so seriously under-estimate the Faith and Order Commission! It is far more important than the Central Committee, although, its membership is expected to be slightly smaller!'[9]

This postcard, written by Oliver in 1952, expresses all his undeviating conviction about the central importance of Faith and Order. For him, what mattered most in the World Council was this. But, for 23 years, he *was* Faith and Order! At first he was assistant secretary to Leonard Hodgson. For five years he was Executive Secretary. For 15 years he was Chairman of the Working Group. But the strange truth is that, whichever position he held, his decisive role remained the same. Long before Amsterdam in 1948 it was clear that the Faith and Order segment of the World Council depended on him for its vitality. Hodgson, Regius Professor in Oxford, was clearly unwilling to stir himself over it, perhaps because he remained at heart unhappy with integration into the WCC. For whatever reason he seems not to have been involved in the theological preparation for Amsterdam. It is worth noting that in October 1947 Visser't Hooft wrote to Bell that it had become very clear Faith and Order needed a full-time secretary and Oliver had 'very obvious' qualifications for the task: 'If that happens we must look for a successor for Oliver' – as Assistant General Secretary. Oliver did, of course, become formally Faith and Order's 'full-time' secretary but he did not relinquish his position as Assistant General Secretary of the World Council. He carried both posts for the next four years and the latter greatly increased his prestige in regard to the former. When he decided to accept the Lincoln Principalship, C. H. Dodd wrote to him in March 1952, 'Your place will be hard indeed to fill in Faith and Order' but, again, in reality he did not give up his 'place' there: he merely shifted the point of control into a newly created position of 'Chairman of the Working Group'! This ensured that he retained the reins of direction in his hands. Probably he did not quite see it like that at the time, but that was what happened. His successor as Executive Secretary, Robert Nelson, carried the day-to-day administrative burden but never exercised anything like the degree of control which Oliver had possessed. Thus, when it came to finalizing a document to submit to the Second Assembly at Evanston Brilioth, President of the Commission, wrote in February 1954, 'I am glad that it is now up to you to try to formulate a definite statement to lay before the Assembly' – the 'you' was a completely personal one. As for the President's own role in Faith and Order it was, Brilioth admitted, 'largely a nominal task'. There is no reason to think that this changed substantially until Oliver laid down his chairmanship after the Bristol meeting of the Commission in 1967, when he was coming up to 60 and had quietly decided it was time to withdraw. Until that moment his authority had simply increased with the length of his experience and mastery of the subject. Nevertheless his leadership was so little obtrusive that even a careful reader of the documents could easily miss its extent.

What we have now to establish is the central task of Faith and Order as he had come to understand it, particularly from the later 1950s. To do so it is best to start by relating what one may call the logic of the Toronto Statement with the logic of Lund. We have seen why the Toronto Statement was necessary. It did indeed represent the foundational stance of Faith and Order as Hodgson, for instance, understood it. Its point was to deny that the World Council had an ecclesiology of its own. Member Churches were committed to a trinitarian doctrine of God but to no particular theology of the Church. Some could, and did, adhere to theologies which 'unchurched' other members of the WCC. This was clearly a necessary position. The World Council could hardly work for unity between all Churches if it declared in advance what kind of unity it believed in. The start of such a process had necessarily to leave out an account as to how it would, hope-fully, terminate. Faith and Order had been in its early phase particularly insistent on this approach – on not evaluating or judging its members as also on not speaking in the name of its members as if it was somehow a super-church. Life and Work had been much more willing to embark on the latter and this was one of the reasons why some in Faith and Order had been reluctant to be linked with it. One sees this approach still clearly in place in the volumes commissioned long in advance for Lund. The volume on *The Nature of the Church*, edited by Newton Flew, in particular, was essentially a matter of compara-tive ecclesiology. Different views were exposed sympathetically but there was no attempt to get beyond them, to criticize or attempt a synthesis, to suggest to the Churches in what terms they should conceive of unity. Faith and Order's purpose was seen essentially as the provision of useful material which the Churches could then employ as they chose in discussion between themselves. This approach had severe built-in limitations which irked more and more as the corporate thinking of the World Council developed. One was natu-rally led on from considering different historically conditioned ecclesiologies into attempting to formulate an account of how the Church's unity should now be conceived. Yet, even if such an account did not become quite officially the WCC's ecclesiology, it was bound to appear as the ecclesiology which the World Council was aiming at. In point of fact, even the Toronto Statement was not simply a denial that the World Council had an ecclesiology which in any way conditioned its membership, because it did go on to claim certain 'ecclesiological implications' involved in the sheer existence of the World Council, such as recognition that 'the Church of Christ is more inclusive' than the membership of one's own Church body and that at least 'elements of the true church' (*vestigia ecclesiae*) are present in bodies one does not recognize as 'churches'. Indeed, the very title, World Council of Churches, could hardly be merely a matter of politeness. In some sense it was accepting that these bodies were either 'churches' or something like churches, and 'churches' has meaning only in relation to 'Church' – the 'One Holy Catholic Church' of the Creed. Of its nature, then, despite the attempt on occasion to deny it, the World Council not only sought an ecclesiology but was already grounded on certain important ecclesiological presuppositions.

While the Toronto Statement, often treated as the WCC's 'ecclesiological charter' could be seen as a minimalist defence of the indefinite continuation of the status quo, it could then also be treated as a stepping-stone towards an extended 'WCC ecclesiology'. In fact, the whole subsequent movement of Faith and Order lay in the direction of defining a new agreed convergence, transcending anything to be found in the status quo. The ecumenical movement and the WCC were felt to render, or show up, every status quo ecclesiology as defective in one way or another. The fundamental step forward was actually taken at Lund when it declared in its opening 'Word to the Churches' that, 'We have seen clearly that we can make no real advance towards unity if we only compare our several conceptions of the nature of the Church.' It agreed, furthermore, that there are 'notes of unity' and one of them needed to be 'visibility'. An essentially invisible unity is simply not enough. Lund's preparatory volumes can, then, fairly be seen as 'the end of a road', the conference itself as the beginning of another. As an official historian of Faith and Order put it: 'At Lund an era of study in comparative ecclesiology ended. A new method was begun.'[10] It was unease with this new method which produced the sharp Orthodox reaction at Evanston. In principle the Orthodox had a valid point, yet if it was accepted there could really be no future and no progress towards the resolution of disunity achievable by the World Council itself. Oliver at least was now wholly committed to presiding quietly over the 'new method' and his concealed impatience with Orthodox reluctance to go along with it, to insist that the WCC remain fixated by the Toronto Statement instead of accepting that their own ecclesiology, as well as that of everyone else, was inadequate, is in retrospect unquestionable. In terms of a minimalist reading of the Toronto Statement his position appears untenable, but in terms of an on-going purpose for Faith and Order, seen as the spearhead for the doctrinal reconstruction of a united church, it was inevitable.

The year after Evanston the new programme began to get under way. At the Central Committee meeting that year Visser't Hooft presented a long paper entitled 'Various Meanings of Unity and the Unity which the World Council of Churches seeks to promote'.[11] The aim was to reconcile Lund with Toronto. 'How,' he asked, 'can we justify the fact that in spite of our intention and promise not to promote a specific doctrine of church unity we continue to make statements about the nature of unity?' The categories of theological thought, he claimed, had simply not caught up with the new ecumenical situation. While the way he himself tried to delineate the theological issue was rather unsatisfactory – it had too much of 'a Protestant colour' Orthodox spokesmen claimed – there was sufficient agreement that the World Council's own theologians must try to fill the ecclesiological gap.

The challenge of Faith and Order in the whole post-Lund period was how to do just that: how to construct an agreed new ecclesiology which went well beyond the existing ecclesiologies of member Churches of the WCC without too flagrantly contradicting the Toronto pledge, so as not to raise the hackles of old-fashioned Protestants wedded to an essentially invisible church or old-fashioned Orthodox and Catholics for whom the visible church was already identified with their own communion. Oliver was not present at this meeting and, in his absence, his latest ally Professor Henri d'Espine, an austere Genevan theologian of the old school who had come to the fore in Faith and Order matters at Lund and Evanston, presented a report outlining a programme of study on how far the World Council could go 'beyond the Toronto Statement'. This turned effectively into a prolonged study on 'The future of Faith and Order' chaired by Oliver in the Working Committee. The aim was both to get beyond Toronto in establishing a shared concept of what unity really meant and to rejuvenate the actual functioning of Faith and Order within the World Council.

The Working Committee presented interim reports to the Central Committee at Nyborg Strand, Denmark, in August 1958 and Rhodes, Greece, in 1959 before presenting a definitive report, approved by the full Faith and Order Commission which had just met, at St Andrews in August 1960. Oliver was not present at these meetings before St Andrews and it is noticeable that in the middle years of the 1950s the discussion of Faith and Order matters in the Central Committee had been subsumed under the Report of the Division of Studies. Faith and Order was distinctly unhappy to be so placed. Its stalwart supporters felt they were being steadily downgraded within the World Council and this was widely recognized as being the case. Thus at Nyborg the Bishop of Guildford remarked that, 'Many say that the WCC has over-emphasized service and has forgotten Faith and Order.' For Bishop Newbigin, 'The WCC has grown, and Faith and Order does not occupy a place commensurate with the importance of Unity.' Visser't Hooft did not accept the truth of this but his argument failed to convince. At Rhodes d'Espine insisted that the basis of the new proposals was a 'conviction that Faith and Order is not in a position within the World Council from which it can adequately fulfill its task', having been reduced to a mere unit within the Division of Studies served by a single staff member. 'Give Faith and Order fair play,' cried Bishop Dibelius in the name of a group of Germans. The consequence of all this could be seen at St Andrews where Oliver presented the final 'Report on the Future of Faith and Order' while d'Espine presented a linked one on 'the Role of the World Council of Churches in regard to Unity'.[12] The core of the two reports was identical. This was a particularly important meeting of the Central Committee for several reasons. It was 50 years after the Edinburgh Conference of 1910 and there was an evocative service in Edinburgh at which Joe Oldham, now 86 years old, read the second lesson. It was also only a year before the Third Assembly was to be held, this time in New Delhi. Moreover, the Secretariat of Unity had just been established in Rome and Mgr Willebrands was himself a Catholic observer at St Andrews. It was undoubtedly a moment of new beginnings and an appropriate one for Faith and Order to stage what one may well call a 'come-back', what Professor Alivisatos hailed as 'the revival of the Faith and Order movement', after years of marginalization. Oliver's report appealed for a genuine recognition that Faith and Order must truly be returned to the centre of the World Council's life as a major element in its organization: 'To promote the original intention of the founding of the WCC that the concern for unity should be at the very heart of its life and penetrate all of its activities, the structural position of Faith and Order in the organization of the WCC needs to be reinforced as well as its staff and financial resources strengthened.'

This surely represents an implicit rebuke to those who in the post-Evanston years had allowed the Faith and Order element within the World Council to be progressively diminished. Visser't Hooft had himself presided over this development. Why it is not easy to understand but it may have gone with his belief that the Church's essential unity was an invisible one given by God, while the need for a visible 'manifestation' of that unity was now being fulfilled, not inadequately, by the World Council over which he presided. Faith and Order of its nature challenged any such measure of self-satisfaction. It is noticeable how little mention he makes in his *Memoirs* of the two great Faith and Order conferences – Lund and Montreal – held in his time as General Secretary. If this was now in some way to be gently reversed, it was largely due to Oliver's careful leadership. At the same time the two reports presented at St Andrews offered a new definition of the unity sought whose shorthand became an almost magical phrase 'all in each place':

> The Commission of Faith and Order understands that the unity which is both God's will and His gift to His Church is one which brings all in each place who confess Christ Jesus as Lord into a fully committed fellowship with one another through one baptism into Him, holding the one apostolic faith, preaching the one gospel and breaking the one bread, and having a corporate life reaching out in witness and service to all; and which at the same time unites them with the whole Christian fellowship in all places and all ages.

Most of this passage including the phrase 'all in each place' went back to the report as presented at Rhodes the previous year. Rhodes in its turn had drawn the phrase 'in each place and all places' from Newbigin's *One Body, One Gospel, One World* published in 1958.

In the privacy of his journal Oliver was able after the St Andrews meeting to table a considerable achievement:

> We have now succeeded...in getting first of all the full Faith and Order Commission and then the whole Central Committee to accept our 'Future report' – the greatest point being the inclusion of a definition of the meaning of church unity which goes beyond anything *explicitly* said before by either Faith and Order or the WCC. If it is further accepted by the Assembly at New Delhi, it will be even better. We have also got authorization for a staff and budget more nearly adequate for the job.

The 15 months between St Andrews and New Delhi would be very busy ones. In late November he was in Dublin giving a series of lectures on unity. In March he made his retreat. In April he was back in Dublin for a three-day meeting of the British Council of Churches. A week later there was Convocation; and in June ten days in Switzerland – a Faith and Order Working Committee in Geneva, followed by a week's holiday with Ursula in the Valais. After a meeting of the bishops in early October and 'lots of tidying up in the diocese' Oliver and Ursula left by boat for India with the 'blessed thought' of three weeks at sea! Given that this was only his third year at Bristol, the amount of time he felt able to spend outside the diocese is remarkable.

New Delhi was an immensely important assembly of the WCC. It brought into it at long last the International Missionary Council. Lesslie Newbigin, the IMC's General Secretary, delivered the inaugural address. It brought into it too the Orthodox Churches of the Soviet bloc – Russia, Rumania, Bulgaria and Poland – ensuring that the Orthodox presence would be far weightier, and often more awkward, than hitherto. It brought in also a number of Churches of the southern hemisphere, while its very location in India, linked with marriage to the IMC, helped make clear that from now on the WCC really would be a worldwide fellowship. It was, again, the first Assembly to have observers from the Roman Catholic Church. New Delhi represented in these various ways a genuine new birth for the World Council, but no less important was the fact that it fully endorsed the St Andrews Faith and Order statement about the nature of Church unity. Officially Oliver co-chaired the Assembly section on unity with David Moses, representing the host church of North India. Effectively he chaired it, steering a course through some very rough waters. 'It is his guidance of that large and motley sector at New Delhi which I chiefly remember,' wrote his new Faith and Order staff member, Patrick Rodger, 'the combination of the authority conferred by long experience and deep conviction with a patient listening to contributions and objections from many quarters of the globe'.[13] This was the first major public example of Oliver's greatest skill – the presidency of a meeting. This was not something he had to acquire in the course of his episcopate. It was there, already matured, from the start.

Oliver's hope for New Delhi as expressed at St Andrews was wholly fulfilled. 'All in each place' became afterwards almost the New Delhi signature tune and was taken up also in the Assembly's 'Message to the Churches' – 'Let us find out the things which in each place we can do together now', an appeal to local ecumenism and one reminiscent also of the Lund Principle. Kathleen Bliss chaired the New Delhi message committee. It is remarkable that Newbigin, Tomkins and Bliss, Cambridge SCM members together in 1930, and all three influential at Amsterdam in 1948, were no less so at New Delhi in 1961. In fact, it was a Cambridge four because Frank Woods, now Archbishop of Melbourne, was included with Bliss as a member of the small Executive Committee inside the Central Committee. For each of the four New Delhi was in World Council terms as much a beginning as a point of fulfilment, but for none more so than Oliver whose forthcoming plans for the developing work of Faith and Order both worldwide and in Britain were remarkably expansive.

## Montreal

Once New Delhi was past, Oliver's sights were fixed on Montreal. The plans for a fourth World Conference on Faith and Order to be held in July 1963 were already well advanced. The New Delhi committee on Faith and Order, chaired by Hanns Lilje and serviced by Paul Minear, Lukas Vischer and Patrick Rodger, outlined the preparatory study needed. The new unity formula 'All in each place' was, of course, to be examined in its varied implications but, more unexpectedly, the main stress was laid on the wider development of a new sort of 'theological discourse'. Faced with a 'rapid drift towards the various forms of materialistic secularism and sophisticated nihilism', the Churches, it was urged, must be persuaded to face the need for 'a radical revision of theological language'. The central Christian doctrines, it claimed, 'have become increasingly unintelligible to the contemporary European mind and their reformulation has become an urgent and inescapable task'.

This suggests a far more subtle and wide-ranging programme than Faith and Order had hitherto attempted and one less narrowly ecclesiological. It was as if, having established over many careful years an agreed account of what church unity implies, it now felt free to undertake a complete rethink of the entire field of Christian theology on the assumption that church divisions were inextricably bound up with all sorts of out of date mental attitudes. Whether it was wise to be so ambitious is disputable; what is clear is that the agenda proposed by New Delhi would in point of fact prove central to much of the more radical thinking of the 1960s. Thus John Robinson's *Honest to God*, published 18 months later, fits exactly with such a pursuit of a new 'theological discourse'. Again, the New Delhi Faith and Order committee requested its working group to take on board another hot potato of coming decades, 'the theological, biblical and ecclesiological issues involved in the ordination of women'. Clearly, the fourth world conference on Faith and Order was likely to prove an exciting occasion, expressive of a very considerable change in the atmosphere. Minear, representing Faith and Order at a Central Committee discussion in 1962, described the change as 'a willingness to build bridges, however slender, across the deepest chasms rather than to be satisfied with more easily built and substantial bridges across lesser cleavages.'[14] Such 'adventurousness' could be seen in many places: 'Some were surprised to find that the supposedly irreconcilable is not so, and that very great difficulties begin to yield.'

Crucial to this new kind of bridge building was what was going on within the Catholic Church in the run-up to the Second Vatican Council. At New Delhi a wish had been expressed that Faith and Order undertake a history of the councils and the concept of councils, a concept which involved the whole notion of 'tradition', a notion soon to be battled over in Rome. The two sides – WCC and Roman Catholic – were being pressed to examine quite the same questions and were helping each other to do so. It is striking, for instance, how a reshaping of ecclesiology by both owed a great deal to the impact of the liturgical movement. The continuity between the two was further assisted by the fact that Vischer who did much to mastermind the Montreal agenda was one of Vatican II's most fluent official 'observers'.

Montreal was the first city chosen for a major ecumenical conference to be situated within the Catholic rather than the Protestant world and its very geographical location would prove of considerable significance, whether or not it was chosen for this reason back in 1961. But the Catholic impact on both the World Council and the theological world in general was building up quite extraordinarily in these years. The first session of the Vatican Council was opened by Pope John on 11 October 1962. It was still quite unsure at that date what it would lead to. On the one side were numerous eirenic statements by the Pope, together with the founding of the Secretariat of Unity, the activity of Cardinal Bea and Mgr Willebrands, and the fact that observers from other Churches, as also the WCC, had been invited to attend. On the other hand was the fact that the Roman Curia as a whole had not changed, it was the Curia which had dominated the conciliar preparations so that the draft documents distributed to the Council fathers were, for the most part, manifestly reactionary in tone and could well leave relations with other Christians worse off after the Council than before. Pope John seemed unaware of the contradiction and many Catholics keen on reform were decidedly pessimistic about what the council would bring. However, what the first session witnessed was an amazingly rapid upsurge of anti-curial feeling led by a group of northern cardinals – Liénart of Lille, Frings of Cologne, Alfrink of Utrecht, Suenens of Malines and Döpfner of Munich. In an epoch-making vote on 20 November 1,368 fathers opposed the draft on the two 'sources' of revelation, scripture and tradition, while only 822 were in favour. The pope ordered it to be withdrawn next day. It suddenly became clear that something not entirely unlike a religious revolution might be building up, as Cardinal Ottaviani, the principal leader of the curial conservatives, angrily suggested. The degree of wider support for a 'progressive' approach associated especially with Bea was clearly enormous. It called for a more biblical, less scholastic, theology; for an ecumenical awareness of what other Christians thought; and for a pastoral reform of the liturgy with much greater use of the vernacular in place of Latin. The effect of all this on attitudes within the World Council was considerable. While no document of any sort was approved in the first session, everything being sent back for redrafting, an atmosphere of great theological excitement had been generated which considerably affected the preparations for Montreal.

In this new atmosphere in which the building of bridges over the deepest of chasms at last seemed possible, Catholics could be incorporated almost organically within both the preparation and the actual discussions at Montreal, but only perhaps because Oliver was quietly so determined that they should be. This was done initially by holding a meeting at Bossey in March with a group of Catholic theologians. Oliver led a strong Faith and Order team, including Tom Torrance, Max Thurian, J.-L. Leuba and Donald Allchin to discuss the documents prepared for the conference one by one with a no less strong Catholic team. The latter was led by Willebrands and Hamer while Congar, Villain, Couturier's disciple and biographer, Dumont from Istina, Dom Olivier Rousseau from Chevetogne and Maurice Bevenot from Heythrop were among the members – several of them old friends of Oliver from conferences of more than a decade earlier. Ostensibly the Catholics were there as members of the non-official Catholic Conference for Ecumenical Questions. In reality it was a team fielded by the Secretariat of Unity, still a little shy of coming fully into the open, but, in consequence, it was a conference, in Oliver's cautious words, 'of a somewhat different order from anything that has been held before'.[15] Effectively, it was the first in a long line of ecumenical discussions subsequently carried on between the Roman Secretariat and Christians of many other traditions. Oliver was struck at once by Roman ecumenical professionalism – they were 'on the whole better briefed' on the Faith and Order documents than the Faith and Order team! He also admitted to 'a certain shade of embarrassment' that the documents hardly seemed good enough, given that they were meant to represent ten years of Faith and Order work since Lund! In general, the meeting made him ponder once more the right relationship between the World Council and the Roman Catholic Church now that the latter actually wanted a relationship. He continued to think it 'both inconceivable and undesirable' that the latter should be a member of the WCC in the same sense as other churches, yet 'On our Faith and Order side, the thing that struck me most forcibly was the way in which one now sees more than ever clearly the unreality of discussing these great themes with so large a part of the mind of Christendom absent or only able to make an intermittent contribution, external to the process of thought in itself.'

At Montreal not only was there a distinguished group of officially appointed Catholic observers, there were also 15 further Canadian and American Catholic 'guests' plus a host of other Catholics disguised as journalists (including Villain). Moreover, Raymond Brown, the distinguished New Testament scholar, gave one of the conference's principal public lectures, the first time a WCC Conference had been addressed by a Catholic. Montreal thus represented a quite new level of theological sharing between the World Council and Catholics, something which would soon become normal but was still, at the time, quite remarkable. Of course there were sturdy Protestant voices warning against believing that Rome might change and perhaps such a degree of ecumenicity was only possible in 1963 because the Archbishop of Montreal, Cardinal Léger, was one of the council's leading progressives, someone genuinely delighted to make Faith and Order welcome. When Léger invited some 20 people from the conference to dinner at the Archbishopric and Oliver found himself sitting on the cardinal's right with Wim on Léger's left and the Greek Orthodox Archbishop of North America and the Salvation Army Commissioner opposite, he could not but realize that something quite new in the pattern of Christian behaviour was taking place. Even more exciting was an 'Ecumenical Gathering' in the great Hall of the largely Catholic Montreal University with an amazing mix of church choirs and speakers before Léger ended by leading the whole assembly in a remarkable ecumenical prayer: 'Blessed art thou, God, the Father of our Lord Jesus Christ. We have sinned against thee, we have introduced divisions into thy work of unity. Even in our proclamation of thy truth we have often been narrow, exclusive, and lacking in love. We have forgotten the beam in our own eye in order to judge the speck in our brothers' eye.' How incredibly different all this was from the last great ecumenical gathering in North America, at Evanston nine years before, when the Cardinal Archbishop of Chicago forbade any Catholic to be present.

No less important was the very considerable Orthodox presence. It was the first Faith and Order conference to which Orthodox theologians really contributed from within rather than standing on the sideline and denouncing. They were numerous and capable enough to do so. In consequence the discussion looked at times more like a Protestant–Orthodox confrontation, with each side having to reappraise, but also stand up to, the other. That was another fruit of New Delhi.

Oliver had led the team which prepared the conference and he was immediately elected its chairman with much applause. It was to be the highest point in his international career but chairing it was by no means easy. There may never have been a modern theological conference with more cut and thrust, abler and more wide-ranging in its membership, more vibrant in debate, grappling with an impossibly varied and complex range of ideas. It was almost as if the central theological debate of the four long sessions of Vatican II was compressed into two exciting but impossible weeks. The most creative themes proved to be tradition, worship, local church, and the relationship of church unity to global unity – close indeed to the central themes of Vatican II. The conclusions, such as they were, of the one could prove surprisingly close to those of the other – of course in July 1963 Vatican II had as yet come to no conclusion but its debates and revised drafts showed the way the wind was blowing. The marked re-evaluation of the idea of 'tradition' (at one point the sober Catholic theologian Georges Tavard had even to warn against adopting a 'sola traditio' formula, starkly in contrast with the 'sola scriptura' of the Reformation – Max Thurian and Ernst Käsemann said the same) and insistence upon eucharistic unity as constitutive of the Church, both local and universal, brought to World Council theology a far more catholic note than had been customary hitherto. This was undoubtedly due in part to the mere fact of active participation by a considerable number of Orthodox and Roman Catholic theologians but, still more, to the creative interaction of all traditions at a privileged moment in time. The very radicalism which made of John Robinson's *Honest to God* the most popular buy in the conference's bookshop actually made it easier to go 'back' to a basically more traditional ecclesiology: 'The unity of the Church is to be found not only in the merger of denominational structures but even more profoundly in the *koinonia* of true eucharistic worship, where the whole Catholic Church is manifest.'

Oliver presided over all this with aplomb. It was all, he felt, 'a most promising chaos'.[16] When the first draft of the conference's 'A Word to the Churches' came under heavy fire, he rewrote it on his own during the night, after which it was quickly approved. The heat of Montreal in July was excessive, especially in the Winter Stadium where the plenary meetings were held. Garments were gradually stripped off, perhaps symbolizing the discarding of theological prejudices. The hymn 'As pants the hart for cooling streams' was sung twice in the first two days of the Conference. On Monday 22 July Oliver had to preside over no fewer than five sessions wearing headphones in a temperature of over 90°. For some the conference was a 'failure'.[17] There was no way that such theological conundrums could be massaged satisfactorily into agreed reports within a couple of weeks. There were just too many chasms to bridge, in particular Protestant–Orthodox disagreements as also liberal–conservative ones (on the biblical side the conference undoubtedly tended to identify with the moderate Catholic Brown against the more Bultmannian Käsemann, whom Visser't Hooft was quite alarmed to find had been invited even though in New Testament studies circles Käsemann was correctly seen as a critic of Bultmann's undue scepticism – his invitation was an indication of how, theologically, Oliver's approach was considerably more inclusive than Wim's). Yet the value of Montreal lay precisely in jerking people of many orientations out of a certain contentedness with previously almost unchallenged agreement inside their own neck of the woods. The theological 'chaos' produced by so wide a range of participation was such, Oliver concluded in retrospect, that 'the "ecumenical reality" is now too big, too diverse, and too fast-moving to do anything like justice to it in the traditional Faith and Order manner. Perhaps it was worth holding a "World Conference" if only to make clear that this is so!' Moreover, the 'Ecumenical Gathering' in Montreal University's Great Hall, with a degree of public fraternization with Roman Catholics which hitherto had been unimaginable, gave him the impression of 'an almost unbearable apocalyptic – "a door opening in heaven" revealing the potentialities of the Una Sancta on earth'.

'A Word to the Churches' spoke of '"an ecumenical reality" which takes shape faster than we can understand or express it'. In the weeks after the conference Oliver all the same endeavoured to express it for as wide a public as possible by hastily writing a little book on the main issues as he saw them, *A Time for Unity*. 'I thought that after Montreal you would have collapsed rather than write a book,' wrote Wim admiringly from Geneva. Oliver's determination to do this, while still in Canada awaiting the Anglican Congress in Toronto, demonstrates the way the rapidly changing 'ecumenical reality' had seized him at this period and he was determined to make the most of it while the mood lasted. Cool as he appeared, he felt a huge personal responsibility to help the churches meet the *kairos*, indicated by the signs of the times, as he read them: the decolonization of Africa, Vatican II and so on. He was convinced that this was the time, God's time, to unite: 'There is no time to play with. History is not on the side of our divisions, because God is not. Can we unite in the freedom of love, and quickly?' It is not surprising that he says nothing in his journal or elsewhere about the Anglican Congress. He was far too polite to say so publicly, perhaps even to admit privately, but that was too much an exercise in denominational reaffirmation, something which had actually to be overcome if Oliver's commitment to 'all in each place' was to bear fruit. Perhaps in his book he was little more successful than the Montreal Conference itself in sorting out a 'chaos' of creative ideas. 'If only I was better equipped to do the thinking,' he complained to himself the following year. He was not a theologian and did not, perhaps, always grasp the theological side of things in their full complexity, any more than in his discussion of the 'non-Theological

Factors' he always got his history quite right. But who did? He certainly saw things whole in a way few managed. His role was essentially presidential as he appealed to the churches, his own especially, to look again at all the issues in the lively belief that something could actually be done. Such was the spirit of 1963.

The Commission of Faith and Order met every three years. Its last meeting had been at St Andrews in 1960 but the Working Committee sensibly decided that Montreal would need a year to sort out so the Commission was postponed to 1964 and met in August at Aarhus in Denmark to review the conference and set out a new programme of study in its light. Lukas Vischer was now Director of Faith and Order and the very extensive and mostly effective series of studies carried out over the next few years owed a great deal to his theological expertise and forcefulness of direction. Oliver's position in this the final phase of his Faith and Order leadership was presidential rather than directive. The Commission's constitution was revised and plans were successfully laid to bring Catholics into full Faith and Order membership, a daring proposal accepted both by Rome and the fourth General Assembly, Uppsala, in 1968. The study programme itself had attained a theological complexity and sophistication for which he was not suited and had not the time to supervise, but he continued to chair the Working Committee which met at Bad Saarow in Eastern Germany in 1965 and at Zagorsk near Moscow in 1966, two remarkable experiences. It was, however, absolutely fitting that the next triennial meeting of the Commission should be at Bristol in 1967 (29 July–9 August). Reports were presented on God in Nature and History (a particularly impressive one), Scripture and Tradition (including a study of the conciliar process in the early Church), the Eucharist, and the Church and the Jewish People. Both Oliver as Chairman of the Working Committee and Professor Paul Minear who had been Chairman of the Commission since Montreal had decided to resign. The question was raised whether one person should not in future fill the two positions (given that the division had been initially created to enable Oliver while still quite a junior person to continue effectively to direct Faith and Order after ceasing to be its secretary) but it was felt, on his advice, that the work could be too burdensome for one person. Bishop Harms of the German Evangelical Church took over as Chairman of the Commission and Professor Nelson, who had succeeded Oliver as secretary in 1953, as Chairman of the Working Committee.

Oliver preached on the opening day at a service in the cathedral which was followed by a reception from the Lord Mayor. On the last afternoon he and Ursula gave a garden party at Bishop's House after which he delivered a valedictory address on the Future of Faith and Order. He could look back on 'twenty-two years of direct Faith and Order work'[18] and far longer on his first attendance at one of its meetings, plenty of experience on which to draw. He commented on three paradoxes: first, 'the toughness of institutions and the fluidity of ideas' – institutional patterns had altered remarkably little in that time while the intellectual climate had experienced 'startling changes'; second, the 'daily more obvious' need of Christian unity yet 'a baffling indifference to it'; third, the growing cohesion of the ecumenical movement contrasted with a growing difficulty to define the role of Faith and Order. He ended a masterly review of the way he saw that role with wistful reference to combining it 'with all the diffused longing for human solidarity' voiced by the Beatles in their song 'Eleanor Rigby'. Lukas Vischer thanked both Minear and Oliver as they retired from office, noting particularly 'the unusual combination of distance and presence possessed by the Bishop of Bristol' uniting an objective perspective with intimate involvement in the issues. That was true to the end. His involvement had not lessened but objectivity had convinced him that it was time for a change, of an exhaustion in what he could personally offer. Perhaps, too, there had been a note of veiled disappointment in his words. Hopes, just tenable at Montreal, had not been fulfilled; instead he sensed a 'baffling indifference'. There might be a 'promising chaos' in the world of ideas but ecclesiastical structures remained largely impervious. His heart was with the one but, for the future, his work had to remain within the other.

What had Oliver achieved in his long leadership of Faith and Order? First, he had revived its functioning after the war and Amsterdam, where its existence was pretty shadowy, and organized the Lund Conference. Second, he had held it together in existence during the 1950s after Lund when pressure was again considerable to wipe it out almost completely. Life and Work had sunk without trace as a separate entity within the expanding activities of the World Council. Why should Faith and Order not do the same, as Oldham had urged back in 1937? For many, its absorption within a 'Division of Studies' seemed eminently sensible and that is almost what happened. It was largely, one suspects, due to Oliver's quiet but tenacious leadership that it did not. In this he proved faithful to the mantle of Hodgson, successfully defending a course of which Hodgson himself had seemingly despaired. Faith and Order fought back and greatly flourished in the 1960s, to the considerable benefit of the World Council as a whole. Oliver presided over this revival, choosing an excellent staff team, ensuring its continued independence, setting out specific goals, and proposing alterations in method. It was actually of assistance in much of this that he was not a member of Central Committee, seldom attended its meetings under any guise, and thus maintained a useful measure of independence. It was an independence comparable to that he possessed as Assistant General Secretary through not residing in Geneva. Finally, he enabled Faith and Order to pioneer new relationships with Catholics at every stage, almost always ahead of any other branch of the World Council, and set the scene for their full entry at Uppsala into this one privileged area of WCC work. Surely that was enough.


## Nottingham 1964

'Britain seemed almost the only country where no progress was being made towards organic unity,' wrote Ernest Payne of the early 1960s.[19] That may be an over-statement but it certainly seemed odd that while so many British Christians, like Payne himself, were busy leading the ecumenical movement elsewhere, in Britain so little was done. The Church of South India, hailed as the model for organic unity, had largely been designed by British clerics like Michael Hollis, Lesslie Newbigin and Leslie Brown. In almost all the unity projects being canvassed in Africa, British missionaries were much involved. In Geneva too Britain had always been over-represented and yet in Britain itself very little had been attempted beyond a few desultory conversations, despite a multiplication of local councils of churches. Oliver had for long been acutely conscious of the gap between his high international ecumenism and the home reality. It was why he had felt bound to leave World Council employment in the early 1950s and return home. So it is hardly surprising that after his formula for organic unity had been approved at New Delhi, he should feel it vital to get the bandwagon moving in Britain. Hence the September 1964 Nottingham Conference on Faith and Order.

Who initially proposed it is not absolutely clear but plans certainly developed very quickly in the aftermath of New Delhi. It was discussed in Oliver's Interchurch Group at its meeting in Cumberland Lodge in February 1962. Kenneth Slack, General Secretary of the British Council of Churches, and John Weller, secretary of the BCC's Faith and Order department, of which Oliver was Chairman, were members. It was for the BCC to sponsor such a conference, for Weller to organize it and for Oliver to chair it. Slack had been at New Delhi and Weller at Montreal. Probably still more influential was David Paton, Secretary of the Church of England's Missionary and Ecumenical Council and Oliver's closest ecumenical ally. Paton had been at both New Delhi and Montreal, had written up the latter's official 'Diary', was secretary of the Interchurch Group and produced the final pamphlet in preparation for Nottingham, *One Church Renewed for Mission*. New Delhi, Montreal, and now Nottingham constituted a single well thought-out strategy in which the centrepiece was the Delhi statement on the 'Unity we seek'. While this was clearly a strategy for which a group of people was collectively responsible, there can be no doubt that the quietly presiding role throughout was Oliver's. He chaired the New Delhi section on unity, the Interchurch Group and both the Montreal and Nottingham conferences.

The preparation for Nottingham was considerable, with numerous regional conferences and the publication of an extensive series of pamphlets beginning in the summer of 1962. Each one printed the New Delhi statement on its opening page and it is interesting to note that the pamphlet specifically entitled *All in Each Place* was written by Horace Dammers who, after training at Westcott House, spent some years in the Church of South India before becoming vicar of Oliver's old parish of Millhouses in Sheffield. The tradition of localizing ecumenism had thus continued at Millhouses and the central purpose of Nottingham was to spread the practice far and wide. Dammers had been incorporated into Oliver's ecumenical team and it was he who would propose Nottingham's dramatic 1980 resolution. Never before had there been such a considerable British ecumenical gathering. Indeed, it may be claimed that there has never been a conference so representative of British Christians as a whole within their varied traditions with as many laity as clergy among its 500 participants. Many of the Churches' principal leaders were there too. Archbishop Ramsey joined it for the Sunday. The excitement matched the time. It felt like a wonderful moment for religion in Britain. John Robinson's *Honest to God*[20] had been the best of sellers the year before and continued to generate a huge discussion. Vatican II was rolling on: its second session, coming after Montreal, had demonstrated that the great Catholic shift of direction had outlasted Pope John. The ecumenical climate really did seem to have changed. Not that the Catholic dimension would matter so much here. Ten places had been offered but no more than six Catholics received permission to come. Bishop Ellis of Nottingham was one of the least ecumenically sympathetic of the English Catholic hierarchy so there could be no repetition of Léger's welcome at Montreal. In this field English Catholicism remained far behind, at least in its leadership, but their observers, including the veteran Dominican ecumenist Henry St John and the Jesuit Bernard Leeming were well received. Oliver would not have desired or expected more than this. The aim of the conference was certainly not Rome-orientated and it was far less theological than Montreal – where Catholics were needed at the intellectual level to make a specific contribution – but far more practical. What was wanted was to get the boat moving towards organic unity between the Church of England and the Free Churches. Too much consideration of relations with Rome could only be distracting and, even, inhibiting.

The discussions at Nottingham produced three particularly memorable proposals. The first was a resolution asking the Churches to recognize that, while there were still important doctrinal differences between the Churches within the BCC, these were not sufficient to stand as barriers to unity. David Jenkins, a young Oxford theologian who had been one of Oliver's students at Lincoln, had had much to do with formulating this proposal. The second was an invitation to those same churches to covenant together to work for the inauguration of union by an agreed date. Essentially this was a resolution about covenanting but to it was added an exciting specification which may actually have obscured the main point: 'we dare to hope that this date should not be later than Easter Day, 1980'. The third was a request that the Churches 'designate areas of ecumenical experiment' in terms of an organized sharing of ministries, buildings and mission. The Easter 1980 proposal took Oliver by surprise – and everyone else too. It flowed out from the enthusiasm of the conference participants (despite some opposition) but it still represented in principle exactly what the conference had been intended to do: bring New Delhi's 'all in each place' firmly home. Unity should not be put off by further temporizing. The third was a practical way of moving further in this direction, by allowing some places to take a lead and go well ahead of others. This was what he had begun to do back in Millhouses in the 1940s. It made ecumenism 'local' and led quite quickly to the designation of numerous 'areas of ecumenical experiment' in the next few years. Essentially an attempt to apply 'the Lund Principle' – Oliver's very own – in any place where people were ready, it focused on congregations rather than on the larger units of diocese or denomination but the plan was, of course, that successful local unity would generate an élan which could be carried through to the higher levels. While there had been local congregational cooperation long before Nottingham, there was far more of it afterwards. By the end of 1966 no fewer than 170 local ecumenical 'projects' had been designated. In theory Oliver was entirely in favour of LEPs, as they came to be called. In practice, however, he was not a man happy to let go of control here or anywhere within his diocese. There was a continual tension within him between the desire to encourage, and identify with, youthful and prophetic enthusiasm and the anxiety to follow regulations and remain personally in control. In practice, the latter usually won. Yet in Swindon Old Town an LEP combining Anglican, Methodist and Congregationalist churches soon became something of a model.

For more than one participant at Nottingham, nevertheless, all this was a dangerous and mistaken approach. Bishop Moorman of Ripon attended with evident reluctance. He had little liking for all such conferences and considerable misgivings about this one. In general he saw little to be said for advancing unity between Anglicans and Nonconformists, especially if that could result in further distancing the former from Roman Catholics. He always saw one as in potential opposition to the other. The day before going to Nottingham he had read through the latest draft of the Vatican Council's decree on ecumenism and found it an exciting advance on previous ones: 'If this goes through,' he commented in his diary,[21] 'it will put Roman–non-Roman relations on an entirely new footing.' Having attended the first two sessions of the Council as the leading Anglican observer and seen the latest draft decrees, he was in a better position than anyone else to realize just how remarkable the developments in Catholicism now were. It is understandable that, in consequence, he looked on what happened at Nottingham rather differently from most other participants, being always anxious to stress the existence of the 'other ecumenical movement' whose quickly growing reality must completely alter earlier ecumenical logic. Of the opening session on Saturday, 12 September, he noted: 'Too long. Oliver spoke first – rather the same old stuff. Then Visser't Hooft telling us why the Ecumenical Movement doesn't advance.' The next day, Sunday, there was an open communion service but he was fortunately able to absent himself, celebrating in a parish: 'I don't think I should much have enjoyed the great inter-communion free-for-all being celebrated in the Great Hall.' Moorman was especially anxious to make a speech about relations with Rome and to propose sending a message to the Secretariat of Unity but felt that Oliver was avoiding both it and him. 'I have been much worried about the speech which I want to make and which I am finding it so diffi-cult to get a chance of making. I wrote twice to Oliver (Bristol) before we came and have now made 3 verbal attempts to get him to say that I may make it,' he wrote on Monday. In fact, he discovered, a telegram of greetings had already gone to Rome, somewhat spiking his guns, but he felt that that was not sufficient and wanted something more substantial. The next day things went better. Oliver, who was doubtless overwhelmed with responsibilities of every sort, asked to see him in the course of the morning and, when they talked, seemed to approve of the speech which he was to deliver that evening. Moorman was somewhat jaundiced in regard to Free Churchmen. While acknowledging that his speech, expounding the meaning of Christian unity as a whole rather than local unions, was well received, he could not help adding 'no doubt most of the applause came from the Anglicans'. However, his dislike of the conference proceedings mounted. Day after day he described as 'uncomfortable', particularly disliking 'a determination on the part of the young (especially nonconformist young)' to force through a resolution that 'union in Great Britain should be achieved by 1980'. To add to his distress Oliver announced that no further message would be sent to Rome: 'I am sorry to say,' lamented Moorman, 'that this was greeted with wild applause by one section of the Conference. So my little attempt to send a message of fraternal greeting to our fellow-Christians in Rome was torpedoed.' The next day (the 18th) was the formal vote on the 1980 resolution: 'Those of us who voted against it will be regarded, no doubt, as reactionaries, lacking in zeal and in faith. But I'm afraid many of those who voted for it will be disappointed when the time comes – unless by then they have learned sense.' He was one of 53 people regis-tering a negative vote. Declining to take part in any discussion on how to follow on from Nottingham, he withdrew to his room to read *The Trial of Oscar Wilde*. All this may appear depressing. Undoubtedly John Moorman had his prejudices and far less ecumenical experience than Oliver, yet his judgement was realistic enough; moreover he had already seen, perhaps more than Oliver, what huge implications the changes in Rome were bound to have for everyone else. The Moorman approach to Rome was, however, a consciously Anglican one, encouraged by the special reference to the Anglican Communion in the Decree on Ecumenism. Oliver, on the contrary, always saw himself as representing a far wider constituency and that was probably behind his reluctance to accede to Moorman's suggestion that a further message be sent from Nottingham Romewards. He feared it would introduce division and argument. With this, the Catholic observers agreed. They were anxious, as Oliver wrote to Michael Ramsey as soon as the conference was over, 'that we should not, in the short time available to us, run into any kind of acrimonious discussion without having time to resolve it'.

Oliver was intensely busy throughout the conference. All we get in his journal is 'Sept 12–19 = Nott'm F & O = No time to record it!' Even he was running out of breath. He knew the 1980 resolution would catch the headlines and prove hard to sell. It seemed absurdly Utopian yet still encapsulated the true point of his campaign. And he was a sober man. In his closing address he tried to gloss its meaning: 'I believe that it is best interpreted as being a poetic rather than a prosaic way of expressing our determination. By that I do not for a moment mean that it is to be taken less seriously. There are many circumstances under which poetry is to be taken more seriously than prose, for it contains a dimension of truth which prose can never portray.' In his letter to Ramsey of 22 September he suggested that, 'It is best thought of as a sort of eschatological gesture. Just as you fail to understand apocalyptic as soon as you take it literally, so I think this date must be seen.' While the resolution in question was really an appeal to the Churches to covenant together to work for unity, the tacking on of the 1980 date acquired a power of its own, for Oliver as much as for the Bishop of Ripon. But the result of the resolution was that he had yet another committee to chair – on covenanting!

Six weeks later, 5 November, he presented to the Church Assembly a report on the three Faith and Order meetings of Montreal, Aarhus and Nottingham. This may well have been the most significant speech he ever made there. He was not a great intervener in its debates, or later, in those of Synod. He was not in fact a debater at all. But in presenting the Faith and Order report he could, for once, within the Church of England in a way preside, which is what he was good at. What strikes one is the way he presented the three meetings as so closely linked. Nottingham gave him the chance to speak to a British Anglican assembly about Montreal and Aarhus – all in all, 'more than thirty days of conferring'. Moreover for him they were all a follow-up to New Delhi which was itself the culmination of years of work in the Faith and Order Working Committee. He talked with reference to Montreal about the changing understanding of tradition, with reference to Aarhus about a much wider sense of unity emerging in relation to the whole of creation, and with reference to Nottingham he picked out the report on Faith put together largely by David Jenkins, which focused on why the theological disagreements so often cited as grounds against uniting could be seen instead as good reasons to do so: only within a united church was it likely that 'balanced and integrated answers' would ever be found. But, above all, in addressing General Assembly he stressed 'a humble, glad but terrifying sense that God was at work faster and wider than they could keep up with: terrifying because this shifted familiar landmarks, destroyed old certainties and left them naked in faith'. It is hard to get that sort of feeling across to a gathering like the Church Assembly, where it seems his tone tended to irritate as schoolmasterly – perhaps its members really did not like to hear someone speak out of an experience and conviction incomparably beyond their own – yet he confided to his journal that he found 'the response very encouraging' despite some Anglo-Catholics still looking nervously beneath the bed for 'the old bogey of the "Pan-Protestant bloc"'. He felt he had managed to convey 'something of the sense of God being really on the move' and continued, 'It is *this* aspect I must begin to think about now'. The four-year advance from New Delhi to Nottingham was, undoubtedly, the high point in Oliver's public ecumenical leadership. It had coincided with a wider moment of religious and cultural excitement, symbolized by Pope John, the Beatles, *Honest to God*, the return of Labour rule. After addressing the Church Assembly Oliver went on to the House of Lords, 'getting the flavour of having Labour on the Government benches'. There was indeed a rather optimistic millennialist note in the air but was it God who was 'really on the move' or only a flip in western culture?

## The succession to Visser't Hooft

Already at New Delhi in 1961 Visser't Hooft announced that he wished to retire as General Secretary in 1965 when he reached the age of 65. He had been General Secretary for over 20 years and no one could easily imagine a World Council not led by Wim. He had shaped the job in his own image as one of masterly leadership and imaginative power. In the summer of 1963, meeting in Rochester in America, the Central Committee began the process of finding a successor and appointed its Executive Committee as a Nomination Committee. In consequence the process of selection remained in the hands of the Chairman and Vice Chairman of the Central Committee, Franklin Fry, an American Lutheran, and Ernest Payne, General Secretary of the British Baptist Union.[22] They had both been in these positions since Evanston so they knew the working of the World Council inside out. As the Chairman of the Central Committee and the General Secretary are the WCC's two most important posts, Fry rightly believed that they should not both be held by Americans. As he was himself an effective and popular chairman, this seemed to rule out an American General Secretary: it certainly did so in his mind. Two views emerged in the coming year as to the sort of person they were looking for. One view was that it needed to be someone young, dynamic and able to stay in office for a long time – perhaps rather in the image of Wim himself when first appointed. The second view held that major changes were inevitable, especially in the rapidly altering circumstances of the 1960s, and that this could best be managed by a senior figure who would not stay too long but would preside over a rethink in strategy and structure necessitated by the departure of Wim. The first view proved at the start the more popular and in February 1964 the Executive Committee agreed to invite Lukas Vischer. In many ways Vischer appeared ideal. As a Swiss, he was unlinked to any power bloc. He had a grasp of languages comparable to Wim's, a clear mind and a sound knowledge of theology. However, he declined, despite being pressed quite hard by Fry and Payne. The reasons were obvious. He was young, only 37 when approached, and had worked for the World Council in Faith and Order for less than three years. He felt himself quite unready for such a heavy organizational responsibility.

It was on 1 April 1964, while the Executive Committee was endeavouring to persuade Vischer to agree, that Roger Schutz, the Prior of Taizé, and a representative of the other viewpoint, wrote to Oliver to say that everyone at Taizé and many other people too were confident that he should be Secretary General. He was, Schutz wrote, the right man for the job, 'l'homme de la situation', with the experience and wisdom to give the World Council 'un élan tout neuf'. Oliver felt 'shattered' when this arrived and kept it, unhappily, under his hat, hoping no more would come of it. He did mention it to Michael Ramsey but the latter was firm that Oliver should stay in Bristol and devote himself to influencing the Church of England. Ramsey was never much convinced of the point of doing anything else. The Executive Committee did not, anyway, follow up Schutz's approach. Instead it turned to another young man, this time Patrick Rodger. He was not as young as Vischer but he too had only been three years in World Council service. It is striking that both those chosen should have been within the tiny Faith and Order team, Oliver's own appointments. At the meeting of the Executive in August 1964 there was a unanimous vote to invite Rodger and he was summoned by telephone to meet Fry in Munich where he was asked for an immediate response. Naturally flabbergasted, he insisted on returning to Geneva to consult his wife. Placed under great pressure he felt he ought to answer yes.

Oliver heard of these latest developments from Fry on the 7th and commented in his journal:

> This seems to me a daring but wise proposal. He is comparatively untried
> but am confident that he has the potential. I am glad of the day that I dug

him out of the sheep-folds of Kilmacolm for Faith and Order! I am glad too that I am spared the fearful disturbances implicit in Roger Schutz's suggestion! I am too old to start such a job – if nothing else against it – and am convinced I can serve the Oekumene better from where I am.

A week later, on the way from Copenhagen to Aarhus for a meeting of Faith and Order, he sat beside Wim who told him there was 'considerable resistance' to Rodger's appointment among younger WCC staff. He claimed too that Fry had 'forced' the unanimity and that the Presbyterians were opposed on the grounds that Rodger had been brought up a Presbyterian and become an Anglican at Oxford (in point of fact the Church of Scotland repudiated this opinion as contemptible). Wim was not supposed to have anything to do with the selection process and how reasons for Rodger's unsuitability could already be marshalled by him within a matter of days remains mysterious. He seemed already to be backing away from actually giving up. In his *Memoirs*, while insisting that 'It was clear that I should not express any preferences concerning the choice of my successor' he also admitted that 'I do not pretend that I made no mistakes. It was a situation in which it was impossible not to make any mistakes. To have remained completely passive would also have been wrong.'[23] Tension and uncertainty were certainly increased by Wim hinting that he would be willing to stay on at least until 1966 or even 1968. Much of the trouble arose from the mistake, for which Fry was responsible, of allowing the news to reach the staff, and then the general public, before the Central Committee had been informed. The emergence of two parties put everyone, but Patrick Rodger most of all, in a very awkward position in the months leading up to the next meeting of the Central Committee only due to meet in January 1965, this time in Enugu, Nigeria. It was preceded by a meeting of the Executive which reaffirmed its recommendation to appoint Rodger. At the Central Committee, immediately afterwards, Payne took the chair to leave Fry free to present the Executive's recommendation. Numerous sessions, much discussion and growing confusion followed. The conclusion was a mysterious vote, passed 40 to 37, to 'take no action on the executive's recommendation'. It seems that if the recommendation had been formally rejected Fry would have resigned, while if it had been accepted a number of WCC staff would have done the same. It appears, however, that a number of Central Committee members were confused as to the real significance of the vote and one member at least, from Ethiopia, voted on both sides. A new selection committee was then appointed, to be chaired by Bishop John Sadiq of Nagpur. Wim announced his decision to stay until 1966 but no longer, while Pat Rodger naturally withdrew his name from the exercise. It may be noted that in 1967 he was appointed Provost of Edinburgh and Bishop of Manchester in 1970. In 1974 he was offered the Archbishopric of York. It does not look as if the confidence of Frank Fry and Oliver that he would have made an excellent General Secretary was misplaced.

Kathleen Bliss, a member of both Central and Executive Committees, wrote to Oliver at Bishop Sadiq's request on her way home from Enugu to explain what had happened in her usual clear-minded and forthright way:

> There was too great a confusion of motives and opinions for it ever to be sorted out. The Russians just said 'We want Visser't Hooft' if not for ever then till 1968 etc! There was unfortunately a good deal of lobbying, starting before the meeting and mounting through it. Some of the members of staff were embroiled in this, including Wim himself. The executive was – as we knew we would be – in a very difficult position and all of us including, and

especially, Frank Fry, fell over backwards to allow the opposition to Pat's name full expression… The way Pat stood up to it all is beyond praise and almost beyond belief. His loneliness and his isolation from Margaret who was going through torments in Geneva made it all the harder to bear. Worst of all his own colleagues on the spot, holding meetings, signing letters (shown to Wim) etc etc. It was a miracle that somehow or other the ecumenical movement has taken a firmer grip of people's loyalties during all this: it emerged as something greater than the persons who have made or now carry it. That on the good side but on the reverse side a demoralization among the staff that affected all our subsequent work. The shoddiness of the work of the secretariat on some of the reference committees was really shocking, and Wim himself though he was riding high on the succession issue had almost no grasp at all on the subsequent business. Geneva is going to be a pretty grim place to work in for a while and Wim by being so deeply involved is unlikely to be the one to pull things together – though having written that I reflect that he can pull a good many rabbits out of hats when he really tries!

Sadiq had asked Bliss to approach Oliver about becoming General Secretary, but then also wrote directly himself. Oliver received his letter and actually wrote straight to her before she was able to finish her own. Reluctance to ask him, coupled with distress about Enugu, had held her back. On receiving Oliver's letter she continued, 'How awful for you!… I do think that for you and Ursula and the girls and the diocese we must try every other alternative possibility. The trouble is that in a sense you are the most acceptable person in many quarters.'

Sadiq wrote on 26 January to say the new Nominating Committee had held two sessions before leaving Enugu. 'There is a general and widespread feeling that at this juncture a senior person already known who can serve 5–10 years during the period of transition is to be preferred.' Among various names discussed, Sadiq continued, 'yours is one of the most important ones and I have no doubt that it will receive warm support in the Committee, the staff and the Central Committee… The WCC is at a critical juncture and those of us who believe in it must do all we can to save it from disintegration.' Would Oliver be available if invited?

He hated the idea. He discussed it with Kay Bliss, with Ursula and, briefly, with Michael Ramsey. All three encouraged him to decline. After 'much prayer and even more worry' he felt clear he should do so. He did not agree that an 'older man' was right. 'Pat Rodger, I believe, was right in principle as well as in particular.' Second, even if they wanted someone older, he was too old, not far off 60. He felt inadequately in touch with the complex web the WCC had become and he lacked adequate language skills (though in point of fact, almost all business was handled in English). Third, he felt that Nottingham had reinforced his 'sense of vocation to unity for renewal and mission in the C of E'. He felt reassured that Ursula, Kay and Michael were all agreed that, quite apart from the third point, the first two were sufficient: 'I find it hard to be objective just because I so love my present work that I tend to feel I *ought* to offer the harder way simply because it is harder.'

Was he right? After his highly successful presidency of the conferences at Montreal and Nottingham he stood head and shoulders above anyone else and could hardly claim convincingly to have become remote from the world of the WCC. Ramsey's advice was predictable. He had been at Enugu himself but largely failed to connect with its business or even to be supportive towards Rodger in his need. For him it was all boring. He could see no sense in a successful diocesan bishop moving to such work in Geneva of all places. Ursula's was predictable too. She was immensely happy in Bristol and knew that Oliver was as well. To give it up for the strains of the General Secretaryship would have been hard indeed, especially as she had never lived abroad. Kay Bliss is more hard to fault. No one knew the World Council better but Enugu had deeply distressed her. It was the WCC's all-time low and she found it next to impossible to urge Oliver that this merely increased the responsibility to rescue it from itself. Moreover for both Kay and Oliver it must have been distasteful to think of Oliver accepting a job which had just been, in their view, improperly denied to their younger friend and colleague. Yet Oliver's central argument does not quite make sense. For a man of 56 in excellent health and vigour to turn down so weighty an invitation on account of his age when those responsible felt that what was needed was precisely an older man seems unconvincing, especially when he suggested Leslie Brown instead, someone with far less relevant experience and only two years his junior. It suggests at least a lack of audacity. Perhaps he feared in his heart that that was true. Nevertheless his third reason, though almost set aside in his own summing up of the case, had considerable validity. Only three months earlier, in November, he had as we have seen presented in Church Assembly a Faith and Order Report on the three meetings at Montreal, Aarhus and Nottingham – seen almost as one. He had spoken on them at length with enthusiasm, moving a motion that diocesan bishops explore means for implementing the Nottingham resolutions in their dioceses. To withdraw to Geneva from leadership of a specifically British endeavour to move forward with local ecumenism just as it might be getting under way could give all the wrong signals about what really mattered most.

In due course the Nominating Committee proposed Eugene Carson Blake, an American Presbyterian and a member of the Central and Executive Committees. He was older than Oliver. Fry offered his resignation but it was not accepted so at this fairly crucial period the World Council was indeed briefly led by two Americans. The only attempt to cover over American domination with a figleaf was to elect as an extra vice-chairman an Indian theologian, Russell Chandran. As Chandran was at the time a professor at Union Theological Seminary, New York, it seems a poor figleaf. When Blake was appointed, Oliver felt reassured that he had the qualities needed to clear up the mess in Geneva, 'qualities of tycoonship and even ruthlessness which I certainly lack', yet when visiting Geneva again in May 1966 'all the old self-questionings about whether I was right to refuse to stand for the WCC General Secretaryship' were stirred up once more. 'It was my last chance to do something a little mad,' he admitted. He prayed for peace – by forgiveness if he had been wrong, or assurance if he had been right, and claimed at the end that 'I no longer get all churned up inside when I think about it' – an admission that it had meant much more to him than the initial refusal might suggest.

Even ten years later, when attending a meeting of the Central Committee, on which he was by then a member, in Berlin in 1974, he could still find himself asking: '*If* I had stood for General Secretary in 1964, *if* I had been chosen instead of Gene Blake, what sort of WCC would it be today? Should I have kept it clear of these (partly justified) charges of being primarily political – and selectively so?... Could my body have stood the pace – and would it have been worth dying for?'

Who can answer such questions? Certainly there were many people at the time who had hoped he would say yes, and it seems a little strange that he brushed so easily aside the opinion of Taizé. Certainly a refusal to be considered for the top job in the work to which he had dedicated the greater part of his life reflected his perennial modesty and lack of ambition. The fact remains that he had a better claim than anyone else – in experience, in maturity of judgement, in the ability to lead without dominating. Perhaps he and Ursula had both simply come to love Bristol too much to feel it could be God's will to leave and move to the harder life of Geneva. But perhaps, if he had allowed himself to be persuaded, the World Council might have achieved a mature balance which many felt continued to evade it. 'The fact is,' he could only conclude as he sat pondering these questions in the warm evening air of a Berlin August, 'I am still Bishop of Bristol and now I must finish *that* course to the best of my ability – and leave God to judge.'

## Romewards

In November 1964 two months after Nottingham, the Vatican Council approved two extremely important texts – *Lumen Gentium*, the Constitution on the Church, and *Unitatis Redintegratio*, the Decree on Ecumenism. Oliver had hitherto remained notably cautious in his assessment of what was happening at the Council. But with the decree on ecumenism passed, it had become clear that major changes really were taking place. An English translation of the decree was published already in January 1965 in the pages of the *Furrow*. Oliver obtained and retained a copy, marking it carefully. That same month Visser't Hooft, on his way to the World Council's Central Committee meeting in Enugu, went first to Rome to see Cardinal Bea and Mgr Willebrands to settle arrangements for the establishment of a Joint Working Group, as it came to be known, between the WCC and the Secretariat of Unity. The age of regular 'dialogue' between Rome and every other side of Christendom had begun and Oliver was bound to be part of it.

It seems strange, given his long ecumenical career, that he had never hitherto been to Rome. This had now to change and that April he spent ten days there, accompanied by Ursula. Before setting out he made his usual annual retreat at Cerne Abbas with the Franciscans, during which he found time to read Pope John's *Journal of a Soul*. Like many another reader he was struck by the unmitigated spiritual conservatism there revealed in the shaping of the man who would let loose the Council: 'Individualist, pious, counter-reformation – a Jesus–Mary piety which is supposed to be out! It only shows that Our Lord can ride into triumph on any kind of ass, so long as the ass is willing.' Here he recognized 'a hard-won victory against even venial sin willingly entertained' which in rather typical Oliver fashion he felt he must contrast with his own 'puny efforts – scatty and sketchy prayer, reluctance to be *decisive* in matters of discipline like non-smoking, the censoriousness which is hard on others whilst indulgent to myself'.

And so this self-indulgent man, having completed his retreat 'largely through reading of that holy man', set off to see 'the Rome which must be forever different because he was Pope'. There was plenty to do and see: attending mass in the catacomb of St Priscilla, walking on the Janiculum below the statue to Garibaldi, an outing to the monasteries at Subiaco, solemn vespers in St Paul's Basilica, a visit to St Peter's to find Pope Paul being carried aloft on the *sedia gestatoria*, long hours in the Vatican Museum and the Sistine Chapel. Perhaps the Castel Sant'Angelo made the sharpest impression:

> An overwhelming combination of power, pride, cruelty and piety – it's this kind of image of the Papacy which it will take many Pope Johns to

obliterate...there was the little guide in the Salon of Apollo, decorated with classical scenes for Leo X (Medici), who plucked me by the sleeve to show me proudly the 'pornographia' in the ceiling – some of the lustier scenes from Roman mythology. Also, an intriguing marble bathroom, centrally-heated, built for Clement VII, another of the Medici, and in the room next door, two trap-doors in the floor for popping the bodies of murdered guests straight into the Tiber.

The important business, however, was a series of meetings – with Mgr Willebrands, Cardinal Bea, the Pope himself. When Oliver spoke of the Abbé Couturier, the Cardinal replied: 'Yes, first prayer *for* unity and now prayer *in* unity, we must get on with it.' Longer, more informal conversations with members of the Secretariat staff, like the American John Long, or over lunch at the English College or the Foyer Unitas all helped make clear how much was changing and how quickly: 'we talked the same language on all essentials' he felt with Long, 'the young men are bursting with ecumenical and reforming ideas' he discovered at the English College, while the mass at the Foyer Unitas was 'really astonishingly reformed'. The private audience in Pope Paul's study, alone with an American chaplain to interpret when needed, remained the moment that mattered most: 'Paul VI is transparently good – a sensitive man to whom opposition is pain and decisions a labour – he sees too clearly all points of view.' He found him a very tired man with dark-rimmed eyes and wondered whether he ever had a holiday.

'How I long to be "reconciled"' was Oliver's concluding feeling on return from Rome.

> History is tough material – and unless the pattern of civilization in the West is totally destroyed, Rome must now forever have a unique place in Christendom. How gladly I could accept him as supreme 'Pastor pastorum' in the total episcopate. Please God 'collegiality' will lead on to possibilities of corporate reconciliation for Ecclesia Anglicana which need not imply a total repudiation of our corporate past – and how important to remember how I feel vis-à-vis Rome when thinking of relations with Methodism and Presbyterianism. Attitudes change so fast in some RC quarters, that *nothing* can be excluded from the work of Him who does so exceedingly abundantly!

All Oliver's experience of contacts with French Catholics 15 years earlier was now reactivated in a way he had never anticipated could happen. In Lyons in 1949 when he had suggested inviting Fr Boyer from Rome to join their planned ecumenical conversations, Congar had brushed the idea aside – how could one invite the Gestapo to sit down to dinner with the Resistance? Yet now he had been sitting at dinner with old Boyer, listening to his lengthy discourses in inaudible French, and reflecting that ecumenism in Rome itself had now passed Boyer by. In practical terms all this meant that Oliver had to fit two more continental meetings a year, as member of the Joint Working Group, into his already overburdened schedule. In consequence he was back in Italy that November, at Ariccia above Lake Albano, beginning the discussion whether the Roman Catholic Church should apply for World Council membership and, if not, why not – all part of the long task ahead of working out the implications of Vatican II (at that point not yet quite over). In Geneva the following May his impression was, once again, less of what had been achieved, than of what mountains lay ahead: 'One realises how slender an advance column is the Unity Secretariat still, compared with the vast solidity of old institutions like the Holy Office. But at least it is now an advance column of the whole body and no longer freedom-fighters dropped behind the lines.' Moreover he sensed that, cautious as the authorities remained, there was a torrent of popular ecumenism building up in the Catholic Church, especially in North America, 'which nothing can stem'.

Archbishop Ramsey had made an official post-conciliar visit to Paul VI in March 1966 two months earlier than Oliver's Geneva meeting. It proved an enormously important and symbolic event, all the more so because Ramsey had a considerable personal antipathy to Roman Catholicism to overcome. He stayed in the English College, meeting the Pope first in the Sistine Chapel and finally at St Paul's-without-the-Walls where a Common Declaration was read committing them to inaugurate 'a serious dialogue' between their two communions. In a final amazing gesture Paul took the episcopal ring off his finger and gave it to Ramsey, who wore it to the end of his life. John Moorman accompanied the archbishop and was appointed by him as Anglican chairman in the coming dialogue. Oliver was not there and his suggestion that Michael might take with him a Free Churchman, such as John Weller, had not proved acceptable.[24] Ramsey went to Rome, he insisted in reply, as Archbishop of Canterbury and President of the Lambeth Conference. He wanted to stress the international, rather than the English, dimension to prevent Cardinal Heenan from having a controlling finger in the subsequent dialogue; he wanted too to build on the specific recognition of Anglicanism in the Decree on Ecumenism. Oliver saw the point but feared, just what Moorman preferred, a stress on the bilateral.

This meant, however, that Moorman and Tomkins were engaged in parallel and near simultaneous talks with the Roman Secretariat, including several of the same people on the Catholic side, such as Willebrands and Bill Purdy. Thus, if Oliver met the latter in late November 1966 near Geneva, the Bishop of Ripon met them six weeks later at Gazzada in North Italy. When a year later the two were somewhat at loggerheads within the Intercommunion Commission it helped that Oliver could tell John he would shortly be going to the next meeting of the Joint Working Group in Moorman's beloved Assisi and was rereading a little book of Moorman's on St Francis 'as a bit of homework'. Had he any special tips? Canon Purdy had promised to snatch an hour or two to be his guide. If Tomkins and Moorman represented consistently differing approaches to ecumenical priorities, they also shared a great deal, and for both of them the growing personal relationship with Catholics like Purdy, Willebrands and Mgr Arrighi was important. While the multilateral approach preferred by Oliver had, theoretically, much to be said for it, he had himself chaired the lengthy bilateral Anglican–Presbyterian Conversations which ended in 1966 with an agreed report, yet little real advance towards unity. But if bilateral progress was hard enough, multilateral was much more difficult. As ecumenical discussions grew ever more numerous, Oliver explained to Ramsey, there was a great need to keep 'this criss-cross of relationships' in touch with each other. Yet in reality there was little danger of not doing so, as so many of the same people were involved wearing a variety of hats. A new ecumenical community was rapidly coming into existence drawn from numerous churches and countries. Its members were 'talking the same language in all essentials'. Much as Oliver still yearned to make ecumenism 'local', the danger of a vast gap between busy ecumaniacs criss-crossing in a multitude of exciting conversations and the unconverted denominationalist in the pew was actually growing. Perhaps he could hardly admit to himself how little all the hard work he and David Paton had put into the Presbyterian Conversations had actually achieved when communicated back to the churches on either side.

One amazingly bold, if probably unrealistic, dream of Oliver's to make ecumenism local needs special remembrance. One Maundy Thursday in the late 1960s Ursula rang Fr Joe Buckley to say that Oliver was deeply disturbed and could he come over at once. Buckley found Oliver pacing the garden, upset by the Catholic plan to build a new cathedral in Bristol (Clifton Cathedral was eventually opened in 1973). It seemed so wrong to waste money when there were already too many churches in the city and in 1966 Oliver actually appointed a special commission headed by Sir Philip Morris to report on the future of Bristol's historic churches, some of which were clearly redundant. Would it not be better for Catholics to take over Bristol Cathedral while the Church of England would move to St Mary Redcliffe? He would do everything he could to arrange it. Buckley replied that Bishop Rudderham would not consider it for a moment and very wisely. If, on the contrary, Rudderham and Buckley had welcomed the idea and put the plans for Clifton Cathedral on hold, could it conceivably have happened? Could the Dean and Chapter, the City Fathers, the Church Commissioners, public opinion have been persuaded? It seems fanciful. Oliver could have become entangled in an impossible and bitter battle while the Catholic diocese in the end could come to feel badly let down. But what a gesture to offer one's own cathedral to another church! And how marvellous it would have been had it succeeded!

## The Commission on Intercommunion

In October 1964 Michael Ramsey wrote to Oliver proposing an Archbishop's Commission on Intercommunion but adding, 'it is difficult to see the chairman unless you take it on'.[25] He did so, immediately proposing Professors Hodges and Lampe as members: Hodges, an old acquaintance, was on the conservative side in the intercommunion debate, Geoffrey Lampe, the Ely Professor of Divinity at Cambridge, on the radical. The commission was constituted in the course of 1965 with a left of centre majority, which included Lampe, John Robinson and Donald Allchin as well as Oliver himself, but there were two 'wings' – a strong conservative Anglo-Catholic one led by John Moorman and a more lonesome Conservative Evangelical one consisting of Gervase Duffield.

Intercommunion was a matter with which Oliver had wrestled all his adult life. For anyone working closely in an ecumenical context with fellow-Christians of other churches it could only be painful, and even seemingly absurd, not to be permitted to share together the 'sacrament of unity'. The more one both sees that communion in the body and blood of Christ is at the heart of the life of the visible church and experiences a real unity of faith and mission with one's colleagues, the more intolerable it becomes never to share the sacrament with them because, in denominational, institutional or 'organic' terms, one belongs to separated churches. Again and again it has been asked: is sharing in the eucharist really only a sign of unity already achieved and not also a means to unity to be achieved? Almost every conference Oliver ever attended argued over these questions. On the whole 'Catholics' insisted that shared communion must wait on institutional union while 'Protestants' argued that it should come earlier and be a means towards unity. Sometimes it could seem that Protestants argued like this because they had a 'low' view of communion, especially in ecclesiological terms, while Catholics stressed the integral relationship theologically between Church and eucharist, each constituting 'communion'. On the latter view, to share communion while remaining within separated churches could be claimed as intrinsically contradictory. Yet it could also seem that the Protestants were arguing like good Catholics, and the Catholics like Protestants, in that the former were adopting a concept of sacrament as potentially causative of something, while the Catholics were reducing it to a symbol acceptable only when what it symbolized was already achieved.

The Church of England had come to adopt a rather restrictive position formalized in some resolutions of the House of Bishops dating back to 1933 which allowed non-Anglicans to be received to communion in exceptional circumstances but did not envisage any in which Anglicans in England should communicate in other churches. That is to say limited 'open communion' was permitted but not reciprocity. These resolutions had, however, no strict canonical authority and some Anglicans would always have disregarded them. They derived chiefly from insistence on the necessity for an episcopally-ordained ministry for eucharistic celebration. The Orthodox and Roman Catholic Churches had been still firmer in rejecting any possibility of 'intercommunion', while most Protestant churches were already committed to a practice both 'open' and 'reciprocal'. It is noteworthy that even at the inauguration of the World Council of Churches in Amsterdam in 1948 an Anglican Communion Service was held at which only Anglicans were expected to receive communion though other members of the conference were 'warmly welcomed' to attend, while at a service of the Dutch Reformed Church all conference members communicant in their own churches were invited to partake.

With the impetuous upturn in ecumenical activity in the early 1960s pressure for intercommunion greatly increased both from ordinary church members and from many theologians. In November 1961 32 theologians led by Geoffrey Lampe appealed in an open letter to the archbishops of Canterbury and York for change and in many places Anglican priests were finding it pastorally impossible not to welcome members of other churches to communion and wanted too to be able to reciprocate. In particular the negotiations for full unity between Methodists and Anglicans had advanced so far that many on both sides felt the time had come to share communion. Such feelings were further stimulated by liturgical renewal in almost all the churches which brought their rites far closer together, the liturgical proximity implying proximity in eucharistic belief. While eucharistic theology had been a prime ground for division in and after the Reformation, this had ceased to be so, at least for a lively minority of ecumenical activists. What continued to divide were variant doctrines of the ministry, from the papacy downwards, coupled with the sheer fact of the existence of a multiplicity of denominational institutions.

No one felt all this more than Oliver and he had written on the subject of intercommunion on a number of occasions, notably his lengthy contribution on 'Intercommunion in the Ecumenical Movement' in the Lund volume on *Intercommunion* and, more recently, a chapter 'The Challenge of Intercommunion' in his post-Montreal appeal *A Time for Unity*. He very much wanted the Church of England's regulations to change. He regarded them as outmoded in the new ecumenical climate and yet, an intensely law-abiding man, he still felt the 1933 resolutions, limited as their authority really was, must be obeyed though he had also convinced himself that where 'a determination to seek visible unity' had been demonstrated it was now legitimate to practise reciprocal intercommunion on some occasions.

Two occasions in 1962 illustrate his dilemmas. In July he chaired a session of the Anglican–Presbyterian Conversations in Durham at which the issue arose among Anglicans with some intensity. He celebrated himself on the first day, having given an open invitation to the Presbyterians to communicate. He had checked this beforehand with both Ramsey and the Bishop of Durham. The next day, as he knew would happen, the Church of Scotland rite was celebrated, also in the college chapel, and Oliver received communion 'after long thought and prayer'. It was actually the first time he had done so. He decided 'to receive as a pledge of my own readiness to give the rest of my time, if need be, to making that anticipation into a realization of full "communio in sacris"'. While several other Anglican bishops joined him, others declined to do so, including the two bishops representing the Episcopal Church of Scotland. When Ramsey heard about it, from numerous letters of complaint, he wrote to Oliver about 'the distress' caused by the intercommunion at Durham.[26] The 1933 resolutions should still be applied. If Moorman, a member of the Anglican–Presbyterian Commission, had been present, as he was not, he would certainly not have received. However, the Bishop of Edinburgh, Ken Carey, wrote to Oliver that what he had done was 'absolutely right'. Oliver replied to the archbishop, setting out what had happened at considerable length, making clear how almost impossible it was to refuse reciprocity in such circumstances, insisting nevertheless that it had been 'an agonizing and deeply personal decision', yet offering to resign his chairmanship if Ramsey thought it would help. His action was certainly not without precedent. Only two years before Dean Matthews of St Paul's, representing Archbishop Fisher at the centenary celebrations of the Scottish Reformation in Edinburgh, had received communion in St Giles Cathedral.

A month after the Durham meeting Oliver was at Taizé for the dedication of the new Church of the Reconciliation. It was a vast and wonderful gathering bringing French Protestants and Catholics together in common worship at about the most ecumenical place in the world. In the eucharist according to the Taizé rite Bishop Stephen Neill preached brilliantly in French. But Oliver declined to receive communion – though not unhappy that fellow Anglicans, including his daughter Monica, did so. The explanation he gave himself was that 'the reasons for which I felt obliged to take communion from the Church of Scotland – viz as a pledge of the corporate intention between our two churches to unite – did not apply here'. This is really very odd. The Anglican–Presbyterian conversations were not strictly about uniting and there was certainly no pledge, and little intention, by either Church to do so. In the real world, not of clerical negotiations but of ordinary Christian life, there was ever so much more commitment to Christian unity at Taizé than almost anywhere else. Indeed, when the following year Oliver wrote about intercommunion in *A Time for Unity*, it was Max Thurian of Taizé that he found himself quoting again and again.

Where Oliver and John Moorman disagreed theologically was over the status of non-episcopalian ministry in a divided church. For Moorman, whether the Church was divided or undivided, that status was one of invalidity in terms of the apostolic succession. For Oliver episcopal ordination was a necessary part of the character of the ministry in the one church as it should be, but was one of those things, including unity itself, which had inevitably been lost or become dispensable within the divided state of Christianity as it actually exists. He liked to quote Leonard Hodgson who distinguished 'between God's will for His Church in its unity and His will for it in its present divided condition'.[27] Perhaps neither asked himself whether the separation between episcopate and presbyterate might not have emerged in the very early church as an essentially jurisdictional development, stimulated by growth in the number of believers in a single city, and that, in terms of orders, the apostolic succession simply does not have two layers to it, presbyteral ordination being in essence identical with episcopal. This was, perhaps, an unfashionable view in the 1960s, given Vatican II's insistence on the difference in orders between the one and the other (*Lumen Gentium*, 21) but that may well prove one of the

Council's less happy ideas. Nevertheless at Lambeth 1968 Oliver, chairing the 'Principles of Union' sub-committee, actually did tone down the Lambeth Quadrilateral insistence on the episcopate to 'common acknowledgement of a ministry through which the grace of God is given to his people'. This considerably disquieted Ramsey and several other bishops. Clearly, Oliver had to be cautious.

The Intercommunion Commission worked intensely hard. Between October 1965 and May 1968 when its report, *Intercommunion Today*, was published, it met 17 times, 11 of them residential. Oliver set out the issues in advance and steered their discussion with immense clarity, patience and sense of authority. He probably never had a more arduous task. The struggle to obtain a unanimous report entailed modifying what the majority wanted to recommend again and again; yet in the end it still proved impossible to obtain full agreement. The line the Commission followed, Oliver's own, was that almost every-thing depended on a 'serious intention to unite' on the part of the churches themselves. This approach appeared to justify allowing things now which were not rightly allowable hitherto. Where that intention was present 'the majority of us believe that it is right to proceed to a far greater degree of reciprocal intercommunion with both episcopal and non-episcopal churches than has commonly been thought appropriate in the past'. Hence, given the negotiations for union between the Church of England and the Methodist Church and – far more dubiously – with the Presbyterian Churches, the majority recom-mended 'reciprocal acts of intercommunion on specific occasions'. The minority, led by Moorman, disagreed, recommending that unity would actually be jeopardized by such acts 'before the conditions of full communion have been established'. Given the consid-erable pressure for shared communion in the 1960s, a movement which had already spread to Roman Catholics well before 1968,[28] the recommendations even of the majority appear distinctly tame and dangerously conditional upon the assumption that 'organic unity' really did exist in the intention of the churches and would continue to exist.

For Oliver the discussions had proved increasingly frustrating. He was bombarded with abrasive letters by Geoffrey Fisher while battling with objection after objection from both Moorman and Duffield. 'May I as one of the "wings" of your Commission,' wrote Duffield, 'thank you for the patience you have shown as chairman... It must have required a good deal of perseverance on your part at times.' 'I don't think,' remarked Moorman in September 1967, 'that our Report is going to give much help to the Church in making up its mind about the rights and wrongs of Intercommunion unless, and until, it is prepared to say something about the nature of the Eucharist and the Church.' John Coventry, the Catholic observer, wrote to Oliver 'with great reluctance' to express much the same reservation. There remained too much an impression that the argument derived from a kind of ecumenical expediency, judged appropriate within a particular moment of church history – a moment which was, unfortunately, anyway misunderstood.

Geoffrey Lampe wrote at the end of it all thanking Oliver 'that you have steered us through with such skill. I am tempted in pessimistic moments to think that the heavily qualified majority recommendations emerge as a rather ridiculous *mus* after all the para-phernalia of the body of the Report... but I then reflect that even so guarded a concession to reciprocity is a break-through.... You did a wonderful job with your commission, especially in never losing patience with us.' To Donald Allchin, his closest colleague on the commission, Oliver admitted he felt disappointed by the result, to which Allchin replied: 'It was certainly one of the most intensely difficult things that I have ever been involved in, and I think that many of us felt that way about it. We certainly should not have reached any kind of constructive conclusion at all, had it not been for the genuinely supernatural hope and patience which you showed all the way through which was, if you will permit me to say it, one of the most genuinely hope-making things I have ever seen.'

It was only a Report. While its influence on the Lambeth Conference which met a couple of months after its publication was considerable, within the Church of England it became bogged down by standard procedures of procrastination. Sent to the Church Assembly, it was passed on to the Convocations. Eighteen months after its publication, in October 1969, Oliver, addressing the Canterbury Convocation insisted, 'I must say that I believe these steps are an overdue minimum... They represent the least we can do.' Yet they were passed on for reconsideration by General Synod a couple of years later. When the Anglican–Methodist union plan failed to obtain a sufficient majority in Church Assembly and it was necessary for bishops to indicate on what basis immediate Anglican–Methodist relations should be conducted, Oliver's almost sardonic instruction to his diocese in a special Pastoral letter declared, 'I have no hesitation as Bishop in saying that the 1933 resolutions, under which alone I am entitled to advise you, can properly allow us to invite members of the Methodist Church to receive communion in the Church of England "on special occasions..."'. Oliver's rather legalist caution could make him appear more concerned than almost anyone else with the authority of the 1933 resolutions.[29] A great opportunity had come and gone. When he looked back on the Commission's recommendations a few years later Oliver had to admit that they were 'oddly out-of-date already in their formulation'.[30]

## 1968

The year 1968 proved to be an exceptionally tense and memorable one internationally, a climacteric year politically, culturally and ecclesiastically. Oliver was expecting it. The *Diocesan Gazette* for January already labelled it 'A Year of Decision' and announced that the bishop would be issuing a special Pastoral Letter on the subject for Passion Sunday, 31 March. In many ways all that Oliver had been working for over the years now seemed about to come to a head: the final reports on Anglican–Methodist unity and his own Intercommunion Commission were almost ready for publication and, he hoped, acceptance, the World Council's fourth assembly was to meet in Uppsala in July and would be followed almost at once by the Lambeth Conference. The Report of the International Anglican/Roman Catholic Preparatory Commission was also completed at Malta in the first days of January to be ready for consideration at Lambeth. So much, then, was planned to happen and so much of this would closely overlap that it seems best to consider the year's developments as a single whole.

Oliver and Ursula began the year in Uganda. They had flown out just before Christmas to visit their son Stephen, now teaching at Makerere University, and to combine a holiday with what he called an 'Ecumenical Safari' – with Oliver ecumenism could never be left out of things for long. So, besides visits to game parks and other places of tourist interest, there were sessions spent with the Joint Christian Council in Kampala and the East African Church Union Committee in Nairobi offering the advice of a 'consultant', while stressing that he was not 'a travelling oracle' yet noting down what he should later report back to Faith and Order in Geneva. Out of this visit grew a permanent and flourishing 'Companion Relationship' between the diocese of Bristol and the Anglican Province of Uganda, a relationship later shared – given the multiplication of Ugandan dioceses – by

Bristol's neighbour of Winchester. To the Church in Uganda it has always meant a great
deal and it brought Archbishop Luwum to visit Bristol and Oliver only a little before he
was murdered. After Uganda and Kenya there was a final week in Ethiopia, including a
visit to the rock churches of Lalibela and an interview with the Emperor Haile Selassie
reminiscing about his church-going in Bristol when in exile in the 1930s. Ethiopia proved
most memorable – the colourful riders on horseback, the extraordinary churches, the
strange but lovely liturgy, at which he was even permitted to preside, the famed
monastery of Debra Libanos: 'Do you wonder that the place wove itself into my dreams
for weeks afterwards?'

Back to England in early February and further final meetings of the Intercommunion
Commission. After the very last, on 18 March, he commented ruefully, 'I've never had
such a sticky assignment. What with John Moorman prickly with suspicion to the end...
and Cheslyn Jones being completely intractable in supposing that if he argued for long
enough we should all agree with him.' Once that was done, he wrote to each member of
the commission individually. But there was so much else – Bishops' meetings, British
Council of Churches meetings, weeks on duty at the House of Lords. In April both the
BCC and the Anglican Presbyterian Liaison Committee met in Newcastle. Before that he
had preached every day of Holy Week in the cathedral – a course of sermons which in
time developed into his last book *Guarded by Faith* (1971). On 2 May the
Intercommunion Report was published. A week later Oliver accepted yet another
responsibility. *Parish and People* had been founded in 1949 by Henry de Candole, the
Bishop of Knaresborough, to further the liturgical movement within the Church of
England.[31] With the years it had tended in the direction of a rather ritualistic Anglo-
Catholicism, until in 1963 a more radical group including David Paton assumed control.
In 1968 de Candole, now 73, decided it was time to retire as chairman. At a meeting at
William Temple College, Rugby, on 10–11 May, Oliver, hitherto a Vice-President, was
invited to become chairman while the movement itself turned emphatically ecumenical.
Amalgamation with the Methodist Renewal Group was set in motion and all efforts
became concentrated on securing Anglican–Methodist Unity.

As soon as the Rugby meeting was over Oliver had to be in Convocation, first,
to present two other reports which he had chaired – an interim one on
Anglican–Presbyterian Conversations in England and another of the BCC Standing
Conference on 'Covenanting for Union' – and, second, to take part in the debate on
Anglican–Methodist Union. Immediately after Convocation he flew to Germany to take
part in the latest meeting of the WCC/RC Joint Working Group and introduce its discussion on intercommunion. At the same time Gene Blake invited him to chair the 'Message
Commission' at Uppsala. And so it went on. Oliver's Pastoral Letter promised in January
was published in the *Diocesan Gazette* for April. Focused on Uppsala, Lambeth and
Anglican–Methodist union, it sought to suggest the way his diocese should respond to all
this – 'to grasp afresh something of the greatness of what God is doing in His world'. He
insisted that his sense of this had grown out of discussions in the diocesan Bishop's
Council, but the direction and sense of urgency were clearly his own. Above all, everything in this 'year of decision' was to be focused on reunion with the Methodists.

But far larger developments in the political and cultural climate were at work which
would deeply affect the ecclesiastical world. Suddenly the rather comfortable liberal optimism, linking establishments and reformers together, of the early 1960s was replaced by
a far more confrontatory and cynical mood separating the one from the other. The
Vietnam War and the Civil Rights campaigns in America did much to precipitate this. By

1968 there were over half a million American servicemen in Vietnam and tens of thousands of tons of American bombs were raining down on the north. On 4 April Martin Luther King, black leader of the Civil Rights movement, was assassinated in Memphis, Tennessee. He had been billed as the opening preacher for the World Council in Uppsala. Two months later Robert Kennedy, who appeared at the time a hopeful possible leader for a more liberal world, was likewise assassinated immediately after winning the California primary for the presidency. At the same time a violent wave of student demonstrations across the western world, most notably in Paris, reflected both an upsurge of abhorrence among the young for established ways and a final burst of neo-Marxist vitality. Again in Czechoslovakia, led by Alexander Dubcek, there was a brave attempt in what came to be called the 'Prague Spring' to modify the crushing stranglehold of Communist rule and replace it by 'Socialism with a human face' as Dubcek described it. All of this had its effect on reform movements within the Christian Churches, radicalizing their mood and engineering a growing dissatisfaction with the temporizing of those in authority. When the Fourth Assembly eventually met in Uppsala it would be in consequence the most radically politicized of all WCC gatherings. Something of the same spirit would be manifest at the Lambeth Conference and again, in September, at the third great church gathering of that year, the Second General Conference of the Latin American Catholic Bishops at Medellín, the birth moment of Liberation Theology.

Oliver was well aware of this upsurge in secular urgency, especially among the young. One can, admittedly, read his journal and much else that he wrote and find little echo of it. He sympathized with the 'Charles Davis syndrome', as he had come to call it – impatience with the 'structures' and established leaders producing 'creative disaffiliation' from all of them – though he regarded it as disastrous.[32] But he thought a great deal about student unrest and the reasons for it. Thus the sit-in at Bristol University over Christmas 1968 was something he responded to in a variety of ways which included introducing a debate in the House of Lords (23 April 1969) on 'Student Participation in Higher Education' with a remarkably interesting and well-informed speech analysing the slogans of being 'anti-élitist', 'anti-ivory tower', 'anti-authoritarian' and 'anti-power structures' with considerable sensitivity. One wonders how many other bishops at the time could have offered nearly so proficient a piece of social analysis. His sense of urgency to advance Christian unity was never then just for the sake of the Church but precisely so that the Church could speak more convincingly to the world. He really did hold the old ecumenical conviction that unity was a necessary precondition for effective mission. So when, for instance, the introduction to *Intercommunion Today* admitted that 'when the credibility of speaking at all about God is at stake, and men doubt whether the Christian religion has a relevant word to speak on nuclear annihilation or race conflict or mass starvation, the domestic differences among Christians as to how far they can worship God together may seem blasphemously trivial', he at least felt that this was very much the case. Still more do we find this awareness in the *Message* of Uppsala for which he was largely responsible: 'The excitement of new scientific discoveries, the protest of student revolution, the shock of assassinations, the clash of wars: these mark the year 1968' – so it began, Uppsala's most memorable dictum. At least for the month at Uppsala Oliver withdrew from his preoccupations with organic unity to concentrate instead on what the Church should be saying to a world in turmoil.

The Fourth Assembly began on 4 July. It was for the World Council in many ways the start of a new era. Eugene Carson Blake had taken over as General Secretary just 18 months earlier. Visser't Hooft had been so dominant a figure within the World Council

since it began that his retirement was bound to alter its ethos profoundly. But there was
a far wider, fairly sudden, change in personnel. Franklyn Fry, Chairman of the Central
Committee from 1954, died suddenly a month before the assembly. Ernest Payne, the
vice-chairman, presided in consequence over the discussions at Uppsala but did not
continue in office beyond it. The membership of the post-Uppsala Central Committee
was almost wholly new.[33] The senior staff too had greatly changed, removing almost all
Oliver's friends and colleagues from the past: Leslie Cooke, Philippe Maury and Hendrik
Kraemer by death while Francis House had returned to England, Lesslie Newbigin to
India and Patrick Rodger to Scotland. It is true that at Uppsala itself many of these old
friends were present – Newbigin, House, Rodger, Kay Bliss, Frank Woods, David Paton
– as delegates or consultants but for most of them it represented the last point in any
major World Council engagement. It was clearly necessary that after 20 years the generation of people who had led the enterprise at Amsterdam and carried much of the burden
since should be replaced. That was in part why Oliver himself had given up his chairmanship in Faith and Order the year before. Yet, even now, he remained in point of fact
the one great survivor, being elected for the first time to the Central Committee and to its
Executive Committee as well. Indeed, it appears that he was very nearly elected Chairman
of the Central Committee, and would have accepted the post if he had been. In fact, M.
M. Thomas of Bangalore was chosen. As an Indian theologian and a layman he responded
far better to the new face the World Council desired and its turn towards the south. With
the mood as it was at Uppsala, it is remarkable that Oliver was seriously considered,
remarkable too that in the near clean sweep of older staff and Central Committee
members his own role should be not terminated but renewed.

The Fourth Assembly closed at Uppsala on 20 July. The Lambeth Conference opened
with a service in Canterbury Cathedral on the 25 July. Oliver and Ursula were lent a
flat in Chelsea for the following month. The same day Paul VI published the encyclical
*Humanae Vitae* condemning all forms of artificial contraception as intrinsically evil.
While doubtless not so intended the timing of the encyclical could look like a slap in the
face for Anglicans, condemning as it did what an earlier Lambeth Conference had
declared legitimate. Again, while the bishops at Lambeth had been allowed to receive
copies of the Malta Report, completed six months earlier by the Anglican/Roman
Catholic Joint Preparatory Commission, after very strenuous efforts on the part of
Ramsey and Moorman, there was trouble over this as well. It was clear that someone in
Rome, maybe Oliver's old friend, Jérôme Hamer, who had now moved across to the
conservative side in Rome with appointment to the Holy Office, did not like the report,
perhaps because of its references to intercommunion. Despite its unanimous acceptance
by the Catholic members of the commission, including Willebrands and four other
bishops, its publication was never to be officially authorized by Rome. It would seem that
Ramsey, partially converted after his Roman visit of 1966 to pressing forward ecumenically in that direction, had all his old suspicions re-aroused by both *Humanae Vitae* and
Roman backsliding over the Malta Report. The gap between his approach and that of
Moorman had notably increased.

What happened at the Lambeth Conference itself would not help matters. One of three
sections in the Conference was devoted to unity. It was chaired by Archbishop de Mel,
the Metropolitan of India whose province was about to enter the new united Church of
North India. Within this section Moorman chaired a sub-committee on relations with the
Roman Catholic Church and Oliver another on 'Principles of Union', where he
succeeded in massaging the structure of the Lambeth Quadrilateral into harmony with

the new Delhi definition of unity which the conference report then quoted in full. He wanted to avoid the impression that by insisting on episcopacy *eo nomine* Anglicans were approaching union 'through a *diktat* which one part of Christendom imposes upon others'. Michael Ramsey was unhappy with this but had to be content with putting the Lambeth Quadrilateral as such in a footnote.[34] Near the end of the conference De Mel made a speech referring to the British Anglican–Methodist unity scheme and strongly criticizing its opponents. Moorman and others were distressed by what he said and in consequence Moorman absented himself from the final service at St Paul's when De Mel was to be the preacher. He also wrote to tell Ramsey that he had done so. Ramsey in turn was angry. He described Moorman's action as a 'wound'. If the archbishop was somewhat disturbed by the Bishop of Bristol's pressures in one direction, he was very much more upset by the Bishop of Ripon's in another.

It was a trying time. All the bishops at Lambeth had attended a performance of Baron Corvo's *Hadrian VII*, a superbly acted presentation of the sort of papacy they would have liked to see, but just a mirage in the world of *Humanae Vitae* as it had not been in that of Pope John. In the real world the Soviet Union had invaded Czechoslovakia while the Lambeth Conference was meeting, to suppress the liberalization of the Prague Spring. In church and society alike confrontation was now again the order of the day. In the Catholic Church, in particular, a large part of the theological community, the laity in the West and numerous pastoral clergy, would be pitted against pope and curia. In Rome in the meantime Ramsey was regarded as having done a volte-face at Lambeth, throwing his weight behind Oliver's report on intercommunion in an outspoken speech while back-pedalling on any recognition of the papacy. For Anglo-Catholics of the more rigid school Lambeth was encouraging 'a head-first plunge towards ecumenism and unity' which must lead to 'destruction rather than renewal'.[35] Bishop Graham Leonard of Willesden, one of the most uncompromising of their leaders, was known to be in correspondence with the Apostolic Delegate suggesting that if Anglican–Methodist union went through, there would be a great breakaway to Rome. At the same time Bishop Stopford of London, an ecumenically minded bishop who had chaired the Anglican–Methodist Conversations, was enquiring of the Delegate what he should do about the increasing number of Roman Catholic priests wanting to join the Church of England in consequence of *Humanae Vitae*.

Truly the 'Year of Decision' had turned into a year of crisis, in which the entire 1960s movement of ecclesiastical reform and ecumenical convergence seemed suddenly in danger of being blown apart. Reflecting on Lambeth where his own work had been highly successful, Oliver thought it not 'so urgent as Uppsala, but neither has it been so frenetic'. He thought too that this owed much to 'Michael's personality... his dislike of frenzy, his quiet daily guidance of the meditations and his love of depth rather than width'. But he realized too that there were likely to be difficult fights just ahead: 'I sense a similar conflict with us in C of E as now tears the C of Rome. Many of the Lambeth resolutions will precipitate some hard struggles – the Methodist and Inter-communion issues especially. I may have to be ready for some lonely battles.' That sounds rather more dramatic than is customary with Oliver, but he knew he carried more weight on the international than the national front, just as had been the case for Bell. And he was right enough that there were battles to come. Throughout this 'year of decision' he had kept his eye fixed primarily on the urgency of Christian unity and he demonstrated it strikingly enough with a lengthy letter in *The Times* on the nature and need of unity published on its final day, 31 December 1968.

## Anglican–Methodist unity

Throughout the 1960s Oliver's heart was set beyond all else on the achievement in England of Anglican–Methodist unity.[36] Conversations between the Church of England and the Methodist Church began in 1956 and moved forward at a somewhat leisurely pace. An initial report was produced in 1958, proposing union in two stages – full Communion after a Service of Reconciliation would constitute the first stage to be followed at a much later date by 'organic unity'. The division between the two churches had come about almost accidentally and no great doctrinal issues were involved, so in theory their reunion in an ecumenical age should not be too problematic. With no other British church was the Church of England anywhere near to coming into union, so in practical and local terms this became the flagship venture of English Anglican ecumenism. The more Oliver became the principal Anglican ecumenical leader, the more he was inevitably and rightly concerned with the achievement of this reunion. That was all the more the case as he believed that if it could go through, other churches in this country would follow and a great step be taken towards realizing in England the kind of unity proclaimed at New Delhi. Moreover as Anglicans and Methodists both form worldwide communions and both began in England, one could hope that unity between them once achieved at home would help bring about unity all across the globe.

Back at Millhouses in the 1940s Oliver had already established a very special parochial relationship with the local Methodist congregation. When in July of his first year in Bristol, the annual Methodist Conference was held in the city, its President, Dr Eric Baker, was invited to preach at Evensong in the cathedral and as many Anglican clergy as possible were asked by their bishop to attend. That too set Oliver's course for the coming years. When in 1963 the Anglican–Methodist Commission published a further report, approved by the Convocations in July for study in the dioceses, it became for Oliver, once he had returned from Montreal, the focus of his attention and that of his diocese. A strenuous programme for the autumn began at the Diocesan Conference in late October when he and Rupert Davies, Tutor of the Methodist Theological College in Bristol, presented the Report. In September Oliver had already visited and addressed the Methodist District Synod. In November he introduced the Report in each of the Ruri-Decanal Conferences. Meanwhile Rural Deans and Methodist District Superintendents were expected to be making contact to arrange still more local joint discussions. Other organizations like the diocesan Mothers' Union and the Methodist Women's Fellowship were also roped in to hold joint meetings. The Report, Oliver explained in the *Diocesan Gazette*, was 'potentially the most important thing that has happened in English religious life for a very long time… All this presents us with a most exciting challenge. For a long while we have heard about unity as something that might concern folk in South India or Ceylon. Now we are faced with the need of making some real decisions which would affect every town and village in England.' Thus, 1963–4 represented for Oliver the *Kairos*, God's appointed time for unity which, if neglected, might never recur.

Exciting the challenge might be but the procrastination quite to face up to it continued. Five years later, in the autumn of 1968, he and the diocese had to undertake much the same exercise all over again. The final Anglican–Methodist Report had at last been published in April. The summer had been taken up with Uppsala and Lambeth. Now each diocese had six months to make up its mind. Writing in the *Diocesan Gazette* Oliver pointed out that following the discussions inaugurated in October 1963 roughly 75 per cent of the Diocesan Conference had voted in favour of going ahead with unity. 'I have a feeling,' he admitted, 'that perhaps the church as a whole could have gone ahead four or five years ago with more conviction' than now appeared to exist but, as he recognized, the battle had to be fought once more. He and Pauline Webb would present the Report to the Diocesan Conference in October. This would be followed by another round of local meetings and an extraordinary Diocesan Conference on 25 January to vote on four basic questions: Unity in two stages, the acceptability of the proposed new ordinal, approval of the proposed Service of Reconciliation, and the actual inauguration of Stage 1. It was hardly accidental that the day chosen by him for the vote was the last day of the Week of Prayer for Christian Unity. The final votes in Convocation were to be taken in July 1969 with the Methodist Conference voting in Birmingham the same day.

Oliver set out the reasons for his own affirmative answers to all four questions in the January issue of the *Gazette*. While there was just under 75 per cent approval in the Diocesan Conference for the Service of Reconciliation, there was about 82 per cent on the other three questions, including that of asking the Convocations to give final approval for the inauguration of Stage 1. Oliver could only be satisfied with the support he received from his own diocese though he had hoped for nothing less than unanimity.

It had been agreed that a 75 per cent vote in favour was required from both parties to the union. In June a Clergy Referendum throughout the Church of England revealed that over 40 per cent were unwilling to take part in the Service of Reconciliation – a dangerously high proportion, suggesting that a vote in favour in the Convocations might well lead to something like schism. In the dioceses of London, Peterborough and Truro a majority said 'no', and even in Bristol it was over 25 per cent. The decision to hold this referendum was an odd one. Effectively, it undercut the authority of the Convocations. When July arrived, the Methodist Conference gave its approval by 76 per cent but the Anglican Convocations failed to do so. There only 68.5 per cent were in favour. The mostly Anglo-Catholic opposition, led by Bishop Moorman, Bishop Eastaugh of Peterborough and Graham Leonard of Willesden, was sufficient to block it. They were backed by the bishops of Carlisle, Leicester and Sheffield. The objection lay chiefly in regard to an admitted ambiguity within the Service of Reconciliation: did it, or did it not, include the ordination of the Methodist clergy? If that was intended, then Methodists could not accept it; but if it did not, Anglo-Catholics could not accept it. Ramsey had explained that he himself was agnostic on the subject but could leave it to God to provide what was necessary. Union was a good thing on account of which some temporary sacrifices in coherence were justified. He did not think that 'everything in the Anglican–Methodist scheme is all right but... moaning and groaning does not help very much'.[37]

For Oliver, rejection signified 'a shameful day for the Church of England... We are too divided to unite with anyone.' It was 'a failure in moral courage', made all the worse for him personally when, three months later, the Convocations failed to accept the Intercommunion Report. He and the Chairman of the Bristol Methodist District sent out a 'Joint Pastoral Letter' in October on what should now be done locally and announced a joint 'Service of Commitment to Union' to be held in Bristol Cathedral on 2 November. Michael Ramsey decided, moreover, that the matter should be returned for reconsideration once the new General Synod came into existence. So a further vote was taken in May 1972. Once again the Methodists had agreed to unite and Oliver went to cast his vote knowing that the diocesan synod stood behind him with a majority of 79 per cent, about the highest in the country. However, despite two eloquent speeches by Ramsey the national vote was now less than 66 per cent in favour. Anglican–Methodist unity was dead. 'Here I am,' wrote Oliver that night, staying at Westminster with Max Warren, 'after a black day. I am very proud of my Archbishop and very ashamed of the General Synod. I find it hard to see what kind of church I now belong to – its representative governing body has shown complete contempt for moral and intellectual integrity.' 'It is not enough to say that one is in favour of unity but not in favour of this Scheme,' declared Francis House, speaking now as Archdeacon of Macclesfield, 'because in fact this is the only gateway to all possible future schemes in this country.' Whether the 'all in each place' model was really 'the only gateway' to unity may well be questioned but at the high level of reunion schemes, for Oliver and those who shared his view, this could seem the end of the road and, in some sense, the end of Oliver's career, the effective termination of everything central to his work and thinking over 25 years.

Back in March 1966 Kathleen Bliss had asked Oliver 'How long will the present head of steam behind the drive for unity between separated churches last I wonder?'[38] In the May 1972 Synod debate Oliver remarked sadly, 'We could still have made the decision in 1965, when the whole business would have had something of the freshness of a venture of faith.' Instead of that everyone had dragged their feet, dawdling prudently along the ecumenical way, rewriting an awkward phrase here or there, until Bliss's 'head of steam' had indeed faded away. Kenneth Slack, General Secretary of the BCC, wrote a little book entitled *The British Churches Today* in 1960. Revising it in 1969 he found it necessary to remark 'Passage after passage written in 1960 has seemed strangely optimistic and has had to be excised' (ibid., p. xi). The moment of opportunity when the tide was coming in had been lost and some of the blame for this may fairly be laid on Ramsey's shoulders. In 1972 he declared himself 'puzzled' by what had happened but the truth is that for many years he had done nothing as Primate to provide a lead. Even at Lambeth in 1968 Oliver still felt unsure what the archbishop's position really was. When he finally came out in full support – most emphatically only in 1972 – it was when the time of optimistic venturesomeness was long passed and the opposition had hardened. Here as in much else Oliver found Bishops' Meetings '*very* frustrating because of Michael's muddly chairmanship'. Ramsey was never a person really to consult or to collaborate in any regular way – silent at times, a beacon of light at others, but always unpredictable.

Yet one might well argue that it was criminally irresponsible for Ramsey and Tomkins to press ahead after the negative votes of 1969, in particular the clergy referendum. Whatever the validity of their reasoning, the fact that over 40 per cent of Church of England clergy had refused to take part in the Service of Reconciliation was surely a more than adequate indicator that it would be madness to go forward. To ride roughshod over such a vote was no way to unity. Here as in other cases an ecumenically committed leadership had lost adequate contact with its own rank and file and, in consequence, its grasp on common sense.

For Oliver himself the débâcle must have been particularly frustrating because he had never been personally involved in the negotiations nationally.[39] The Church of England's chief ecumenical figure, he had been given almost every other ecumenical responsibility, but denied this one which was unquestionably the most crucial, as his strategic eye saw most keenly. He never seems to have remarked on this – it was not in his character to complain about the way he was treated and he had, after all, been up to his eyes with other responsibilities. In 1968 he did, however, attempt to play a national role in this through his chairmanship of *Parish and People* which had been transformed from a liturgical into an ecumenical ginger group under his leadership. Some 20,000 copies of a pamphlet entitled *A Guide to the Debate on Anglican–Methodist Unity* had sold out by October, to be followed by a 10,000 reprint. Nevertheless his own role in regard to Anglican–Methodist unity was largely confined to his own diocese and to the speeches he made from time to time in Convocation or Synod where he was never at his best when caught in argument. In October 1972 he attended the inauguration of the United Reformed Church, bringing together Congregationalists and Presbyterians, in Westminster Abbey. He found it 'a tonic' to witness how other churches could make a success of unity, to note the warmth of welcome accorded to Michael Ramsey 'Our Archbishop', and to see how well Eric Abbott, now Dean of the Abbey, had arranged the service, but it sadly reminded him too that 'so much of my efforts seem to have led nowhere at all!'

## The later years

In August 1969 Oliver commented in his *Diocesan Gazette* on a plea from the parishes that he and his suffragan bishop spend more time in visiting them – doubtless a plea heard from time to time in almost every diocese. 'There is nothing which both of us would more wish to do,' he insisted, while admitting that 'there seemed to be a widespread impression that a large part of my own absence from the diocese was due to ecumenical commitments.' Oliver was sensitive to this accusation in Bristol as at Lincoln but his response was perhaps less than candid: 'As a matter of fact comparatively little of my time is spent in ecumenical absences.' He stressed instead the amount of time every diocesan bishop had to be away each year attending three meetings of the Church Assembly, Convocation, two or three Bishops' Meetings, two or three duty weeks in the House of Lords. The combination of all this, together with the ecumenical work, as well as further responsibilities such as chairing the Religious Advisory Committee of the BBC and ITA, certainly did limit the amount of energy as well as time remaining for pastoral ministry, especially as he was not one to shirk the details of diocesan administrative chores. Inevitably much of the burden of parochial visiting simply had to be carried by his suffragan, the Bishop of Malmesbury.

It was in 1964 just before Nottingham that he had accepted the chairmanship of the Central Religious Advisory Committee to the BBC and ITA (CRAC), a body which included representatives of all the main churches in Britain – in consequence in itself a usefully ecumenical activity. Michael Ramsey had encouraged the BBC's proposed nomination. Oliver wrote to him admitting that religious broadcasting interested him greatly but added, 'it is a matter of how many extra-diocesan things it is sensible to take on.' He already had his chairmanship of both the World Council's Faith and Order Commission and the BCC's Faith and Order Committee, chairmanship of the Anglican–Presbyterian Consultations and membership of the Commission on Roman Catholic Relations. Then there was the chairing of a further British Council of Churches Standing Conference on 'Covenanting for Union'. To all of this would be added the very burdensome chairmanship of the Intercommunion Commission as well as the twice yearly meetings somewhere on the continent of the Joint Working Group. Hardly had he given up the Faith and Order chairmanship at WCC level than he was elected to both its Central and Executive Committees. While he humbly claimed to the diocese that 'far the greater part of my absence from Bristol is simply part of what every diocesan bishop has to accept', this seriously underplayed the reality of his multiple responsibilities elsewhere since for a large part he was not simply attending meetings but chairing them and, indeed, directing the entire strategy that underlay them. His role had become for some years rather more like that of the Archbishop of Canterbury, whose most significant responsibilities had ceased to be diocesan but were national and international. However, while Ramsey had a moderately large staff both to help him on the wider side and to replace him within the diocese, Oliver had only the support provided for any other diocesan bishop. Jim Bishop who was his suffragan for all the middle years at Bristol (1962–73) reflected that:

> some people thought he was too often out of the diocese. But I remember the Dean, Douglas Harrison, pointing out that he still managed to know his clergy (and often their wives and children) by their Christian names, still managed to read every new book before most of us had even heard of it, and still managed, at Diocesan Conferences or Board meetings, to reveal a depth of understanding of the matters in hand that put the rest of us to shame. For my part, my fellow suffragans, almost to a man, envied me my Diocesan.[40]

In Jim Bishop's opinion, Oliver's work in the ecumenical field should not be allowed to overshadow his pastoral ministry. It was the latter which most endeared him. And yet it was impossible that his almost ceaseless ecumenical cares – in preparation and correspondence as much as in actual meetings – should not have detracted from what Oliver himself would have liked to do on the pastoral and diocesan side. From this point of view Jim Bishop, exactly his own age, was the perfect complement and replacer, a wonderfully pastoral man, especially for the clergy, a *pastor pastorum*. He shared Oliver's profoundly ecumenical spirituality, being drawn more and more into the Catholic Focolare Movement. Eighteen months after retirement, in a mood of retrospective self-examination, Oliver could blame himself bitterly enough:

> I grieve that I failed to gain acceptance as a pastoral bishop. I *did* want really to love them all – but my heart was too small and too cold. And how does one 'love' 300–400 people on my prayer-list – not to mention all the unknown lay people that each parish priest represents? And I was too duty-bound – dictating letters in the desire not to neglect those I was answering; attending General Synod and all those commissions etc because I was *on* them, either *ex officio* or because Michael C. or someone had asked me.

Even ten years later, when reading the life of Leslie Hunter, he could exclaim, 'I wish I had treated any of my young clergy as generously as he treated me in those war years.' Undoubtedly this is unfair. One remembers how, after his parish years in Sheffield, he commented 'I was a poor pastor'. Oliver was only too prone to blame himself and his 'lack of love' where others recognized on the contrary an unstinting willingness to give himself to the overwhelming range of tasks his ability and experience had brought his way. Yet it is true too that he had far too many chairmanships and suffered from such a sense of duty in regard to committees that little energy was left over for experiencing the joy in what he was convinced he wanted most – parish visiting, being 'local'. Fortunately he had Jim Bishop.

In point of fact the balance did begin to change from 1969 and, still more, 1970. Some of the commissions disappeared entirely, others faded into insignificance. Bishop Ian Ramsey of Durham took over the chairmanship of CRAC. In May 1970 Oliver also decided to resign from the World Council's Executive Committee. While he felt 'a twinge of regret at moving a few more steps away from the centre of things ecumenical', he had come to recognize that he and his heart were almost exhausted from persistently exceeding 'the limits of what Brother Ass can bear'. He hoped that 'a new rhythm of moderation' might make it possible 'to go on being useful'. The ageing of his face across the years of episcopate is striking. If 1970 constituted a year of change, shifting from a primarily ecumenical to a more diocesan focus, it went too with a lasting decline in energy. Most unusually he took two full months of summer holiday that year – in Yugoslavia and then at Bryn and in Ireland – which helped achieve a certain recovery: 'I feel the fight coming back into me,' he could write by October but added revealingly, 'I can't help wondering how far the whole business was induced by a sense of defeat in one of my main concerns in life.' It could be added that one almost never feels stirred by anything in his monthly messages in the *Diocesan Gazette* apart from what he has to say that is emphatically ecumenical. It may be that the rest did not bore him but in a retrospective reading it looks like that.

And 1970 was a year of change too in that two daughters, Monica and Ruth, married while Deborah became engaged. Stephen had married already before going to Makerere. This left him with the always fulfilling company of Ursula while providing quite soon an expansion of grandchildren and family homes to visit – something which, hitherto, had hardly existed. All of that was delightful but it added to the rather rapid arrival of an atmosphere of elderliness. Yet in 1970 Oliver was only 62. Just as he had imagined himself entering middle age somewhat prematurely, so did he have a sense of growing old rather earlier than many others might do. It was a sense stimulated both by the continuous overexertions of the 1960s and a resigned recognition that the great central campaigns of his life were almost over without being won.

January 1971, nevertheless, saw him in Addis Ababa for a WCC Central Committee meeting whose main concern would affect him considerably – the Programme to Combat Racism. He had attended the 1969 meeting in Canterbury which launched the Programme and, as an Executive Committee member, he had approved the following year a first series of grants to organizations combating racism, including various liberation movements in Southern Africa, some of them committed to armed struggle. The grants, it was agreed, should only be used for humanitarian purposes, medical and educational. This action produced a very hostile reaction in conservative political circles as also some religious circles especially within the Church of England. Oliver supported the programme in principle but was also worried by it. He felt that the World Council had failed to explain sufficiently what it was doing. He also distrusted a politicizing of the movement and feared for a loss of reputation. He had always been a Faith and Order rather than a Life and Work person. He accepted that racialism in Southern Africa was so oppressive as to justify revolution but was not convinced that the time for this had come. He felt 'ambivalent'. In Addis Ababa he tried to express his reservations and was in consequence dismissed by some as 'an unrepentant colonialist',[11] but he did not vote against what had been done – nobody did – and he always felt that as a member of the Central Committee he should defend the Programme. Archbishop Ramsey, on the contrary, believed it was wrong and said so the following month in General Synod and continued to do so over the years to an extent which surprised many. The movements which received money included the Rhodesian (Zimbabwean) ZANU and ZAPU. The Anglican Bishop of Mashonaland (Rhodesia), Paul Burrough, walked out of the Anglican Consultative Council, meeting at Limuru, Kenya, later in February when it backed the World Council by a large majority, despite Ramsey's wishes. The Rhodesian Council of Churches gave a similar backing – Burrough did not represent their opinion. It was especially white Anglicans, with their profoundly establishmentarian culture, who were offended by the grants, though the Salvation Army could feel as strongly.

The next year the issue of investment in South Africa came up in the Central Committee, meeting this time in Utrecht (August 1972). Oliver's unhappiness with the line being followed had grown. He felt that the very integrity of the World Council was being put into question, that a 'party-line' was being 'relentlessly pressed – the atmosphere has been emotional and too often irrational'. Unconvinced by the case made for disinvestment, he abstained in the vote, only to be further dismayed that 'the few negative votes and abstentions were so resented and so ineffectual'. In 1974 General Synod reduced the Church of England's contribution to the World Council by £1,000 as a token expression of disapproval. Oliver hated to disagree publicly with 'Michael, my Metropolitan' but in this matter he all the same felt obliged to do so, joining Patrick Rodger, by then Bishop of Manchester, David Paton, Ernest Payne, Pauline Webb, Lord Caradon and others in a public appeal to back the World Council's Programme. Given his private reservations, his public loyalty to the Programme remains remarkable.

At Addis Ababa Carson Blake announced that he would be retiring the following year and a committee of nomination was appointed to choose his successor. Oliver was somewhat relieved not to be included. The desire was to choose a General Secretary from the Third World. Oliver shared emotionally in the sense that this was the way the World Council needed to go but he lacked any close experience of southern realities. When Philip Potter was selected he could only be delighted. A native of Dominica who had long experience within the Student Christian Movement in Britain and elsewhere, he combined orientations old and new.

It was characteristic of Oliver that he declined to attend the fifth General Assembly of the World Council at Nairobi in 1975, although still a member of the Central Committee until it met. He was on the point of retiring and wanted a younger person to fill the available place. If he had gone, it would have been as one of the WCC's patriarchs to be honoured accordingly, but such a role was one he always shunned. For him the final truly memorable association with the World Council was at the Central Committee meeting in Geneva in August 1973 when the 25th anniversary of Amsterdam was commemorated. After the service in the cathedral of S. Pierre he stood on its steps with Visser't Hooft and Niemöller recalling the first meeting of the Provisional Committee after the war, in February 1946, and the service held there then. How few of those who built the World Council were still around! Philip Potter preached and the service included 'some startling changes'.

Back in Bristol from Addis Ababa Oliver's 1971 was chiefly memorable for two things: creating Trinity Theological College and publishing his last book, *Guarded by Faith*. There were no fewer than three Anglican theological colleges in Bristol, all Conservative Evangelical – Tyndale Hall, Clifton and Dalton House. The first two were for men, while the third was the only Church of England college devoted specifically to the training of women for the ministry. They had failed to cooperate and various attempts at a merger had fallen through. Their 'ethos', it was claimed, was irreconcilably different, Tyndale being rather more fundamentalist than Clifton. An agreement to unite made in 1969, including the naming of a new Principal, broke down given 'the almost complete disagreement between the two college staffs'. A leading Evangelical, Roger Beckwith of Latimer House, Oxford, wrote to Oliver, who was Visitor to both colleges, that it was 'very sad that Evangelicals are not only unable to agree with a good deal of official policy in the Church...but are even unable to agree over their own domestic concerns'. In consequence, in September 1970 the Runcie Report on future theological education in the

Church of England recommended to the bishops the closure of both colleges. If that happened, Dalton House would almost certainly go as well and there would be no Anglican theological education left in the West of England. The situation was not made easier, given the desire of the bishops to link colleges more closely with university departments, by the thoroughly unsympathetic attitude to the 'ethos' of both colleges of Professor Grayston, a 'radical liberal', head of the Bristol University Department of Religious Studies.

Oliver called everyone involved together for a 'round-table conference' in Bishop's House on 30 December: either a merger is created on the Clifton site (the only one big enough) or all will close. This involved changing almost everyone's mind from the bishops, anxious to implement the Runcie Report unmodified, down. The work of patient negotiation he put into this throughout 1971 was enormous and the wriggling on the side of the parties almost unbelievable. 'I am simply not prepared to go on with this endless haggling,' he wrote in September, while someone in Church House commented, 'What a trying and ghastly time you have had! The whole experience drives me back to Augustine on the perverse captivities of the human will even under grace!' and a leading layman in General Synod declared that it is 'with shame and fury' that Evangelical Anglicans look upon the Bristol Colleges situation. In the end, yet again, patient and skilful chairmanship achieved agreement and Trinity College, Bristol, came into existence, though for years the conflict of traditions and personalities continued within it. Only after the appointment of George Carey as Principal in 1982 was this overcome, allowing the college at last to flourish on the lines that Oliver had justified its retention to his fellow bishops 'as an opportunity for post-Keele evangelicalism, open to the rest of the Church of England, to ecumenism and to secular thinking...an act of faith that the old style self-enclosed conservative evangelicalism would soon be no more than a memory'.

As a bishop Oliver felt it incumbent to teach. After retirement he retained the drafts of more than 500 separate sermons he had delivered during his years in Bristol. Their centre-piece was a series he had given in the cathedral in Holy Week of 1968 and repeated at greater length as Lent Lectures in both Bristol and Swindon in 1969. These became *Guarded by Faith*, a simple but effective paperback on the meaning of faith in the contemporary world as understood by someone combining great pastoral concern with an emphatic sense of being 'a modern man'. He is, he says, 'trying to walk on a tight-rope instead of sitting on the fence'. Each chapter opens with a quote from George Herbert's *The Temple* while the book itself ends with a very lengthy passage from Teilhard de Chardin's *Le Milieu Divin*, thus representing throughout the Oliverian approach. Some months after giving these lectures he reflected in one of his more sombre moods that, while they had been 'an attempt to honour a bishop's obligation to teach the faith...the degree of support showed that not a *great* many people expected me to be of much help at that point!' He could be hard on himself. As a teacher or theologian Oliver had a great maturity, perhaps unrivalled among his fellow bishops,[42] but he knew that he had neither the biblical learning of Coggan nor the charisma of Ramsey. Meanwhile the calls of administration and committee meetings continued to produce a 'growing weariness with what cannot be avoided at the expense of what matters more'.

His chief ecumenical concern after the rejection by Synod in May 1972 of union with the Methodists was to advance things on the local scene. In a sense nothing else was left. Immediately after the vote he wrote uncompromisingly that 'Areas of "Ecumenical Experiment" will need not only unrestricted reciprocal communion but exchange of ministries'. Yet here again reality proved less amenable. For one thing there were far fewer

such areas than ecumenical enthusiasts had hoped for – only seven, for instance, in the
Bristol diocese. If, by the end of 1966, just 16 months after the Nottingham Conference,
there were already 170 nationwide, the figure had risen to no more than 289 ten years
later. By then, too, they had been rechristened LEPs (Local Ecumenical Projects), a less
challenging formula – the dangerous 'experiment' word had been excised. Bob Jeffery,
their principal pioneer, appealed in 1977 to bring the number up to 1,000, only then might
parent denominations take serious note of the degree of unity achieved at local level but
the likelihood of such growth by then was slight indeed. Even Oliver, so committed in
principle, had his problems in practice. A profoundly law-abiding person he had to admit
to himself that 'almost all that Areas of Ecumenical Experiment wish to do is strictly
illegal'. Donald Coggan feared that what was being encouraged would simply turn into a
new 'epoch of lawlessness'. In a brave moment Oliver was prepared to remark that as
Anglo-Catholics had been lawless in the past they at least had no right to complain about
another kind of lawlessness now, but such an approach did not suit his own temperament,
which was one of control. Even quite slight liturgical innovations by his clergy could
upset him. While liberal Catholic priests on the continent who sat lightly to Roman
instructions in some way pleased him, he could not help asking 'What will be the effect
of this contempt for "authority"?'

Moreover, he only really believed intercommunion was acceptable where there was a
group commitment to organic unity and, as this had been rejected, it was hard on his own
principles to see how one could press for 'unrestricted reciprocal communion'. Again,
while he had no doubt that LEPs needed monitoring, in fact this seldom happened. There
was little wider evaluation and quite a number practically collapsed when one or another
ecumenically enthusiastic minister moved elsewhere. For Oliver this was all very trying
but there was little one could now do except insist on prayer and the example of the Abbé
Couturier, encouraging everyone to keep the Week of Prayer for Church Unity each
January.

There was, however, one final great event: the South West Ecumenical Congress held
in Colston Hall, Bristol, in a May weekend in 1973. It was a jamboree without any institutional agenda but it brought together 2,000 delegates from the South West of England,
generating remarkable enthusiasm. Ursula undertook the huge responsibility of arranging
their accommodation. It was the first time, in England, that a large ecumenical gathering
had taken place with the fullest Catholic participation. Indeed the idea had come chiefly
from Joe Buckley. Bishop Rudderham, never a personal convert to ecumenism, was in
hospital and thus excused from attending. 'It's an ill wind,' he remarked enigmatically to
Buckley. Cardinal Suenens of Malines and Archbishop Ramsey both took part. To see a
cardinal preaching in a local Baptist church would have been, as Oliver told his diocese,
'inconceivable only a few years ago'. Something of the spirit of Montreal had, ten years
later, arrived in Bristol to gladden its bishop's heart before retirement. When Rudderham
retired in 1974 he wrote movingly to Oliver 'I cannot tell you how warmed at heart I was
by your most gracious letter... You know me well enough, as you say, to realise that I
did not find it easy to adjust myself to the alterations which the ecumenical movement
brought about.' If institutional schemes had slipped, the great advance lay in the growing
strength of the Roman Catholic presence at a popular level in British ecumenism.

For Oliver, nevertheless, the personal battle was almost over. Less than two years after
the fateful vote of General Synod he was taking the decision to retire. He was tired, unable
to cope as he wished with the punishing workload he imposed upon himself: 'It's time to
leave. I can no longer keep two steps in front of the Archdeacons.' Even a country walk

could tire him exceedingly. This much he could admit to others. The almost unmention-able sense of deeper ecumenical failure to push the Church the way he believed it ought to go was, perhaps, still more decisive. *Never glad confident morning again.* Many years later he could still refer to this 'sense of mute failure at the end of my time in Bristol'. 'Mute' is here a key word. Probably the most memorable passage in *Guarded by Faith* is 'the hardest lesson I have learned as a bishop is the toughness of the material out of which institutions are made. The amount of spiritual and intellectual energy which has to be generated before one cubic foot of institutional life can be changed seems to be prodigious.'

Yet he remained extraordinarily innovative on all sorts of fronts in these latter years other than the ecumenical, where his presidential role and concern for the common good were no less effective. Thus in 1972 he set up and chaired an unofficial public enquiry into the intention of the Ministry of Defence to close the Royal Navy Depot at Copenacre. His panel included Frank Cousins, former General Secretary of the TGWU and Minister of Technology, 1964–6, John Garnett, Director of the Industrial Society, and Derek Whitcroft, former personnel director of Imperial Tobacco. Evidence was taken, including from several MPs, the arguments for closure were exposed as unconvincing and, eventu-ally, the Ministry of Defence reversed its decision. Oliver also presided in 1972 over a working party set up by the Lord Mayor on the local employment situation. In 1974, after consulting Prince Philip, from whom he received a long and helpful letter, he joined a deputation to the Prime Minister, together with the city's chief executive, to press that the production of Concorde be not abandoned – 11,500 jobs were at risk. As late as July 1975 he set up a new informal dining group, linking some 20 interested MPs with a group of bishops and other church officials to keep the former better informed of ecclesiastical matters, a group whose convening was then taken over by Robin Woods. Even that August he was writing to the Prime Minister about pay differentials. There was no winding down of activity in the last years of bishophood.

In 1974 when Donald Coggan moved from York to Canterbury, it proved unusually hard to find a new archbishop for the northern province. Given Oliver's still thoroughly effective leadership in these years, it is hardly surprising to find Ken Carey, the Bishop of Edinburgh, writing to him in August 1974 'I think the C of E has gone mad! I know that you want to retire fairly soon but I can't imagine why "they" (whoever "they" are nowa-days!) haven't persuaded you to go to York for 4 or 5 years.' Oliver, he thought, 'stood out head and shoulders' above almost all his colleagues. But the decision to retire was quite irrevocable. 'This has been a *lovely* job,' he wrote to Coggan next year, 'but I'm certain I'm right to go now. Ever since the doctors began to bark at me 3 or 4 years ago, I have been able only to sustain a workload which leaves so many important things undone after doing what cannot be avoided.'

Michael Ramsey retired late in 1974 and Oliver set his own retirement date for 1 October 1975, just two months before John Moorman's in Ripon. John Tinsley, Professor of Theology in Leeds, was to be Oliver's successor. Unlike his own prede-cessor he took no part whatever in choosing the new Bishop of Bristol just as, more surprisingly, he had taken no part in the choice of his old friend, Horace Dammers, to be Dean of Bristol two years earlier. Oliver was never one to go a step across the fron-tiers of his authority. In fact he had hardly known Tinsley, though they sat beside one another at Uppsala. But he was happy with the choice. A retirement home was chosen in Worcester where Robin Woods, its bishop, was very welcoming. Bristol University awarded him an honorary doctorate and there was a final Cathedral service of thanks-giving and farewell which both Ursula and Oliver found very moving. 'I feel quite "poured out" ', he scribbled in a brief *Laus Deo* on 1 October, 'deep down, very tired. We've given all we'd got.' A few hours earlier he had written what was probably his last letter as bishop. It was to Philip Potter, General Secretary of the World Council, assuring him, 'On the day before I retire as Bishop of Bristol... that Oliver Tomkins, in his retirement, will continue to work and pray for the Ecumenical Movement and not least for the way in which the World Council embodies it.'

# 8

# Living with retirement

'Lord, there comes a point when all powers diminish: I am growing slower, stupider, weaker, less alive. Grant me to accept this with fortitude. It is good to be brave but it is better to be joyful. All this experience of diminishment can also be a joyful discovery that your strength is made perfect in weakness.'[1]

Oliver's final service to the diocese of Bristol was to be one of the two 'presenters' of his successor, John Tinsley, at his episcopal consecration, just as George Cockin had presented him. It was on the feast of the Epiphany 1976, 17 years to the day since his own consecration. By then he and Ursula were settled in Worcester in 'retirement'. 14 St George's Square was a tall, pleasant house in a leafy Victorian cul-de-sac leading up to the church of St George. It was not here, however, but the cathedral which soon became Ursula and Oliver's regular place of worship. Oliver had no desire to appear episcopal, or even sacerdotal, when not called to a specific job of work. For the first time he and Ursula could simply be a couple together in church week by week, just as they could share domesticity at the sink or in the garden. He liked that. Her companionship meant so much to him and recognition, as he put it in 1983 in her seventieth birthday poem:

> ... That there is fresh delight which even more enriches life
> Than when we shared the raptured night.

The harvest of a lifelong fidelity is reaped for many elderly couples as work and status fade away. So it was for both of them. The retention of Bryn Cottage and regular holidays there, with or without other members of the family, further sustained the sense of domestic continuity. At the same time the fact that his old friends, Robin Woods and Tom Baker, were respectively, bishop and dean – and worked well together, unlike some bishops and deans – made Worcester deeply congenial. Baker had been his deputy at Lincoln while Woods he had known since Cambridge days. He later wrote the life of his father, presented him at his consecration in St Paul's, and borrowed the Woods cottage on the Welsh coast before he was able to buy one of his own. Oliver became an assistant to Robin and in his earlier Worcester years did much for him, taking confirmations as required. Beyond that he was a member of the 9.30 Sunday family service congregation at the cathedral as well as, quite soon, Anglican President of the Worcester Council of Churches, to which he gave a great deal of time, retaining thereby a gently presidential role. He often presided too at the weekly service of healing in the cathedral crypt. And he continued to display enthusiastic support for Taizé and all it stood for. On leaving Bristol the rather taut side of his character committed to the efficient control of things could give place to the apparently more languid listener with a gentle smile and fatherly kindness. Not that people in Bristol had found him unkind – the unanimous memory is precisely how kind he was – but that internally he felt the demonstration of love constrained by the requirements of office.

Through the Council of Churches he made many friends and was able to exercise a personal pastoral ministry in his own right. He and Ursula were continually hospitable both in St George's Square and by lending Bryn to anyone needing a holiday. It was the quality of his kindness, gently reserved and unsentimental but quite unfailing, which most enduringly impressed all who knew him in Worcester. In Worcester as in Bristol the word 'kind' keeps coming back. If there was plenty to do, pressures were no longer great. There was time. Time to read quietly, to visit the family, to take extended holidays – in the Holy Land, the west of Scotland, Florence, Norway, or just Bryn. Time simply to be. Time to celebrate in a light-hearted way the relationships of love he enjoyed so much. Thus when his daughter Ruth turned up on her 39th birthday in February 1985, just after he had undergone a hernia operation, he could celebrate it poetically:

For Ruth
Our very caring daughter, 7 Feb. 1985

Forty seems a frightening age
Until you really reach that stage
   And find it's not so bad!
But you are in your thirties still
And bring a wife and mother's skill
   To cheer your battered dad.

So – thank you for your loving care
And all the goodies that you share
   To help us on our way.
It's fun to have our little girl
Descend upon us in a whirl
   Upon her natal day!

Or, again, when that same year a great-nephew was given the name 'Oliver' he responded with a 'Chanson d'Oliver':

Oliver David Matthew Smeeth
You enter a tribe who all bequeath
A range of gifts for you to store:
There's Oliver Twist who asked for more
And begged you 'Consider yourself at home'.
The 'Song of Roland' is an Oliver tome
Where Charlemagne's paladins join in strife:
Oliver Goldsmith's tip for life
Was 'he who fights and runs away
May live to fight another day',
A sentiment you'll not detect or
Hear from O. the Great Protector,
A soldier much maligned, but when
Beloved was called 'Our First of Men',
Not to mention a host of others
Whom you inherit as namesake brothers,
So, let the least of them offer a wreath
Of *peaceful olive* to Oliver Smeeth.

The poem was accompanied with notes about 'The Olive Tree'. It belongs to a large family, cultivated since pre-historic time and lives to a great age. Olive Oil is used for giving light, healing, anointing, crowning, not to mention cooking, oiling the wheels and being poured on troubled waters, while the Olive Branch became an emblem of Peace – of national and domestic plenty. All things Oliver valued greatly. They symbolized himself.

There was greater freedom then to dabble or again express personal convictions without an official tag. Thus he enjoyed a last mild political fling by joining the newly formed Social Democratic Party and he felt free to receive communion from a woman minister of the URC. Nevertheless there were plenty of calls to respond to – retreats and sermons to preach, special invitations to this or that, to attend the golden jubilee celebration for Faith and Order in Lausanne in 1977 or a conference later that year in Sofia of the European Council of Churches. In 1978 he was a member of a three-man group appointed by Donald Coggan to report on 'The future role of the Archbishop of Canterbury' which cautiously recommended diminishing the diocesan side of things to find more room for a 'patriarchal' role (a word which does not appear in the Report but is used by Oliver in his journal). It was a direction that both Runcie and Carey would endeavour to follow. In 1979 there was a less happy experience when he resigned from 'Nobody's Friends', a dining club which brings together senior Anglican clerics and a range of other establishment people, meeting three times a year, usually in the Guard Room at Lambeth Palace. It operated a black-ball rule enabling the prejudices of just two members to block new names proposed. Although, under pressure from Oliver and others, the rule was changed from two to four, he still felt it was wrong in principle, given the amount of work which went into the selection process before the final members' vote. A close friend had been blocked and he knew of other cases: 'Too many good men have been hurt'. Being, as he described himself, 'temperamentally a compromiser', it was a hard and unusual decision to set his face against something so close to the inner core of church and state and it further saddened him that the Club's officers would not agree to read his very mildly worded letter of explanation at the next dinner, but he had always found the excessively establishment nature of the club somewhat irritating. The person in question was in fact elected to the club a few years later.[2]

1980, on the contrary included the particularly happy occasion of leading the retreat at Canterbury in March for Robert Runcie and 20 other Primates of the Anglican Communion prior to Runcie's enthronement as Archbishop. Once again, as many times in the past, he based his instruction on his favourite text on the ministry – II Corinthians 4. He had used it first in 1935. He treasured particularly the memory of Lindy Runcie after the service deeply worried at having missed her music professor and his lame wife in the crowd, 'a fact that worried her far more than being due to give tea at the Old Palace to the Prince of Wales'. Two years later he could rejoice in Pope John Paul's visit to England. Watching him on television visiting first the Anglican and then the Catholic cathedral at Liverpool he found it 'a gesture of truly miraculous transfiguration of relationships ... a vindication, such as I scarcely dreamed to see, of the vision which has inspired so much of what I have striven for for fifty years'. Again, in 1984, he was delighted to see his old student David Jenkins appointed Bishop of Durham and to be one of the presenters at his consecration in York Minster. It was the last time he would perform that role.

As soon as he retired Oliver began to plan a book. He had things on his mind which friends and publishers encouraged him to develop. Already in December 1975 he had sketched out quite an ambitious plan of reflection upon the major mutation of history he felt himself to be living within and its effect upon the form of the Church. Later it turned more into a study of spirituality, entitled *The Ring of Light*, that side of the ecumenical movement inspired by Couturier which had not faded away. There were charming pages on some of his favourite topics – Van Gogh, Dame Julian, Rublev's Trinity. But there was no central theme quite strong enough or original enough to hold the book as a whole interestingly together for the wider reader. Publisher after publisher turned it down to Oliver's considerable distress. Ten years later he was still hoping to find someone to take it, explaining that 'the many, many hours that I have been obliged to spend in church unity discussions which had apparently had no fruit, needed to be justified by showing that visible unity is a necessary fruit of taking seriously the Holy Trinity'.[3] Earlier than that he had confided to himself that 'I am beginning to think that the motive for writing at all was to compensate for a sense of mute failure at the end of my time in Bristol'. Oliver felt painfully the rejection of his book and never quite understood why it should be. It was the principal failure of his years of retirement but perhaps, in the odd ways of sanctification, it too was needed to prevent him finding too easily the mirage of a spiritual escape route from the ecumenical cul-de-sac in which, as he saw it, the central ecumenical enterprise of his life had ended. In truth, it had not. The book's best pages were in fact published in 1986 as a pamphlet by the Fairacres Community, *Prayer for Unity*, a meditation on John 17 and Rublev's icon of the Trinity. The ecumenical community over which he presided at Worcester, symbolized by the inspired transformation of St Wulfstan's crypt beneath the cathedral into a chapel of unity, was proof of victory, not defeat, and of victory precisely at the local level which he had always seen as the most important. The consciousness of more and more ordinary Christians had changed irrevocably. Youth, he reflected at the Lausanne jubilee, now 'behave as though the barriers were not there'. He delighted to find himself in the cathedral of Lausanne concelebrating with the Moderator of the Swiss Reformed Church and giving communion to a dozen Catholic choristers while Lukas Vischer administered the chalice. Oliver did see that the movement to which he gave his life had not in the reality of people's lives lacked fruit but he could not quite shake his mind free of the conviction that it was the achievement of 'organic unity' which separated success from failure.

If *The Ring of Light* did not reach publication, another smaller work completed in the Worcester years eventually did so – his book of prayers. Perhaps he never thought of it as publishable but, after his death, his daughter Deborah realized that it was. The sensitive immediacy of these prayers reflects what was freshest in Oliver's personal spirituality in a way that the slightly ponderous presentation of *The Ring of Light* fails to do. People who knew him well, especially his priests, have found in these prayers an enlightening guide, not only to the uses of prayer, but also to an understanding of Oliver's own inward nature.

One cause which came close to his heart in these years of retirement was the ordination of women and he wrote a powerful little plea for this in 1984, *A Fully Human Priesthood*. In it he remembers that already 50 years earlier, when in Sheffield, he had said to himself 'Clearly women ought to be ordained but the time is not ripe.' That long remained his opinion. As a bishop he advanced the ministry of women in many areas, especially of university and hospital chaplaincy, but was not in the vanguard of a campaign for their ordination, being well aware that a step forward here could prove a step backward ecumenically, given Roman Catholic and Orthodox opposition. Only in retirement did he feel a new freedom to speak out, becoming chairman of the local group for the ordination of women though even in 1978 when General Synod turned down legislation to allow it he was only able to comment 'I *think* I should have been among the bishops voting to proceed'. But when, nine years later, the first ordination of women to the diaconate did take place, he was delighted to be able to lead the Worcester diocesan deaconesses in their pre-ordination retreat, held at Stanbrook Abbey, and then preach in the cathedral at the ordination ceremony.

In 1988 Oliver was 80, but still fit enough to make several weighty further contributions to the ecumenical conversation. The first was for the fortieth anniversary of the World Council's opening assembly. In its commemorative volume Oliver's chapter comes first, 'A Personal Retrospect and Assessment'.[4] He was in fact Amsterdam's last major survivor and his memories of that exciting spring time 40 years earlier remained remarkably fresh. The second was a survey of 'The Contribution of Anglicanism to the Ecumenical Movement' for an Italian symposium, and the third an opening paper at a conference at Cuddesdon in April on 'The Lambeth Quadrilateral and the Ecumenical Movement'. The conference, chaired by Henry Chadwick, was celebrating the centenary of the Quadrilateral. The fourth, most moving, piece, in this Indian Summer of ecumenical writing, was an address delivered at Bristol in May for the 250th anniversary of John Wesley's conversion – 'A Church Strangely Warmed'[5] – on the Anglican debt to Methodism. It was a deeply felt account at once of the eighteenth-century debt and of his own long personal association with Methodism. These four papers well suggest, not only how entirely committed to the Ecumenical Movement in all its dimensions Oliver remained to the end, but also how completely on top of his subject. In regard to the 1980s he welcomed particularly the stress by the Vancouver World Council Assembly in 1983 on the 'eucharistic vision' of Church unity, and Faith and Order's Lima Statement on 'Baptism, Eucharist and Ministry'. Oliver remained confident that 'The Ecumenical Movement still moves'.

Life seemed increasingly shaped by commemorations, funerals, memorial services, books about the dead. Martin Niemöller died in 1984, Wim Visser't Hooft in 1985, Dick Milford in 1987, Michael Ramsey in 1988 and Kathleen Bliss in 1989.[6] Reading Owen Chadwick's life of Michael Ramsey, Oliver would stop and say to himself, sometimes out loud, '*Dear* Michael, *dear* Michael': 'How marvellously he evoked our love above and beyond the occasional irritations'. He went with Ursula to Swanwick in 1990 for the obsequies of the BCC and its replacement by a 'Council of Churches in Britain and Ireland' to include Roman Catholics, invited as one of a group of 'oldies' to witness the great change. He easily won 'the old age stakes' as having come to an SCM Swanwick already in 1926 and walking through the gardens he felt around him 'a hundred beloved ghosts'.

The first draft of Ursula's birthday poem for 1988 was headed '2. Cor. 4.16: though the outward man perish the inward man is renewed day by day'. Yet again he had returned to his favourite Pauline chapter.

7<sup>th</sup> April 1988 To my darling<br>For Ursula on her 75<sup>th</sup> birthday

Machines wear out. And so
Do bodies. It has been
A simply wonderful machine,
But now is marked 'Go slow'.

Machines do not have eyes, nor yet
   A sense of humour

> To beget a rumour
> Of eternity beyond the limping gait.
>
> Eyes are windows of a soul;
> Laughter has its hidden springs
> Replenished deep within the whole
> Complexity of silence.
>
> Sings an April blackbird 'New, new, new
> Are these diamonds of dew!
> Although the outer must decay
> The inner is renewed each day!'

Oliver's retirement years proved far more important than is generally the case for someone retiring about 67. His influence flowered anew just because he felt no longer constrained by the requirements of office and he is remembered in Worcester as warmly as in Bristol.

Living on their own at Worcester, however, became too much of a struggle and in 1989 the decision was taken to move to Dorking to be as close as possible to their daughter Ruth. At the same time, tidy as ever, Oliver had been through his papers, selecting what was to be kept, distributing some across various libraries, destroying the rest. But he knew that what he retained would be studied by others and he intended that to happen. Problems in selling the house delayed their move for almost two years in a way that Oliver, with quickly deteriorating health, found confusing. They actually moved to Dorking on Shrove Tuesday, 1991. Canon Winifred Young recalls their last meeting in Worcester, on 25 January, the close of the Unity Octave and always a special day for Oliver. They had a pub lunch with Tom Baker and Oliver amused them reflecting on one of his favourite topics, the manifold English pronunciations of '–ough'; she remembers him a very frail figure walking slowly and courageously up the garden path of 14 St George's Square amid swirling flakes of snow. 'There can always be new beginnings even near the end of the road', the message on Oliver and Ursula's change of address card was defiantly positive but the end of the road in earthly terms was even nearer than expected. For a few months there were still books to read, people to write to or even visit, twice to 'dear old' David Paton struggling to 'reach him through the cloud of his impeded speech and often confused mind'. All in all David had been the oldest and closest of his allies. Good news came when Terry Waite was released from his long imprisonment in Beirut. Oliver was utterly delighted. Waite had worked in the Bristol diocese and Oliver had recommended him to Archbishop Runcie so he always felt some responsibility for what followed. Now that Terry was freed, the video of his coming off the plane on return to England was watched by Oliver almost obsessively.

The opening entry in the journal for 1992 is for Lent: 'Still unsure, after re-retirement, what I am for!' He could not quite accept that presence and prayer could be enough in themselves and was still struggling to compose something, in fact a meditation upon the Lord's Prayer 'Pater Noster Pondered'. It ended on the line 'Thy will be done', with words borrowed from Charles de Foucauld: 'Do with me what you will. Whatever you do, I thank you: I am ready for all, I accept all. Let only your will be done in me, and all your creatures. I wish no more than this, Heavenly Father. Into your hands I commend my soul. I offer it to you with all the love I can. For I *do* love you, in spite of all the failures. I do love you, and need to give myself to you; to surrender myself without reserve into your hands, in complete trust, for you are my Father.'

Books could still be read: *The Old Curiosity Shop*, Konrad Raiser's *Ecumenism in Transition* and *Twelve Sayings of the Mystics* were the last titles to be listed, but there were 60 in all for 1992 including John Mortimer's *Rumpole and the Age of Miracles* and a couple of Agatha Christie novels but also Vernon White's *Incarnation and Atonement* – the mix was much as it had always been. Reading Edward Carpenter's life of Fisher reminded him of the 'often abrasive letters to me from Trent Rectory rejecting the notion of *Organic union*' and raising 'the whole business of "reconciled diversity" now so fashionable'.

There remains a striking harmony between the Oliver of these last months and the Oliver of 30 or even 60 years earlier; the same questions, the same sort of reading matter, the same underlying certainties and uncertainties, the same circle of friends even if most were now 'beloved ghosts', the same urge to be useful. In June 1992 there was a lovely last holiday in Guernsey made possible by Monica's attendance as care-taker and chauffeuse. On returning home he quickly felt ill, an inoperable cancer was diagnosed and he had to make ready for the final 'new beginning', through a series of rather miserable admissions to hospitals in Crawley, Guildford and Reigate – the consequence of commitment to a creaking National Health Service – and then for a blessed last three days in the Princess Alice Hospice, Esher. In hospital he was pleased by a visit from Terry Waite which he had been longing for ever since Terry's release. At the hospice the only non-family visitor was Mary Tanner who had in her way taken over Oliver's ecumenical mantle, becoming Moderator of the World Council's Faith and Order Commission and now received his final blessing. Even in bed he still needed to feel in control, checking up that he had received the right medication and recording it in a little notebook. All his life he had been in control, able to minister responsibly and gently to others, to whom, even his children, he seemed a very Superman. Only ministering to his own need remained, the very need to feel he was ministered to in the fears engendered by dying. One night he dreamt that he had pressed and pressed the buzzer by his bed. No one had come, instead a printer churned out for him page upon page of 'The Patient's Charter'. He woke in a sweat and did indeed press his buzzer. A nurse came over and Oliver explained his dream and his fear of being alone. He squeezed his hand saying 'It's all right, I am here if you need me.'

> Olive branches promise peace
> And your oil is matter for the healing sacrament.
> Olive trees of Tuscany,
> There is still work for you to do.

Thus Oliver ended the poem on the 'Olive Trees of Fiesole' written on a visit there while Ursula was drawing and painting in 1983. The time had arrived for final anointing with his own Olive Oil.

Bishop David Wilcox of Dorking, one of his old Lincoln students, came to do so in the hospice. After reading a piece from *Pilgrim's Progress* he anointed his old teacher ending with the words 'Go forth upon thy journey, Christian soul'. Suddenly Oliver looked up alert demanding to know where Wilcox had got the anointing prayers from. From the latest ASB additions, he replied. After Bishop David had gone, Oliver gave his daughters a little lecture on how long it had taken the Liturgical Commission to come up with an agreed version, given Evangelical objections to prayers for the dead. He added that they were much impoverished by refusing to use the traditional liturgies. His daughters were quite taken aback by this sudden upsurge of the episcopal teacher, still anxious to explain things to others on his own deathbed. Two days later, 29 October, he died with Ursula and his four children around him. They prayed and sang and then Stephen said: 'Let's go and have a sherry'; there were five glasses, no longer six. The bare numerical alteration struck them all. 'Dying seems so often more difficult than it should be. God grant that Oliver soon gets over to the resurrection side of things', David Jenkins had written to Ursula and she was thankful when it was over. But it was encouraging to receive that firmly orthodox assertion of resurrection at the moment of death from a bishop theologian whom others had denounced for a dangerous liberalism but whom Oliver had always deeply trusted.

Oliver Stratford Tomkins was buried at Bristol on 9 November 1992. Bishop Bell's mitre and a wooden shepherd's crook lay upon the coffin. Two months later, in the Week of Prayer for Christian Unity, Mary Tanner gave the address at the memorial service in St Margaret's, Westminster. Oliver's favourite Rublev icon, symbol of the circulating life of God in which humanity is called to share, was placed before the congregation. He had so wanted it to adorn the cover of *The Ring of Light*. Mary Tanner recalled its symbolism as she recalled too Oliver's meeting in 1949 with the Abbé Couturier, principal source of the Week of Prayer's universal appeal, and the Abbé's words murmured and passed on from lip to lip, 'la charité c'est tout, la charité c'est tout'. On Oliver's tombstone beside Bristol Cathedral are the simple Gospel words from John 17.21 which had defined his work throughout life, 'May they all be one'.

# 9

# A time for snowdrops?
# Reflections on the enterprise

In March 1976 Oliver wrote a long letter to Philip Potter commenting on the current state of the ecumenical movement in the aftermath of the Nairobi Assembly. Much of it had to do with the rather poor state of relations between the Church of England and the World Council stimulated by widespread dislike in Britain of the Programme to Combat Racism, a programme which Oliver had defended publicly but distrusted privately. Towards the end of the letter he raised a point about which, he said:

> [It is] more difficult to be objective. It is related to a remark of yours I saw reported somewhere about Nairobi marking the end of an 'élitist' phase in the life of the WCC. Belonging, as I do, to that condemned élite... I find it hard to describe the change of ethos which made the post-Uppsala phase baffling. It is not simply the end of the era in which the white westerner dominated; that I welcome and have tried to interpret positively. It has more to do with what in the widest sense I can only call 'liberalism'... a whole cultural temper which valued thought above slogans, consensus above confrontation, self-criticism above propaganda, tolerance above crusading.

He added, however, that reports from Nairobi suggested to him that a new openness and mutual trust were now developing within the World Council.

In reply Potter confessed that he found being General Secretary of the World Council gruesomely hard, particularly for someone who did not want to exercise 'power' and was in consequence blamed for failing to provide 'leadership'. Taking up the issue of élitism, he insisted that he himself belonged to 'the élitist group' which had dominated the ecumenical movement for two generations ever since he was drawn into it by Oliver and others in the mid-1940s. He was not an outsider even if, as black, he might not have been wholly accepted. He then went on to admit that:

> the old élite or club had two precious characteristics which no longer exist to any significant extent – however hard our debates, we were all committed to the ecumenical cause beyond our own ambitions, and we were loyal to each other. It is a tragic fact that this double loyalty has practically evaporated. Secondly, the ecumenical movement has no future unless the churches and the people are involved. That means that we cannot go on behaving as an avant-garde who will be followed in due course. Wim used to say that it takes ten years for an idea to be taken up. We were the producers of ideas, and went on producing ideas in the hope (assumed, but not fostered) that our precious ideas would be taken up one day.

That second point was something of which Oliver had always been acutely aware: the ideas of the avant-garde had got to be localized or perish.

The truth is that in all sorts of ways the 1970s witnessed a transformation, which could look gloomily like a collapse, of the ecumenical movement as Oliver had known and served it all his life. An analysis of that transformation can well put first the change of personnel, the passing of that quite small 'élite' group to which Oliver had belonged from the mid-1930s. It was partly a sheer matter of ageing. They could not go on for ever but it remains striking how a few dozen people had so largely controlled the World Council until Uppsala and how ill at ease they already felt at Uppsala. The core of the group had been British. When it went, a certain sense of intimate, almost club, loyalty, went too but the change was not just a matter of replacing a founding élite, it was more profoundly a matter of culture and continent. The departure of the old hands went with a massive and rapid shift within the World Council from north to south. The Programme to Combat Racism and the tensions it generated were little more than a totem pole for a far wider shift in the World Council's staff and preoccupations. Given that hostility to the Programme was so notably in the Church of England, it was the more ironic that the crucial decisions had been taken at a meeting in Canterbury which Oliver among others had attended. At the time he does not seem to have felt the reservations which later privately disturbed him. But the underlying point remains that a very different crew was now in control of the ship which had been manned ever since it was first launched by a single group of rather upper-class, mostly Anglo-Saxon, whites. The collapse of the SCM in Britain in the 1960s also helped to ensure that the British ecumenists of the next generation, people like Horace Dammers, Bob Jeffery, Mary Tanner and Martin Reardon, never enjoyed quite the same wide backing or occupied positions of comparable authority either in England or in Geneva. Patrick Rodger was the last Anglican to possess such a double belonging. Oliver had no real successor. The sole British replacement in the top WCC echelon was, characteristically for the new age, a woman and a Methodist, Pauline Webb.

All of this sadly contributed to the widespread loss of interest in Britain, at least among Anglicans, in the ecumenical movement in so far as it was centred in Geneva. Given the key position of the World Council within Christian history from the 1930s to the 1960s and the immense role that British people had occupied in that history from the time of Temple, Oldham, William Paton and Bell, it is extraordinary, even distressing, to see how both the British presence in the WCC and the WCC presence in British religious consciousness had been marginalized by the 1980s. Perhaps it was part of the disorientation, pettiness and crude nationalist phobias of a post-imperial age.

In regard to the achievement of unity Oliver had been throughout primarily a multilateralist, something necessitated by his deep involvement in the World Council which could not, as such, concern itself with negotiations between just two churches or traditions. Oliver, however, himself always saw the one as preparatory to the other in a way that Visser't Hooft almost certainly did not. For Wim the fundamental unity of the Church was given by God. It did not need in any way to be negotiated. What was needed was that it should be better reflected in the behaviour of the churches and that there should be at all levels a more fruitful interaction between them. This could be achieved by the World Council. For Wim, one feels, if the WCC worked well, nothing much more was required. For Oliver that was not the case. Faith and Order was crucial to him as it was not to Wim, and Faith and Order meant in his mind preparing the way theologically for some sort of 'organic unity', of which the model remained that of the Church of South India. The integrated unity of 'all in each place' defined by Newbigin and tenaciously adopted by Oliver was central to all the unity schemes of the period. It was what he hoped to bring about in Britain through the stimulus provided by the Nottingham

Conference and the achievement of Anglican–Methodist unity as a core around which a still larger unification could be realised. When Nottingham took place the message put out was that similar schemes of organic unity were about to be realized in Sri Lanka, Ghana, Nigeria, Zambia and elsewhere. Only Britain lagged behind. Seven years later not only had the British Anglican–Methodist scheme collapsed but so had most of those in other countries. Where a United Church had come into existence, as in Zambia, Anglicans had not joined it (any more than had the Dutch Reformed, the Baptists or the African Methodist Episcopal Church). The only truly significant sequel to South India was the Church of North India and Pakistan inaugurated in 1970.

It is hard in retrospect not to conclude that the ideal of 'organic unity' of 'all in each place' was unworkable, a too simplistic attempt to straighten out the complexities of Christian history, practice and life style, at least when closely tied in reality to its model, the Church of South India. It required the imposition of local uniformity and the abandonment of denominational traditions well beyond what most ordinary Christians could welcome in places where denominations had lived side by side for generations. For ecumaniacs when Oliver was young 'denominationalism' was almost a sin. He never had much patience with Archbishop Fisher's position, put forward again and again after retirement, that all the denominations should be in communion with one another but should otherwise continue on their own lines, at least so long as they conveniently took 'episcopacy' somehow into their system. It was not a very satisfying position from the viewpoint of creatively overcoming the schisms of the past and demonstrating that Christians really could live and work as a single body, drawing together on what is best in each tradition. Rather it seemed to canonize all the often one-sided stresses of particular denominations. It lacked the spirit of repentance and, almost equally, that of renewal. Ecumenicists wanted to draw together the best from every tradition within a new synthesis, yet faithful to the simplicities of a New Testament model. Good as so Utopian an ideal is, once it becomes a matter of joint commissions drawing up lengthy documents for a new 'organic' unity, it turns into something far more bureaucratic through which it seems virtually impossible to preserve the best in each tradition. Rather is one or another likely to prevail in what may seem to become no more than yet another 'denomination'. By the 1980s 'denominationalism' was, however, much better regarded and the health of the world church was seen even by ecumenically minded people far more in terms of an open, interactive development of numerous worldwide communions – Anglican, Methodist, Lutheran, what Lutherans have called 'reconciled diversity'. The logic of CSI had been instead that all such denominationally named communions would cease as such to exist once in each place a single organic unity was established.

Oliver once referred to the fact that as a bishop he could appreciate far better 'the conflict of loyalties that is involved in being both a bishop of the diocese and a bishop of the Church as a whole' experienced by George Bell: how to be a thoroughly Anglican bishop and at the same time a leader of the ecumenical movement. It was clear, for instance, how in 1963 the Faith and Order meeting in Montreal mattered to him vastly more than the Anglican Congress in Toronto the following month, while for Michael Ramsey it was the other way round. For Oliver it was always a secret strain to hold together two such deep loyalties -- to Anglicanism and to the ecumenical church. On his basic theoretical model the worldwide Anglican Communion needed to die for the ecumene to thrive, but increasingly he found this difficult to admit to. No one can reconcile all the antinomies. The paradox in Oliver was how deeply he belonged to the centre of his own tradition and yet how genuinely he was a frontiersman.

When confronted with the argument that the organic unity of 'all in each place' required uniformity, an unecumenical quality, Oliver would argue that diversity would survive between places. It was, anyway, never clear what 'place' really meant. Was England a 'place', or London, or just Worcester, or something even smaller? Even the claim that this had been largely achieved in South India was really a delusion. People in Britain tended to point to it as the example of an achieved local Christian unity, as if a new 'national' church had come into existence in the southern half of the sub-continent. Nothing in reality was further from the truth. The oldest, largest and most indigenous groups of Christians in South India took no part in the CSI, that is to say the Syrian Churches, the Lutheran Church and, most numerous of all, the Roman Catholic Church with its three rites (the Syro-Malabar, the Malankara and the Latin). Even the Mar Thoma Church was not included. It is ironic that when a South Indian Christian came to head the WCC in the person of M. M. Thomas, he was not a member of the CSI but of Mar Thoma. Despite Newbigin's persuasive powers, South India had actually demonstrated that an 'all in each place' model of organic unity was too narrowly conceived to unite Christians. It could only unite groups already rather close to one another and, even then, with considerable strain. Denominational tradition was simply too strong. A realizable unity could not, in this sense, be 'organic'. Already in 1971 Eric Kemp, one of the stoutest supporters of Anglican–Methodist unity, while describing the opposition of John Macquarrie, Lady Margaret Professor of Divinity at Oxford, to the whole idea of organic unity as 'somewhat irresponsible', added in a letter to Oliver, 'We all agreed with him that organic union is not necessarily the right answer in every situation, and to that extent I think we did not wholly accept the arguments put forward at Lund and New Delhi about all in one place' (27 July 1971). Oliver himself seems never quite to have faced up to the unworkability of the formula he struggled for so valiantly, but he was quite flexible over ways of implementing it and did, for instance, at one point suggest rescuing Anglican–Methodist unity by switching from a two-stage to a single stage scheme. But others, probably rightly, insisted that it was far too late to start rewriting the proposals.

There was, however, another factor which helped ensure the collapse of the ecumenical enterprise in the form that it had taken in the 1940s through to the 1960s, and that was the entry into the field of the Roman Catholic Church. Up till the time of Pope John it was perfectly reasonable for ecumenists to express distress over Rome's negative response to their endeavours and then go on to attempt to bring about the unity of all non-RC Christians. In reality even this was always a highly fragile enterprise, especially in regard to the principal Orthodox Churches. Their always rather limited willingness to cooperate owed over much to understandable but fairly opportunistic political motives. Then came the Vatican Council to create a profoundly new situation. It was for some time difficult for ecumenical leaders to decide quite how new. Oliver himself was notably cautious though no one had proved himself more anxious to develop good relations with Catholics. However, by the time the Council was over and the Secretariat of Unity busily at work setting up bilateral dialogues in all directions, it was becoming clear that the underlying presuppositions of the ecumenical movement as a whole required rethinking. Even if it were possible to achieve the unification of numerous Protestant bodies into 'one' larger church, could that really answer to the underlying theological and missionary rationale which had brought the ecumenical movement into being? If the Roman Catholic Church was in any way prepared to cooperate in the achievement of unity then – given that Catholics constituted something like half the world's Christians – there could be little sense in pressing forward towards some lesser and easier goal which would exclude them.

Such a line of thought appealed particularly to many Anglicans such as John Moorman. This tended to irritate Oliver who, so far as one can see, did not quite recognize until after retirement how profoundly the scene had changed. In May 1991, near the very end of his life, he commented on 'what Kenneth Greet called the "cul de sac" of my generation of ecumenists' with the remark that 'the *determining* factor in the change of key was when Rome, after Vatican II no longer just said No, No, No!'[1] It soon became obvious that many of the most committed and thoughtful ecumenists were in fact Catholics. Nevertheless it was in no way clear what the aim should now be. While Catholics had moved a long way and, initially, Genevan old-hands could pursue ideas of somehow incorporating Roman Catholicism within the framework of the World Council and its existent ideals (something which actually did happen in Oliver's own patch, the Commission of Faith and Order) it came gradually to be accepted that this was neither desirable nor workable. Catholics had entered too far into the ecumenical world for the latter to continue with its basic goals substantially unchanged, but not far enough to offer any alternative model for unity which most Protestants or the Orthodox could conceivably accept. Beneath the new cordiality a profound impasse was reached in consequence, an impasse temporarily hidden by the World Council's enhanced political preoccupations in the 1970s.

When the Anglican–Methodist project finally collapsed in 1972 Oliver could at first see no way forward other than that of the Local Ecumenical Projects officially launched back at Nottingham. Yet here too, despite an initial enthusiasm to get them going in which he shared, the problems were enormous and often irresolvable, given the anxiety of almost all church leadership to retain a considerable degree of control over what developed. The fact is that this sort of way forward could only work if it really was free to experiment, yet the word 'experiment' was rapidly and deliberately dropped. By and large the LEPs have achieved less and been fewer than Oliver and his ecumenical colleagues hoped. Nevertheless they did help both to stimulate and to symbolize a basic reality: the quiet advance of ecumenical consciousness at the local level of ordinary Christians in almost all churches, Oliver's favoured 'grass roots'. Few people might want to abandon their own denominational characteristics entirely but they did, increasingly, regard them as less decisively important. It can well be claimed that if the middle phase of the ecumenical movement, that of Oliver's lengthy ministry, failed in its institutional aims, it succeeded both intellectually and spiritually more than most people realized. A new consciousness was emerging irresistibly. That success was bound to come slowly and look partial and patchy. Oliver had himself always insisted that what mattered was what was local and seemed at times almost neurotically anxious to become 'local' himself. For a leader it was hardly practicable. Perhaps only in retirement with no wider responsibility than the honorary presidency of the Worcester Council of Churches could he really stimulate personally the 'local' advance he had so much desired. The problem remained, and remains, how to replicate at local level the kind of experience which the SCM generated inside universities in the 1930s or the WCC itself generated for people like Oliver who regularly attended its gatherings. By far the best way of doing this is shared prayer but for most Christians, particularly Catholics, Orthodox, Anglicans and Lutherans, by far the most regular and important form of public prayer is the celebration of the eucharist. Full participation in the eucharist means communion and, if Christians of different traditions are to come effectively and regularly together through prayer, that can hardly not mean sharing communion together: eating together the body of Christ to become together the body of Christ. So we return to the issue of intercommunion, a matter over which

Christians actively represented in the ecumenical movement struggled from the 1937 Edinburgh Conference onward. Oliver's commission on the subject in its majority recommendations distinguished fairly firmly between the admission to holy communion of individuals on pastoral grounds as something exceptional even if common and 'recip- rocal communion' as 'a corporate matter which involves churches as such rather than their individual members and must be considered in relation to the intention to achieve organic union or full communion'.[2] If the acceptability of intercommunion is circum- scribed in this way it has rightly to be refused when there is no such corporate (i.e. institutional) intention. As a matter of fact, however, when General Synod failed to ratify that corporate intention, Geoffrey Lampe, the leading academic theologian in Oliver's majority, at once declared that he would now simply back intercommunion regardless of such conditions. Many Anglicans agreed with him. Oliver's preferred position, one in which institutional control was not foregone, was thus undermined. The issue has since become acute also for Roman Catholics and it remains so for Orthodoxy.

In retirement Oliver soon came to recognize that the position on intercommunion proposed by his commission was out-dated. Within the anomaly of Christian disunity, he told a Catholic priest in the 1980s, if you receive communion outside your communion you are witnessing to the unity that already exists, while if you refrain from so doing you witness to the great work of reconciliation still to be achieved, and both are witnesses to the gospel. Oliver fell back here once more on his both-and-ness, able thus to make sense of, but also transcend, the pain of that occasion in 1962 at Taizé when the new Church of the Reconciliation was dedicated with such fervour but he had not gone up to communion while his daughter Monica and other fellow-Anglicans had done so. Then he had felt impaled on the horns of an either-or. Now it had come to seem another case of both-and.

It seems reasonable to suggest that it was mistaken theologically to make the matter turn principally on the corporate intention of particular 'churches' rather than on the rights and duties of individual Christians. Could it not be the case that there really is, after all, only one Church and only one baptism? Everyone who receives baptism is baptized primarily into the one Church, the body of Christ, and only quite secondarily into one or another denomination. Baptism and Eucharist are, or should be, bound indissolubly together. One is baptized into the visible body of Christ in order to share the full communion of the sacramental body of Christ. That sharing relates one not only to Christ but also to all other members of the one body. This would seem to be the most basic right of Christians which cannot be taken away by one or another church authority but only forfeited on grounds of a manifest lack of faith or grave public sin. If someone can say a genuine 'Amen' to the eucharistic prayer, it is hard to see how she or he can be convicted of faithlessness. What seems to follow is recognition that there actually is a right to intercommunion for all the baptized, which 'churches' do not have the authority to deny, or concede to, their members. There are, admittedly, personal and pastoral circumstances in which its exercise can cause scandal or hostility contrary to the spirit of love which the sacrament of its nature should promote. We may simply not be ready in mind and heart to accept the implications of our baptism vis-à-vis our fellow Christians. That can be a reason to abstain but it is one less likely to be valid today.

A divided church is, of course, as Oliver called it, 'the great anomaly'. It is unques- tionably part of the anomaly to have any measure of intercommunion involving Christians belonging to 'churches' between which there is no collegial communion in the ministry (although, once again, in practice an informal collegiality now very often exists between the bishops or chief ministers of theoretically non-communicating churches: Oliver practised the closest collegial relationship with the Chairman of the local Methodist District). Nevertheless this remains a lesser anomaly than to admit a common baptism while refusing to allow sharing in the sacrament to which baptism should necessarily lead. 'The great anomaly' is reduced considerably once it becomes one focused only on the ordained ministry and authority – important as they are – and not also on the sacrament of unity itself and its grounding in baptism. Pastorally, moreover, a growing practice of intercommunion, just like a multiplication of LEPs, must help to put pressure on church authorities to restore a basic collegial unity at the level of governance. At the Reformation the bond of communion did not break down at once. Locally sacramental unity struggled to survive well after the breakdown at the level of governmental and theological dissension. It seems right that reunion too should be something separated communities grow into almost organically. That could be the true 'organic unity'. In fact between the Latin and Greek Churches there probably never was a complete breakdown of eucharistic communion at local level.

This reflects too the fundamental nature of a sacrament, a sign which both effects and symbolizes. To argue that sharing in the 'sacrament of unity' should only come after a full restoration of unity is to eviscerate the nature of a sacrament and effectively deny what is most characteristic and encouraging in traditional Catholic theology. Communion is given to make sinners into saints, not as a reward or symbol of sanctity achieved. It is odd that it should be traditionally minded Catholics who defend most strongly this essentially anti-Catholic position. If the eucharist is indeed the sacrament of unity, then it should be allowed to create unity between Christians and not only symbolize it. The 'eucharistic vision' of Christian unity proclaimed at Vancouver, as indeed it was proclaimed at Vatican II, needs to be taken *au pied de la lettre*: the eucharist actually makes church unity in a way that nothing else that is visible can do – not institutions nor agreements nor theological texts. We are one body by sharing the one bread. Out of that sacramental oneness alone can come the institutional 'conciliarity' so much talked about in ecumenical circles from the 1970s.

Christians at the beginning of the twenty-first century have arrived at a situation in which the twentieth-century ecumenical movement to which Oliver dedicated so much of his life and energy, coupled with Vatican II, have created a consciousness of Christian community transcending denominationalism miles beyond anything which existed in the world he knew when young. To that extent the victory has been won. Yet at the same time the institutional battle was largely lost, perhaps even fortunately lost, and there is at present no plausible way to resurrect the type of scheme for reunification, with all details worked out by a multitude of committee meetings, which was so popular in his time. From that point of view we are back near to the start of things and this, too, Oliver himself recognized in his last years with the cheerful hope which was so much part of him. 'All this talk about "the winter of ecumenism"... makes me look again at the snowdrops in my garden. Perhaps God's time-scale was longer than we reckoned.'[3] He had been too easily persuaded in the excitement of the post-Montreal, post-Nottingham years, when he felt God moving faster than man could keep up, that the very summer of ecumenism had been reached. Now, instead, it was actually only February and snowdrops. But snowdrops are still signs of hope. 'Perhaps God's time-scale was longer than we reckoned.'

# Notes

## Chapter 1

1    According to an alternative, more gruesome account, Tamate was clubbed on landing but Oliver witnessed the cutting up of his body and its distribution for eating. He himself was killed next day. (O.S.T.'s journal, Easter Monday, 1951.)
2    Norman Goodall, *One Man's Testimony*, SCM Press, 1949 and 1985, p. 76.
3    G. K. Chesterton, *The Collected Poems*, Burns, Oates and Washburne, 1941, pp. 179–80.

## Chapter 2

1    Forty years later he told 'Nobody's Friends' in his 'justification' for admission that he was now REVILO LOTSIRB.
2    Late in life Oliver recorded an incident in one such evangelistic campaign in the north of England: 'At the close of the first night's pitch, we said we would leave a box into which any question could be placed (so that any shy enquirer need not be deterred). My audience had been small, but supportive at least in the person of a large workman in the front row who interjected an occasional "Allelujah" and "Praise the Lord" during my halting discourse. The next night I opened the box and read out the question on the one scrap of paper in it. "How do you induce the spirit of prayer when you feel it to be lacking?" it read. "What a good question," I said approvingly. "Aye," said the large gent in the front row, "Ah put that in – just to encourage thee – and in case tha don't know t'answer, ah've written it on t'other side."' 'A Church Strangely Warmed', *Epworth Review*, 16, 2, May 1989, p. 57.
3    Elspeth Waddilove, in *O.T. By His Friends*, p. 5.
4    See John R.H. Moorman, *B.K. Cunningham: A Memoir*, SCM Press, 1947.
5    Mervyn Stockwood, *Chanctonbury Ring*, Sheldon Press, 1982, p. 23.

## Chapter 3

1    Letter of Oliver to Ursula, 8 July 1941.
2    Francis House, *A House Family Chronicle*, unpublished manuscript, 2/25 Lambeth Palace Library.
3    Richard Fox, *Reinhold Niebuhr: A Biography*, Pantheon Books, 1985, p. 181.
4    J. Davis McCaughey, *Christian Obedience in the University*, SCM Press, 1958, p. 19.
5    John Mackay and Alan Booth, in *Robert, Your Life and Ours*, unpublished booklet, April 1979; see also Nansie Blackie, *In Love and in Laughter: A Portrait of Robert Mackie*, Saint Andrew Press, 1995.
6    Ruth Rouse and Stephen Neill (eds), *A History of the Ecumenical Movement, 1517–1948*, SPCK, 1954, pp. 701–2.
7    Sir Walter Moberly, born 1881, Vice-Chancellor of Manchester University 1926–35, thereafter Chairman of the University Grants Committee.
8    Sir Alfred Zimmern, born 1879, Montague Burton Professor of International Relations, Oxford, from 1930, author of *The League of Nations and the Rule of Law*, 1936.
9    R. H. Tawney, born 1880. Professor of Economic History, London School of Economics, from 1931, author of *Religion and the Rise of Capitalism* (1926) and *Equality* (1931).
10    A. D. Lindsay, born 1879, Master of Balliol from 1924, author of *The Essentials of Democracy* (1929).

11    Ernest Barker, born 1874, Professor of Political Science, Cambridge, from 1928, author of *Political Thought in England from Herbert Spencer to Today* (1915).

12    Lord Lothian, born 1882, Under-Secretary of State for India, 1931–2, Ambassador to the United States, 1939–40.

13    T. S. Eliot, born 1888, poet and playwright, author of *Murder in the Cathedral* (1935), and *The Idea of a Christian Society* (1939).

14    Robert Cecil, born 1864, one of the founders of the League of Nations, Nobel Peace Prize, 1937.

15    John Foster Dulles, born 1888, American Secretary of State, 1953–9.

16    *The Student Movement*, XL, February 1938, p. 135. Over 50 years later one participant recalled this conference as 'a totally fresh experience for me' and 'a heady discovery for a theological student'. Eric Saxon, *Careering about Manchester*, Adelphi Press, 1993, p. 21. In correspondence Saxon connected this experience quite explicitly with Oliver.

17    The best example of the way he thought and spoke at this time may be his speech on 'The Modern Mood: Intellectual Difficulties' at the Church Congress, Bristol, October 1938, see *The Gospel to this Generation*, Maurice Fitzgerald (ed.), Hodder and Stoughton, 1938, pp. 98–103.

18    *New Directions in Faith and Order, Bristol 1967*, Faith and Order Paper No. 50, World Council of Churches, Geneva, 1968, p. 161.

19    Journal, 2 August 1948.

20    Keith Clements provides a long account of the Moot in *Faith on the Frontier: A Life of J. H. Oldham*, T & T Clark, 1999, pp. 363–88.

21    For Newbigin's attendance at the September 1938 meeting of the Moot, reactions to it and feeling 'that Oldham did not want my viewpoint', see Lesslie Newbigin, *Unfinished Agenda*, SPCK, 1985, pp. 48–9.

22    *The Moot*, file of papers in the Special Collections, the Brotherton Library, Leeds.

23    Christina Scott, *A Historian and his World*, Sheed & Ward, 1984, p. 133.

24    27 February 1939, Lambeth, 3409.

25    'Amsterdam Still', *The Student Movement*, November 1939, pp. 32–4.

26    Oliver Tomkins, *Youth in the World Church*, 1947, p. 17.

## Chapter 4

1    Charles Wilson, *Australia, The Creation of a Nation 1788–1988*, Weidenfeld and Nicolson, pp. 128–9.

2    John Betjeman, *Letters*, Vol. 1, 1926–1951, Candida Lycett Green (ed.), 6 March 1948 to Roland Pym, p. 440. She commented much later on the poem which had delighted her when Betjeman wrote it: 'It really was remarkable the way he imagined it all. Actually, all that about the subaltern and the engagement is sheer fantasy, but my life was very like the poem.' *Sunday Times Magazine*, August 1965.

3    The Theological Club lasted until 1955. Eric Saxon was its secretary 1941–55, and its members included Daniel Jenkins, Ronald Preston, Francis House, Alec Whitehouse, Tom Torrance, David Cairns, Gordon Rupp, Raymond George and, latterly, David Jenkins.

4    Leslie Hunter, *The Mission of the People of God: Being a Picture of an English Diocese and a Visitation Charge in AD 1960*, SPCK, 1961, p. 34.

5    Mary Walton, *A History of the Diocese of Sheffield 1914–1979*, Sheffield Diocesan Board of Finance, p. 63.

6    Sheffield City Archives, BHP 1/10, David Paton to Leslie Hunter, 16 October 1975.

7    Lesslie Newbigin, *Unfinished Agenda*, p. 46.

8    Tim Gorringe, *Alan Ecclestone: Priest as Revolutionary*, Cairns Publications, 1994, p. 76.

9    Sheffield City Archives, Hunter papers.

10    Gorringe, *Alan Ecclestone*, pp. xx–xxi.

11    Sheffield City Archives, Bishop Hunter's Letters, BHP 1/6, 6 November 1944.

12    Yale Divinity School Archives: 45 Mott Papers, box 93.

13    Hunter did in later years develop considerable ecumenical links with the Scandinavian churches, see Lars Österlin, *Churches of Northern Europe in Profile: A Thousand Years of Anglo-Nordic Relations*, Canterbury Press, 1995.

14    Later Professor of Metallurgy and Pro-Vice-Chancellor of the University of Sheffield.

15    Later Dean of Manchester.

## Chapter 5

1    Norman Goodall, *Second Fiddle*, SCM Press, 1979, p. 71.
2    Ruth Rouse and Stephen Neill (eds), *History of the Ecumenical Movement, 1517–1948*.
3    Ibid., p. 705.
4    W. A. Visser't Hooft, *Memoirs*, SCM Press, 1973.
5    Ibid., p. 82.
6    See Keith Clements, *Faith on the Frontier: A Life of J. H. Oldham*, pp. 347–51.
7    E. Jackson, *Red Tape and the Gospel*, Selly Oak Colleges, 1980, p. 239.
8    Robert S. Bilheimer, *Breakthrough: The Emergence of the Ecumenical Tradition*, Eerdmans, 1989, p. 28.
9    *Dictionary of the Ecumenical Movement*, ed. Nicholas Lossky *et al.* (eds), WCC Publications, 1991, p. 1083.
10   This is all the odder given that in John Munsey Turner's entry on Paton in the *Dictionary* (p. 780) it is stated that 'With W. A. Visser't Hooft he became associate general secretary of the provisional WCC in 1938'.
11   See W. Visser't Hooft, *Memoirs*, pp. 168–9, and Eleanor Jackson, *Red Tape and the Gospel*, pp. 294–5.
12   He is described as no more than 'staff, London Office'! It is somewhat ironic that he presented Oliver with a copy of the book which so hugely disregarded his achievement inscribed 'with gratitude for the comradeship on the ecumenical road', but Oliver was the last person to take such things amiss.
13   *God's Apprentice: The Autobiography of Stephen Neill*, E. M. Jackson (ed.), Hodder & Stoughton, 1991, pp. 214–15.
14   *A House Family Chronicle.*
15   Nansie Blackie, *In Love and in Laughter: A Portrait of Robert Mackie*, pp. 122 and 109.
16   Robert S. Bilheimer, *Breakthrough*, p. 74.
17   *German Resistance against Hitler: The Search for Allies Abroad 1938–1945*, Clarendon, 1992.
18   *The Observer*, Profile 'World Churchman', 6 April 1958.
19   *The Church Times*, 25 November 1966.
20   Cf. his obituary tribute to the Cardinal, *Blackfriars*, May 1943, pp. 165–8.
21   Ronald Jasper, *George Bell, Bishop of Chichester*, Oxford University Press, 1967, p. 295.
22   The Bell Papers, Volume 46, contain a very full documentation of this tour, though they can still be supplemented by the unedited 18 pages of close handwritten account in Oliver's journal (1937–50, pp. 81–98).
23   Kenneth Slack, *George Bell*, SCM Press, 1971, p. 103.
24   SCM Press, 1951. This is nowhere mentioned in the published report but is clear from a letter from Ramsey to Oliver, 27 March 1950 (WCC archives 42.5.052).
25   While Hodgson was the author of several papers in the pre-Lund reports, they were mostly written many years before. It is worth noting that his five-page appendix to the pre-Lund report on *The Church*, entitled 'Modern Thought-Forms and the Doctrine of the Church', ended with the words 'we need to say not "either... or" but "both... and"'. Oliver's perennial aphorism was thus comfortingly confirmed by a Regius Professor of Divinity.
26   Oliver Tomkins, 'A Personal Retrospect and Assessment', *Commemorating Amsterdam 1948: 40 Years of the World Council of Churches, The Ecumenical Review* 40, 3–4, July–October 1988, p. 320.
27   From Oliver's poem 'Amsterdam 1948' written in September and published in *Theology*, October 1948.
28   Bell Papers, Box 103 contains much crucial material. See also Owen Chadwick, 'The Church of England and the Church of Rome, from the beginning of the nineteenth century to the present day', in E. G. W. Bill (ed.), *Anglican Initiatives in Christian Unity*, SPCK, 1967, pp. 73–107, Alberic Stacpoole, 'Cordial Relations between Rome and Canterbury, 1944-54', *One in Christ*, 23,3, 1987, pp. 212–32; William Purdy, *The Search for Unity, Relations between the Anglican and Roman Catholic Churches from the 1950s to the 1970s*, Geoffrey Chapman, 1996. However, all these published accounts are somewhat misleading in that they concentrate on Anglican–Roman Catholic relations while omitting any reference to the near simultaneous and largely overlapping development of WCC–Roman Catholic relations, for which see Lambeth Palace, Tomkins Papers, MS 3411 and much other Tomkins and WCC material.
29   Maurice Villain, 'A Supplementary Note', *The Universal Church in God's Design: An Ecumenical Study Prepared under the Auspices of the World Council of Churches*, O. Tomkins, (ed.), 1948, p. 175.

30   Maurice Villain, *Abbé Paul Couturier*, 1954, ET, 1959, p. 16. Oliver marked this passage in his
     copy. He wrote an article on Couturier for *The Times* a quarter of a century later 'The founder
     of the "invisible monastery"' (*The Times*, 15 January 1977) and often preached about him in
     retirement. For Couturier's influence, see also Patrick Rodger (ed.), *Ecumenical Dialogue in
     Europe: The Ecumenical Conversations at Les Dombes (1937–1955) Inspired by the Abbé
     Couturier*, Lutterworth Press, 1966.
31   Later reprinted by *The Times* as a booklet entitled *Catholicism Today* (1949).
32   *Vers l'Unité Chrétienne*, No. 22, April 1950, quoted by Oliver in R. Rouse and S. Neill (eds),
     *A History of the Ecumenical Movement*, p. 693.
33   It was printed, with some revision, as an article in *The Ecumenical Review*, IV, Spring 1952.
34   In January 1976 Oliver wrote to me, 'I looked again the other day at the chapter I wrote about
     1950 on "The RC Church and the Ecumenical Movement". It is *incredible* that so soon after
     so much is changed!'
35   In his *Memoirs*, p. 217, Wim gives the impression that this statement was first drafted after the
     Executive Committee meeting in February 1950. This is certainly mistaken, the first draft
     being dated the previous October.
36   For what follows see the Groser Papers in Lambeth Palace Library, 3432, and also a consid-
     erable file of Oliver's own papers, the two to some extent overlapping; see also an article of
     reminiscence by Oliver in *The Times*, 7 September 1990.
37   Lesslie Newbigin, *Unfinished Agenda*, p. 131.
38   His best account of it from a personal point of view is 'Lund 1952 Re-visited 25 Years After',
     *Mid-Stream*, XVII, 2, April 1978, pp. 169–75.
39   *The Third World Conference on Faith and Order*, Oliver S. Tomkins (ed.), SCM Press, 1953,
     pp. 161–73; it first appeared in *The Ecumenical Review*, October 1952, pp. 15–26.
40   See Robert S. Bilheimer, *Breakthrough*, 1989, pp. 102–3.
41   Its enduring importance for him is suggested by his article in *The Times*, 18 September 1982,
     'Lund Principle, 30 years on'.

## Chapter 6

1    Edward Carpenter, *Archbishop Fisher: His Life and Times*, Canterbury Press, 1991, p. 228.
2    Ibid., p. 226.
3    Owen Chadwick, *Michael Ramsey*, Oxford University Press, 1990, p. 118. Temple, he added,
     was 'hopeless'. This was, it seems, in regard to staff, but in general one wonders as to its
     correctness. Temple was largely responsible for Fisher's own appointment to Chester and then
     London; he appears to have expected Fisher to succeed him: was that hopeless? Again, Temple
     was very good in picking out young talent, such as Ramsey himself and Oliver. Fisher's judge-
     ment appears over-cautious.
4    Norman Goodacre, who had been at Westcott with Oliver, wrote an article for the *Church
     Times* entitled 'Bishops at Thirty'. Decades later, after Oliver's death, he admitted to Ursula
     that when he wrote it Oliver was 'the un-named person in my mind... I always felt that
     Oliver was a born bishop' (letter, 4 Feb. 1993).
5    *Oliver Tomkins by his Friends*, Monica Cleasby (ed.). All the quotations in this chapter from
     Jill Sargent, John Yates, Reggie Askew and Paul Oestreicher are from pp. 47–64 of this book.
6    Fifteen or so years later Ursula held a meeting in Bristol, at Bishop's House, of clergy wives
     who had returned to their original work. 'All agreed that... it *was* worth it!' (Letter of UT to
     AH, 31 January 2000.)
7    *Oliver Tomkins by his Friends*, p. 62.
8    Dick Milford, *Belated Harvest*, 1978.
9    Fisher Papers 200, Lambeth Palace Library.
10   Owen Chadwick, *Michael Ramsey*, 1990, p. 85.
11   Nansie Blackie, *In Love and in Laughter*, pp. 118–26.
12   World Council of Churches, *Minutes and Reports of the Eighth Meeting of the Central
     Committee*, Davos, Switzerland, 2–8 August 1955, p. 35.

## Chapter 7

1    This figure could not be maintained. The average for the next five years was 67 and for
     1966–70, 42.
2    Thomas F. Stransky, 'The Foundation of the Secretariat for Promoting Christian Unity',

*Vatican II by Those Who Were There*, Alberic Stacpoole (ed.), Geoffrey Chapman, 1986, pp. 62–87, gives the best account of these developments

3     Edward Carpenter, *Archbishop Fisher: His Life and Times*, Canterbury Press, 1991, p. 710.

4     Michael Manktelow, *John Moorman: Anglican, Franciscan, Independent*, Canterbury Press, 1999, p. 31.

5     Tomkins personal papers, Volume of Reading Lists, 1967.

6     See, for instance, Clifford Longley, *The Worlock Archive*, Geoffrey Chapman, 2000, p. 110.

7     Papers in Lambeth Manuscript 3411.

8     Lambeth Palace Library, 4206. Anglican–Presbyterian Conversations, 2 June 1966.

9     Geneva. 42.5. 052.

10    Meredith B. Handspicker, 'Faith and Order 1948–1968', in Harold E. Fey (ed.), *The Ecumenical Advance: A History of the Ecumenical Movement, II, 1948–1968*, SPCK, 1970, pp. 151, 155.

11    *World Council of Churches, Minutes and Reports of the Eighth Meeting of the Central Committee*, Davos (Grisons), Switzerland, 2–8 August 1955, pp. 21–6, 86–93.

12    *World Council of Churches, Minutes and Reports of the Thirteenth Meeting of the Central Committee*, St Andrews, Scotland, 16–24 August 1960, pp. 9–11, 112–17, 183–9.

13    Monica Cleasby (ed.), *Oliver Tomkins by his Friends*, p. 44.

14    *World Council of Churches, Minutes and Reports of the Sixteenth Meeting of the Central Committee*, Paris, 7–16 August 1962, p. 16.

15    From Oliver's ten-page report on the subject to Michael Ramsey.

16    *The Fourth World Conference on Faith and Order. The Report from Montreal 1963*, P. C. Rodger and L. Vischer (eds), SCM Press, 1964, Foreword by Oliver, p. 7. A splendid account of the Conference was provided immediately afterwards by Patrick Rodger to the Central Committee, *World Council of Churches Minutes and Reports of the Seventeenth Meeting of the Central Committee*, Rochester, New York, 26 August–2 September 1963, pp. 85–9. Most of the Montreal addresses were printed in the *Ecumenical Review*, October 1963.

17    See the long summary of press reporting and subsequent comment, the *Ecumenical Review*, XVI, 2, January 1964, pp. 183–95.

18    *New Directions in Faith and Order: Bristol 1967*, Geneva, 1968, pp. 161–8.

19    Ernest Payne, *Thirty Years of the British Council of Churches 1942–1972*, British Council of Churches, 1972, p. 22.

20    John Robinson, *Honest to God*, SCM Press, 1963.

21    John Moorman, Diary, 1964, Lambeth Palace Library.

22    The best general account of the first part of the selection process is to be found in W. M. S. West, *To Be a Pilgrim: A Memoir of Ernest A. Payne*, Lutterworth, 1983, pp. 133–40.

23    W. Visser't Hooft, *Memoirs*, SCM, 1973, pp. 359–60.

24    Ramsey Papers, p. 107.

25    Lambeth Palace Library 4203 and 4204 contain Oliver's extensive collection of letters and papers relating to the Intercommunion Commission.

26    All the relevant pages are in Lambeth Palace Library, 4206, *Anglican–Presbyterian Conversations*.

27    Leonard Hodgson, 'Anglicanism and Intercommunion', *Intercommunion*, Donald Baillie and John Marsh (eds), SCM Press, 1952, p. 265.

28    Oliver noted in his journal in December 1967 after attending the Joint Working Group in Assisi 'plans to discuss intercommunion next time, using our Report, since in USA, Holland and elsewhere it is a live issue for RC's, in spite of "Directorium" (the Secretariat's official ecumenical guide). No less significant, intercommunion was in fact discussed at the final meeting of the Anglican/Roman Catholic International Preparatory Commission the next month in Malta and its report included reference to it: 'In the minds of many Christians no issue is today more urgent.'

29    It is curious to note how little different was John Moorman's instructions for his diocese, except that he was noticeably more liberal in his formulation – so much so that Ramsey thought it 'very near to indiscriminate intercommunion'! Michael Manktelow, *John Moorman*, p. 129.

30    Letter to Adrian Hastings, 20 January 1976.

31    Peter Jagger, *A History of the Parish and People Movement*, The Faith Press, 1978.

32    Charles Davis, a Roman Catholic priest and theologian and original Catholic observer on the Intercommunion Commission, announced his departure from the Catholic Church very publicly in December 1966, to join no other church. He published *A Question of Conscience*, Hodder & Stoughton, 1967, to explain why.

33   Two old friends and colleagues to be re-elected were Professor Alivisatos, by then in his eighties, and Frank Woods, still Archbishop of Melbourne. Alivisatos died the following year. Pauline Webb, a British Methodist, became one of the two vice-chairmen, the first woman to occupy so senior a position in the WCC.

34   Journal, 18 August 1968, letter of Oliver to R. M. G. Libby, 28 July 1971, and letter of Ramsey to Tomkins, 2 August 1971.

35   James Simpson and Edward Story, *The Long Shadows of Lambeth*, 1969, pp. 269–70.

36   His large and important file on this subject marked 'Anglican–Methodist 1962–69' is still in Bishop's House, Bristol. In fact, it continues well beyond 1969. There is a further file in Bristol Public Records Office.

37   Owen Chadwick, *Michael Ramsey*, p. 37.

38   Lambeth Palace Library, 4203.

39   Apart from being briefly a member of the Joint Committees of the Convocations of Canterbury and York which produced the report *Relations between the Church of England and the Methodist Church* in 1965.

40   Monica Cleasby (ed.), *Oliver Tomkins by his Friends*, p. 76.

41   Letter to Sir John Lawrence, 7 April 1971.

42   See, for instance, 'Words and the Word', part of a paper read to the Bristol Theological Society in 1974 (*The Churchman*, July–September 1974, pp. 200–4).

## Chapter 8

1   Oliver Tomkins, *Asking God: A Pocket Book of Intercessions*, pp. 64–5. Oliver wrote his reflections on 'Living with Retirement', published in *The Reality of God*, James Butterworth (ed.), 1986, pp. 207–15, reprinted in revised form in *Fairacres Chronicle*, Summer 1992, pp. 34–40.

2   Characteristically, Oliver never told him what he had done.

3   Letter to Peter Firth, 30 May 1985.

4   *Commemorating Amsterdam 1948: 40 Years of the World Council of Churches. The Ecumenical Review* 40, 3–4, July–October 1988, pp. 318–25.

5   *Epworth Review*, 16,2, May 1989, pp. 53–61.

6   The entry on Milford in the *Dictionary of National Biography* was one of the last things he wrote for publication.

## Chapter 9

1   Letter to the author, 16 May 1991.

2   *Intercommunion Today*, 1968, p. 126.

3   *The Tablet*, Letter, 24 February 1990.

# Select bibliography

Oliver Tomkins published five books: *The Wholeness of the Church*, SCM, 1949; *The Church in the Purpose of God*, Faith and Order Commission, 1950; *The Life of Edward Woods*, SCM, 1957; *A Time for Unity*, SCM, 1964; and *Guarded by Faith*, Hodder and Stoughton, 1971. There is one posthumous publication: *Asking God: a Pocket Book of Intercessions*, Deborah Page and Andrew Teal (eds), Canterbury Press, 1998.

Among his more important other publications are 'The present position of the Unity Movement', *Theology*, XLIX, 317 (November 1946), pp. 322–31; 'Intercommunion in the Ecumenical Movement', in Donald Baillie and John Marsh (eds) *Intercommunion*, SCM, 1952, pp. 105–37; 'Implications of the Ecumenical Movement', *Ecumenical Review*, 5 (October 1952), pp. 15–26; 'The Roman Catholic Church and the Ecumenical Movement 1910–1948', in Ruth Rouse and Stephen Neill (eds), *A History of the Ecumenical Movement 1517–1948*, SPCK, 1954, pp. 677–93; 'Legitimate hopes and legitimate fears about the World Council of Churches' role in church unity', *Ecumenical Review*, 12, April 1960, pp. 302–9; 'Ceylon and the dilemma of church unity', *Theology*, LXIV, 496 (October 1961), pp. 397–401; 'The future of Faith and Order', in *New Directions in Faith and Order: Bristol 1967*, World Council of Churches, 1968; 'Conciliarity: the way forward? An Anglican contribution', *Churches in Conciliar Fellowship* (Conference European Churches, Geneva, 1978), pp. 8–19; 'Lund 1952 re-visited 25 years after', *Midstream*, XVII, 2 (April 1978), pp. 169–75; *A Fully Human Priesthood*, Movement for the Ordination of Women, 1984; *Prayer for Unity*, The Sisters of the Love of God, 1986; 'Living with retirement', *Fairacres Chronicle*, 25. 2, (Summer 1992), pp. 34–40; and 'Amsterdam 1948: a personal retrospect and assessment', *Commemorating Amsterdam 1948: 40 Years of the World Council of Churches*, *Ecumenical Review* 40, 3–4, July–October 1988, pp. 318–25.

The most important commission report for which he was responsible was *Intercommunion Today*, Church Information Office, 1968, while the essential tool for understanding Oliver Tomkins himself is *Oliver Tomkins by his Friends*, Monica Cleasby (ed.), Low Barth, Dent, Sedbergh, Cumbria LA10 5SZ, 1995.

# Index